T0041922

About the Editor

WOLFGANG SCHIRMACHER, Ph.D., is president of the International Schopenhauer Association (Hamburg) and Arthur Schopenhauer Chair and Professor of Philosophy of Technology at the European Graduate School (Saas-Fee, Switzerland), where he also serves as program director for the Media and Communications Division.

THE ESSENTIAL
SCHOPENHAUER

Key Selections from
The World as Will and Representation
and Other Writings

Arthur Schopenhauer

Edited and with a Foreword by
WOLFGANG SCHIRMACHER

HARPER**PERENNIAL** ⊗ MODERN**THOUGHT**

NEW YORK • LONDON • TORONTO • SYDNEY • NEW DELHI • AUCKLAND

HARPER**PERENNIAL** ● MODERN**THOUGHT**

THE ESSENTIAL SCHOPENHAUER. Copyright © 2010 by Wolfgang Schirmacher. All rights reserved. Printed in the United States of America. No part of this book may be used or reproduced in any manner whatsoever without written permission except in the case of brief quotations embodied in critical articles and reviews. For information, address HarperCollins Publishers, 195 Broadway, New York, NY 10007.

HarperCollins books may be purchased for educational, business, or sales promotional use. For information, please e-mail the Special Markets Department at SPsales@harpercollins.com.

FIRST EDITION

Designed by Justin Dodd

Library of Congress Cataloging-in-Publication Data is available upon request.

ISBN 978-0-06-176824-8

23 24 25 26 27 LBC 28 27 26 25 24

Contents

Living Disaster: Schopenhauer for the Twenty-first Century

Life is not worth living! This is the thought most associated with the German philosopher Arthur Schopenhauer, who was virtually unacknowledged when he died one hundred fifty years ago. Increasingly, however, we understand that behind the mask of a pessimist Schopenhauer was a Zen master and arguably the greatest mystic of the nineteenth century. Schopenhauer roused more than two thousand years of Western philosophy from its delusion about who we really are, by declaring that materiality—the life of the body, rather than the mind—was the driving force of existence.

Schopenhauer has become synonymous with a thoroughly pessimistic worldview. In defiance of tradition, as may be exemplified by Leibniz, he proclaimed we live "in the worst of all possible worlds." Wherever a human being dares to admit the truth about our existence, privately or publicly, we find it is Schopenhauer's brutal honesty that guides such insights. The German composer Richard Wagner, acquainted with Schopenhauer, famously exclaimed: "Finally, I can tell the truth about life!" Schopenhauer is not a philosophical writer whose texts are part of any "Great Books" curriculum, not even at elite universities, since his only interest is in truth itself, no sugarcoating, no political correctness, no respect for precedent. *Do not read*

Schopenhauer! the authorities advise, but the opposite happens. In Germany, Schopenhauer is still the most widely read philosopher, and worldwide it is not only the rebels, nonconformists, contrarians, and outsiders who turn to him but also professionals who have no illusions about the fragility of the human condition and who refuse consolation: physicians, lawyers, writers, artists. Musicians in particular have been drawn to Schopenhauer, who claimed that in music alone are we attuned to the authentic condition of life, without any interference from language.

Very few people are capable of being brutally honest about what it means to be human. Schopenhauer's brother-in-spirit, Spinoza, did not play the game of false consolation and phony rationalization, but rather reminded us death is not to be feared; we have only to fear that we have not lived. Among the brave who accept Schopenhauer's truth are first and foremost the comedians, the true American philosophers, from *The Simpsons* to George Carlin and Jon Stewart. Woody Allen held up Schopenhauer as a hero, even mentioning the philosopher in his work; influential writers, Jorge Luis Borges among them, learned German in order to read the philosopher in the original. The French thinker Georges Bataille admired the capacity for "laughing in the face of death" as a kind of poetry of living.

But Schopenhauer's most constant readers are found not only among such eminent personalities. His most intuitive reader emerges in everyone who goes through adolescence, a time when all those who had held our trust and admiration now come under suspicion and we begin questioning. At this stage, we are the most human we can be. Friedrich Nietzsche, educated by Schopenhauer, called humans the "non-determined species," and Martin Heidegger pointed to Enowning (*Ereignis*) as the existential "openness" that makes us unique. By discovering our authentic self in the turmoil of adolescence, we must leave behind, without regrets, what we are *supposed to be*. Such an "intellectual honesty" (Nietzsche) can lead to suicide, an act which demonstrates that I have the ability to take my own life, that I belong to no one, and that I share with others only the condition "that we have nothing in common," as Jean-Luc Nancy insists. That teenagers and young adults sometimes take their lives without an apparent "good reason" is an integral part of true freedom—the freedom to make mistakes, as America's courageous philosopher Avital Ronell noted. But Schopenhauer also made the most convincing argument *against* suicide. Taking one's own life merely confirms the unbearable condition of life; through it, we capitulate to what we so despise.

In Schopenhauer's ethics, the only worthy task of philosophy is embodied in an incessant struggle until the last breath, with the full knowledge that we can never win the "heroic life project." It was Theodor W. Adorno who not only insisted that "thinking means thinking against yourself" but also stated unrepentantly that "a philosopher never escapes puberty." Many Schopenhauer editions picture on their covers the portrait of a miserable old white-haired man, but this is not the person who wrote *The World as Will and Representation*, his magnum opus. The young man on the back cover of *The Essential Schopenhauer* is the true author and will always be the philosopher for the young, for creative people—of any age—and a constant threat to manipulation and socialization. There would be no Sigmund Freud, no Jacques Lacan, without Schopenhauer, who boldly pointed to the "sexual organs as the true center of the world." Schopenhauer learned early on that the rationality of Homo sapiens is just a poorly spun veil covering the cruelty of the "will-to-live." Schopenhauer spent his entire life, until his death at seventy-two, explaining and augmenting what he understood as a young philosopher.

When he wrote *The World as Will and Representation* he lived in Dresden, a most remarkable Baroque city before its destruction by Anglo-American bombers in February 1945. In Dresden, Schopenhauer enjoyed a charmed life, not unlike any other young man of means in his late twenties. (It is with good reason that the title of the best book on Schopenhauer, written by Rüdiger Safranski, is *Schopenhauer and the Wild Years of Philosophy*.) After Georg Wilhelm Friedrich Hegel, the leading philosopher of the time, succumbed to a cholera epidemic, Schopenhauer ended his brief period as assistant professor at Berlin University, having insulted the authorities by insisting on teaching only "my entire system." A financial crash forced him to live a frugal life using what remained of the inheritance from his father, a wealthy merchant; but at the end of his life Schopenhauer had more money in the bank than at the beginning. A reclusive life of twenty-seven years in the German metropolis Frankfurt am Main allowed him the opportunity to write without being concerned about public reaction. After his death he became known as "the Buddha of Frankfurt," a fitting description, as he had discovered—on the basis of not very reliable but still usable ancient Eastern texts—that he had many insights in common with Buddha, and he also introduced Buddhism into the Western philosophical debate. Given that Christianity, the Schopenhauer family faith, also describes earth as a "vale of tears" and paradise as a mere promise "after death," Schopenhauer's own thought that life is suffering was not presented as revelation. But as Aristotle observed, a philosopher's power lies not in discovering the new, as do scientists, or offering the unexpected, as artists do. Philosophers take the trivial, turn again to supposedly self-evident certainties, thereby revealing their merely dormant validity. The point is that life is suffering, yet we all live as if it were not. The basic truths are always simple and hidden out in the open, unrecognizable as answered questions, shut cases, settled disputes.

The philosopher is the most dangerous member of society, at least according to Nietzsche, because he stirs up what has been put to rest in order to ensure a functioning society. And the philosopher sometimes even recklessly poses questions in a language everyone can understand without the help of self-important experts. Schopenhauer was one of the great German writers, and this comes through even in the English translations. The titles of his books and the excerpts included in this reader are an indication of the hold questions concerning the human condition still have over us: What are the principles of sufficient reason in a world where faulty reason is called smart? What is the basis of morality when ethics become a problem of social engineering or are left to religion? What constitutes the freedom of the will in the age of neurophilosophy? How can the sublime task of the artist and the inner nature of art still be of significance when art has turned into investment? Can we still glean inspiration from unconventional human lifestyles such as those of mystics, saints, and ascetics for the decisive "question to come": "What does it mean to be a human being?" (Immanuel Kant)

Or: Why live at all? The blissful ignorance of childhood ends all too soon and human beings are faced with the never-ending suffering called "life." It begins with the initial disenchantment that your charmed existence, "being one with the universe," Lacan's "ideal ego," appears to have been a fairy tale. You are, rather, an utterly powerless child, at the mercy of parents, siblings, peers, and virtually any adult. You find yourself suddenly aware of being separated from everything you had taken for granted, from warmth to food, and forced to negotiate for what you enjoyed before without paying for it. Life is a business that does not cover the costs, Schopenhauer remarks. Even the most effective method of making one's nonnegotiable wishes known, screaming as a baby, soon loses its power. Once babies all, we wielded the power of the weak (Levinas). In the majority of cases, our screams brought about the "unconditional surrender" to our command. The baby's need was met, the caregiver's need for quiet appeased. But the weak and the strong are one. The other extreme lies in the inability to respond; the baby, the source of the noise, is ignored, even killed. Toddlers may still throw tantrums, but they lack the baby's perseverance, which made all the difference. Parents as well as teachers in nursery schools have many cunning ways to manipulate you; with language you learn to behave "appropriately" and are guided into the process of civilization. To make a human being out of you, as advocated by educators of all kinds, means in effect directing you to your "place in the world" with the insincere promise that through "hard work and study" the future holds for you the chance to make it beyond that station. Western parents will claim you can achieve anything you want if you just set your mind to it; but this does not change your being "thrown into the world," literally and in terms of your fate, as Schopenhauer put it. We are thrown into social circumstances, with a set of genes that decidedly influence appearance, intelligence, and future health, without our consent or the slightest choice. The "David Copperfield kind of crap," J. D. Salinger, a kindred spirit of Schopenhauer, called it in *The Catcher in the Rye*. Often enough the children of the world are born into circumstances they would not wish on their worst enemies, and it is not overstatement to call children the slaves of our time, treated without regard to their humanity by parents and educators alike. Certainly, there are laws protecting children from the most obvious exploitations, such as child pornography, corporal punishment, and child labor, but it still takes the compassionate adult who will stand as accuser and prod the justice system to at least take notice. Children are bound to discover by their teens that they belong to a species that is, quite possibly, the most murderous and predatory in the world. We do not kill out of necessity but out of arrogance, presuming ourselves the "master and owner of nature" (as did Descartes, whom Schopenhauer identified as a "father of modernity").

"The truth dare not appear naked before the people," Schopenhauer pointed out in an effort to explain how religions retain their influence even after the age of Enlightenment. "Dare to think for yourself!" Kant challenged his fearful fellow wo/man, but even today many prefer the truth clothed tightly in ritual, traditions, and tall tales. Our innate trust in life with which we are born is a survival technique we share with our companion species. This "ideal ego" experience of our all-too-brief life before and after birth possesses its own potent rationalization and is the reason why we crave a first principle, a *prima philosophia*. If not a (personal) God of some form, we call such order Nature and attribute, with the help of science, to its laws, which Albert Einstein suggested might all be "false." With Darwin's system of evolution, the "will in nature" (Schopenhauer) provided a name for universal suffering but in the same breath took the sting out of it. Science lies just slightly less than religions which prefer "consolation"; they presume to call "higher truth" to the plain truth of the suffering they help to deny. And compared with pseudo-religions such as political movements or lifestyle trends promoted by advertising, science at least has on its side "facts" which can be "falsified" (Karl Popper) and religion compassionate wisdom.

Why call it a "lie" when people try to find the good side of events, the light at the end of the tunnel, the opportunity in a crisis? What would be the purpose of mourning the end of innocence and indulging in self-pity after the event of language, Lacan's "mirror stage," in which we realize we are separate from the world around us? The English philosopher Thomas Hobbes famously characterized our relationships to our fellow man as "wolf-to-wolf" and offered to relinquish to authorities most of our freedom if they promised to protect us from our neighbors. The police everywhere claim "to serve and protect," but this does not change Schopenhauer's accurate and horrific description: "Every living being is the grave of other living beings." The constitutional right to pursue happiness—as long as you observe the laws of the land—does not change the fact that our pursuit hurts others who had the same prize in mind but came either too early or too late or were born on the wrong continent. Schopenhauer called happiness just a moment between misfortunes and our belief that we are somehow protected from the suffering we see around us the greatest of all lies: Victim and victimizer are one and the same. A hundred years after Schopenhauer, the French philosopher and Nobel Prize winner Albert Camus acknowledged that "he who lives will become guilty" and affirmed that the issue of suicide is a key philosophical question. His answer was the "human in revolt," who like Sisyphus never gives up, even if the negative outcome is not in doubt. Is life worth living? Only if you make it worth living, Camus as well as Schopenhauer concluded. Schopenhauer did not lay down the Zen master's bamboo stick, since he did not believe the people deserved the "truth in the truth" yet, the "turning of the will-to-live." There is a fullness of nothingness, as we learn from Zen; and Schopenhauer hinted at the mystical "it gives" (Heidegger), compassion and love of humanity as a non-teachable way of ethical living.

Schopenhauer claimed one exception to the rule of rational thinking he called "introspection." The insight into what is in me, accessible to me alone, and protected by the sovereignty of being-there (Heidegger's *Dasein*) is the authentic path of the will itself in me. Nietzsche's response to the suffering which is life was the "will to power," often misunderstood as political agenda. But it is instead the aesthetic power, the creation of a humane world, the truth of fiction, the "contra-factual" ethics twentieth-century philosophers from Ludwig Wittgenstein to Jürgen Habermas advocated. Human beings cannot live without lies, declared Nietzsche, Schopenhauer's outstanding student, but these lies are neither intentional falsehoods nor white lies to protect feelings. There are lies which tell the truth, as Virginia Cutrufelli demonstrated for the true poets such as Friedrich Hölderlin and Paul Celan. Plato, poet turned philosopher, called in *The Republic* for the expulsion of the poets from society because he feared insights which are neither philosophical in nature nor sophistic opinions for power brokering. The Übertruth of poetry originates in the singular "introspection" which Schopenhauer received as reward for his bravery.

His entire work is a philosophical elaboration of this introspection, his one thought he sensed was the truth: Life is suffering. Spinoza calls "intuition" an insight that comes with the feeling of certainty. Nietzsche speaks of it as a "truth beyond good and evil" and an "eternal recurrence of the same." But it is not "exactly the same," every "repetition" of love and hate, striving and missing, of life lived is nearly imperceptibly different, as the French philosopher Gilles Deleuze reminds us.

Fearless and fierce, Schopenhauer found in himself the force called will that, blind and merciless, utterly indifferent to any ethical consideration, approaches life as rapaciously as a serial killer. This will to survive, often formulated in the language of competitive sports, is understood as "survival of the fittest" (Darwin), though it is doubtful that any fairness is involved: Even the fittest murderer needs helpful coincidences and lucky breaks. Schopenhauer was unrelenting in his insistence that every human individual be aware of the inescapable and arbitrary suffering which is set off by the very existence of the will and refrain from using the imaginative power of our mind to envision it otherwise. No Hollywood ending to the horror movie of violence and betrayal. But Schopenhauer's introspection held a hidden call to action which he carefully protected by the cardinal rule of the mystics. Literally, "mystic" means "speak not of silence," because introducing the mystical insight into the everyday chatter of the culture industry will transform into idle talk what is potent only as "usage" (Heidegger), the essential act with decisive understanding. The sages of humankind—from the Zen masters to the Arab poets, the Christian saints, and Western philosophers such as Spinoza—abided by the obvious truth of silence: Do not listen to what the saints are saying, follow their examples. Even Karl Marx, arguably the most politically influential philosopher of all time, echoed this intuition in his famous Eleventh Thesis on Feuerbach: "Philosophers have hitherto interpreted the world in various ways; the point is to change it!" It is this life change which can begin only in singularity that Schopenhauer was blessed (or cursed) with and at which he dared only hint. In the end, "the will turns" in all human beings, and "nothing" is the mode of living authentically.

Schopenhauer was not alone in the hermeneutical limitation leading him to conclude that each individual lives within a context shaped by circumstances we, since Hegel, have called "historical conditions" and, following Hegel's critic Kierkegaard, "existential." And how biased philosophers can be is demonstrated by Schopenhauer's notorious essay on women, included in this reader. Nevertheless, Schopenhauer's philosophy of disaster is a genuine and well-thought-out manifestation of the extreme change concomitant with modern technology. The "war against nature" has ended with human beings becoming fully responsible for the human condition itself. It is not Homo sapiens who had to redesign the world to be humane but rather Homo generator, who realizes in ubiquitous life techniques—from media to biotechnology—how to live fulfillingly under any circumstances. Schopenhauer understood the singularity of the event of humanity, the being-with in each of us. There is no will outside, only, by definition, a misleading representation; the will in me opens its eyes and senses fully its actualization. Addressing the book of Genesis with its story of how God looked upon His creation on the seventh day and saw that it was good, Schopenhauer became conscious of how offensive to all sufferers of this flawed creation it must be, and how insurmountable a problem for any "justification of the existence of God" (*théodicée*). Each of us, whether in puberty or life crisis, can be nothing but "disgusted" by the painful misery that life is for all feeling beings. This is precisely the reaction of the will when finally in the "love of humanity" truth reveals itself to the will. The blind will begins to see itself, slowly and with great effort, and it may take centuries before its sight is fully developed and accepts its limit. The deaf will begins to listen to the resonating of our "living with things" and of the beautiful music of "multitude" (Deleuze). The aimless will which only perpetuated itself discovers the aim in itself, a thriving that stays in Being without negating others, as Spinoza envisioned the *conatus*. The indifference of the will fades away into the ethics of compassion which—according to Schopenhauer—cannot be resisted when it suddenly overcomes us.

With respect to the span of an individual lifetime, the multiple turnings of the will, with its overall easing of suffering, will always be too slow to be noticed properly; so there will still be good reason to continue to fight against injustice and exploitation and for the worthy cause. It is through our technologies—bio- as well as digital technologies—that living changes itself. Each new generation is born into a different set of life techniques which can be trusted only when they appear impermanent and barely visible. The toddlers of today will accept as self-evident what for many people born in the middle of the last century would be close to an abomination. Schopenhauer made the desperate suggestion that human beings stop having sex because procreation only prolongs suffering. But he honestly admitted he would not be able to follow it himself. With chemical birth control Homo generator put this debate to rest, and sex is perceived increasingly as what it is in and of itself for us: the most rewarding bodily activity of being-with. Raising children also has an excellent chance of becoming a choice for the many people who are good at it and enjoy mentoring an offspring. But the "biological clock" will finally stop and the "timing" of each Homo generator take precedent. Even for death, the most effective threat to each individual, a turn is underway: A life fully lived, through the bad, through the good days, greets death as its genuine life ending. Currently, though most authorities remain paternalistic and deny us the choice of our own death, one can observe a quiet rebellion in the medical profession: It becomes acceptable if the necessary relief from pain has merely the side effect of speeding up your death. It will not be too long before the "right to die my way" will be an accepted life choice.

Living philosophy is Schopenhauer's mandate for the twenty-first century. His one thought, that life is suffering, granted him "the turn of the body"—it is not the mind but the "reason of the body" (Nietzsche) which feels the pain and compassion with all fellow suffering beings. Sexuality is the chief activity, often shamefully hidden, and governed by the "unconscious" (Freud) as well as chemistry. And what we call life is a killing game in which human beings rule supreme. Schopenhauer refused to contemplate the other side; his cup was full with suffering, and he considered any talk of a "silver lining" detestable optimism. Our ethical disgust "commands" compassion, as the French philosopher Emmanuel Levinas phrased it. It is in such "compassion" which has not pity but self-awareness at its core that we find a "trace" (Derrida) of an "art of living" which needs no preconditions. Schopenhauer learned from the two philosophers he most admired, Plato and Kant, to pay careful attention to epistemology: What can we know? What is real? Reality is not a given fact but rather a "thing-in-itself" that appears for us solely as representation. There is no rational way to find out *how* reality *is* without our thinking coming into play, but it is equally true that our concepts would be empty without the materials which are not us. Against Kant's carefully argued dictum that we cannot know the "thing-in-itself," Schopenhauer was adamant about there being one exception and offered himself as proof of the actuality of "introspection" into the authentic condition of life that is suffering. No argumentation from outside, no matter how professional and well-meaning, can refute such an insight, felt with all senses and absolute certainty. It takes individuals in crisis, bravely facing how things stand, to back up Schopenhauer. Guided by his basic insight, Schopenhauer explained why there is a "metaphysical need" for meaning when death strikes, at any time, with no regard for circumstances. Life is not fair, and so human beings console themselves with tales of "eternal life" where wrongs will be set right. And the scientific revolutions, which Schopenhauer observed in their early phase with keen interest, provided the ultimate consolation: the inherent promise to delay aging, overcome illness, and, one day, even cheat death itself. But science is just an interpretation of the will in nature, cunningly made up by a corruptible mind eager to ease our ethical disgust. Life is a losing proposition but at least its science has beautifully crafted laws, and future events can be predicted to a certain degree.

Schopenhauer's affinity with German Romanticism is manifest in the exception he allowed for art. Different from Plato, for whom "ideas" were by definition not visible, Schopenhauer considered art "materialized idea": You are more or less aware that it presents the condition of life in detail. For Schopenhauer, art is not representation, pointing to something else; it is what it is, an invitation to stillness, and a meditative break where the will is quiet. We watch people die in a film and are moved, but we do not feel threatened. Still, words can interrupt this calm and connect us to the world as representation of the will, drawing us back into the misery of life. This is the reason why Schopenhauer considered music the genuine art and the sound of being. In the playing of and listening to music all our senses, including the sense of the mind, are attuned to the bad and good fortune of living, without music itself becoming a focus of attention. Art is the world mirror and its gift of "lucid stillness" (T. S. Eliot) is ephemeral but—as the Romantics emphatically stated—a way from aesthetics to ethics. After Schopenhauer, Nietzsche and Kierkegaard, the founder of existential philosophy, contended that the aesthetical leap into ethics is inevitable. Schopenhauer maintained that the customary ought-to ethics with its norms and rules is unable to deliver what it promises. Instead of imploring people Sunday after Sunday to be good or threatening them with sanctions or hellfire, we should ask what human beings are capable of. Responsibility, this key concept of many ethics, anticipates an authority which must be believed before it can be effective. But this kind of basic credibility is precisely what was already lost when Aristotle wrote the first *Ethics*—and he knew it: According to Aristotle, it is a sad day for humanity when one feels the need to formulate the way in which every individual should be living: intuitively, without having to think about it. Schopenhauer understood responsibility appropriately as our "ability to respond" to existential situations which need our ethical attention. For example, egoism need not be an ethical problem because properly understood nothing is wrong with wanting something good for yourself. The ethical question arises when malice takes over, deeply rooted in feelings of insecurity, vanity, and hate. Schopenhauer did not believe one can change human beings born with a certain character, a genetic set we would call it today. But he refused to accept the innate character as justification for wrongdoings since no one can be certain about it—on his deathbed the most miserly person could turn benevolent. It is the nucleus of Schopenhauer's ethics that it is involuntary, an event that overwhelms, a compassion that cannot be denied. It can occur at any time and no defense is possible—it just happens. *Tat tvam asi*—this art thou: The sudden revelation of humanity is the founding act of love and the source of ethical behavior. This love of humanity has many layers and shades and is as private as it is public—it is known to all and confused by many. It reveals and conceals the human condition, a "pendulum between suffering and boredom"

(Schopenhauer), the very process in which ethics, mystics, and media coincide. Learning from Schopenhauer, one must be able to respond to disaster, bravely living the turning of the will, and taking pleasure in how unnecessary suffering diminishes. Unrepentant realism will always be called for and we will never be free of unavoidable suffering.

The texts of this reader present the essential Schopenhauer for our century. Beginning with ontology, addressing the most basic condition of being and, at the same time, insisting on the rationality of the difference between will and representation, Schopenhauer proceeds to his philosophy of art. As the "materialized idea" ("*anschauliche Idee*"), art shows us how life is—without engaging us in its suffering. The event of art, for creator and audience alike, is the exceptional state of calmness. But this state is momentous, and we human beings are engaged anew in living the disaster and feeling compassion with fellow sufferers, animals not excluded. Schopenhauer's wisdom can guide us on how to live ethically under such harsh conditions. The love for humanity entails our moral refusal of living according to the "will-to-live." Schopenhauer underscores that this is not a mere metaphysical question but rather that it shapes daily life.

This reader contains a few changes with regard to the original translated texts for the sake of consistency and fluent reading. It is composed of both British and American translations, but American spelling has been adhered to throughout. Though some arcane references and quotes were omitted, many footnotes have been incorporated into the text proper. On occasion, however, a seemingly outdated phrase or usage has been retained for its evocation of the language and context, the time in which Schopenhauer lived and wrote.

Wolfgang Schirmacher
New York and Dresden
February 2010

Schopenhauer Timeline

February 22, 1788 Born in Danzig, a free seaport city and member of the Hanseatic League (after 1945: Gdansk, Poland). His father, Heinrich Floris Schopenhauer, was a successful merchant who married a much younger Johanna Trosiener. Both were from wealthy German families.

March 1793 Family moved to the Hanseatic city of Hamburg after Danzig was annexed by Prussia.

1797 Birth of sister Adele; Arthur was sent for two years to live with his father's friend in Le Havre, where he learned French. He later recalled it as the happiest time of his life.

1799 In Hamburg he attended a private school for future merchants and bankers.

1803 "Devil's bet" with his father: either two years of travel wherever he wished, after which he would become a merchant like his father, or else prepare for university. Arthur decided to travel through the Netherlands, England, France, and Switzerland and wrote a travel diary (*Reistagebücher*).

April 20, 1805	Death (possible suicide) of his father. Arthur continued to respect the wishes of his father and started a business apprenticeship in Hamburg.
1806	Johanna Schopenhauer moved the family to Weimar, becoming a well-known writer of novels and the host of an intellectual salon. Johann-Wolfgang von Goethe was a frequent visitor, as was Christoph Martin Wieland. Arthur, who had stayed behind in Hamburg, became estranged from his mother.
1807	Left the apprenticeship and finished high school (*Gymnasium*).
1809	Entered the University in Göttingen to study medicine but in 1810 switched to philosophy. Studied with Gottlob Ernst Schulze, who encouraged his reading of Plato and Kant. After reaching adulthood, Schopenhauer inherited a third of what remained of his father's estate and became financially independent.
1811	Attended lectures by the philosopher Johann Gottlieb Fichte and Friedrich Ernst Daniel Schleiermacher, a theologian and philosopher, at the university in Berlin. He also took courses in physics, astronomy, zoology, physiology, psychology, history, literature, and poetry.
1813	Due to the Napoleonic war, Schopenhauer left Berlin and moved to Rudolstadt, a small town near the university city of Jena. Schopenhauer wrote *On the Fourfold Root of the Principle of*

Sufficient Reason, submitted it as a dissertation to Jena, and was awarded a doctorate in philosophy in absentia. From 1815 to 1816 he exchanged letters with Goethe on his *Theory of Colours*, which Schopenhauer revised with a version of his own: *On Vision and Colors*.

1814–1818 Lived in Dresden, the capital of Saxony, and wrote his chief work, *The World as Will and Representation*, published 1819.

1818 The young philosopher, having finished his masterpiece, left Germany for Italy, the destination of choice for the writers of that time. Goethe had given Schopenhauer a letter to pass on to Lord Byron, full of praise for the English poet, who was in Italy at that time, but Schopenhauer disliked "peacock" Byron's appearance and the letter was never delivered.

1819 Forced to interrupt his Italian voyage because the family fortune was in peril. In the wake of a bank failure, the Schopenhauers' banker threatened them with bankruptcy if his clients did not agree to only a fraction of their deposit. Schopenhauer's mother and sister accepted this condition, but Schopenhauer refused and demanded full payment with the statement: "That I am a philosopher does not mean I am a fool."

1820 Successful habilitation lecture (a requirement for becoming a professor in Germany) at Berlin University; Hegel was the chair of the Habilitation Committee and curious to meet the young man who had worked with Goethe. During the summer period, Schopenhauer's first and only seminar, on "My Entire System," scheduled exactly and intentionally at the same hour the popular Hegel held his own seminar.

1821	Began love affair with Caroline Richter from the National Theater, which would last many years.
1822–1823	Second sojourn in Italy
1824	The writer Jean Paul praised *The World as Will and Representation* as "bold and insightful."
1825–1831	Residence in Berlin, during which Schopenhauer met with Alexander von Humboldt and Adelbert von Chamisso. His university lectures were announced but never reached sufficient enrollment.
1831	Fleeing the cholera epidemic, Schopenhauer left Berlin and lived in several places, including Frankfurt am Main.
1833	Settled in Frankfurt, where he resided until his death, with a poodle as his only companion. (When he was mad at the dog, he called it "Mensch.")
1836	*On the Will in Nature*
1840	*On the Basis of Morality*
1841	*The Two Fundamental Problems of Ethics*
1844	*The World as Will and Representation* (second edition, two volumes)
1852	First comprehensive review of Schopenhauer's philosophy, *Iconoclasm in German Philosophy*,

was published in England and widely noticed
in Germany.

1851 *Parerga and Paralipomena*

1854 Composer Richard Wagner presented Schopenhauer with a signed copy of the libretto of *The Ring of the Nibelungs*.

1857 Invited to lecture at the universities of Bonn and Breslau. The poet and dramatist Friedrich Hebbel visited Schopenhauer.

1859 *The World as Will and Representation* (third edition, two volumes)

September 21, 1860 After contracting pneumonia, Schopenhauer died a peaceful death. His grave can be found at the Central Cemetery in Frankfurt am Main.

1873 *Collected Works*, edited by Julius Frauenstädt, was published.

One

On the Suffering of the World

If suffering is not the first and immediate object of our life, then our existence is the most inexpedient and inappropriate thing in the world. For it is absurd to assume that the infinite pain, which everywhere abounds in the world and springs from the want and misery essential to life, could be purposeless and purely accidental. Our susceptibility to pain is well-nigh infinite; but that to pleasure has narrow limits. It is true that each separate piece of misfortune seems to be an exception, but misfortune in general is the rule.

Just as a brook forms no eddy so long as it meets with no obstructions, so human nature, as well as animal, is such that we do not really notice and perceive all that goes on in accordance with our will. If we were to notice it, then the reason for this would inevitably be that it did not go according to our will, but must have met with some obstacle. On the other hand, everything that obstructs, crosses, or opposes our will, and thus everything unpleasant and painful, is felt by us immediately, at once, and very plainly. Just as we *do not feel* the health of our whole body, but only the small spot where the shoe pinches, so we do not think of all our affairs that are going on perfectly well, but only of some insignificant trifle that annoys us. On this rests the negative nature of well-being and happiness, as opposed to the positive nature of pain, a point that I have often stressed.

Accordingly, I know of no greater absurdity than that of most metaphysical systems which declare evil to be something negative; whereas it is precisely that which is positive and makes itself felt. On the other hand, that which is good, in other words, all happiness and satisfaction, is negative, that is, the mere elimination of a desire and the ending of a pain. In agreement with this is the fact that, as a rule, we find pleasures far below, but pains far beyond, our expectation. Whoever wants summarily to test the assertion that the pleasure in the world outweighs the pain, or at any rate that the two balance each other, should compare the feelings of an animal that is devouring another with those of that other.

The most effective consolation in any misfortune or suffering is to look at others who are even more unfortunate than we; and this everyone can do. But what then is the result for the whole of humanity? We are like lambs playing in the field, while the butcher eyes them and selects first one and then another; for in our good days we do not know what calamity fate at this very moment has in store for us, sickness, persecution, impoverishment, mutilation, loss of sight, madness, death, and so on. History shows us the life of nations and can find nothing to relate except wars and insurrections; the years of peace appear here and there only as short pauses, as intervals between the acts. And in the same way, the life of the individual is a perpetual struggle, not merely metaphorically with want and boredom but actually with others. Everywhere he finds an opponent, lives in constant conflict, and dies weapon in hand.

Not a little is contributed to the torment of our existence by the fact that *time* is always pressing on us, never lets us draw breath, and is behind every one of us like a taskmaster with a whip. Only those who have been handed over to boredom are not pressed and plagued by time. However, just as our body would inevitably burst if the pressure of the atmosphere were removed from it, so if the pressure of want, hardship, disappointment, and the frustration of effort were removed from the lives of men, their arrogance would rise, though not to bursting-point, yet to manifestations of the most unbridled folly and even madness. At all times, everyone indeed needs a certain amount of care, anxiety, pain, or trouble, just as a ship requires ballast in order to proceed on a straight and steady course.

Work, worry, toil, and trouble are certainly the lot of almost all throughout their lives. But if all desires were fulfilled as soon as they arose, how then would people occupy their lives and spend their time? Suppose the human race were removed to Utopia where everything grew automatically and pigeons flew about ready-roasted; where everyone at once found his sweetheart and had no difficulty in keeping her; then people would die of boredom or hang themselves; or else they would fight, throttle, and murder one another and so cause themselves more suffering than is now laid upon them by nature. Thus for such a race, no other scene, no other existence, is suitable.

On account of the negative nature of well-being and pleasure as distinct from the positive nature of pain, a fact to which I just now drew the reader's attention, the happiness of any given life is to be measured not by its joys and pleasures, but by the absence of sorrow and suffering, of that which is positive. But then the lot of animals appears to be more bearable than that of man. We will consider the two somewhat more closely.

However varied the forms in which man's happiness and unhappiness appear and impel him to pursuit or escape, the material basis of all this is nevertheless physical pleasure or pain. This basis is very restricted, namely health, nourishment, protection from wet and cold, and sexual satisfaction, or else the want of these things. Consequently, in real physical pleasure man has no more than the animal, except insofar as his more highly developed nervous system enhances the susceptibility to every pleasure but also to every pain as well. But how very much stronger are the emotions stirred in him than those aroused in the animal! How incomparably more deeply and powerfully are his feelings excited, and ultimately only to arrive at the same result, namely health, nourishment, clothing, and so on.

This arises primarily from the fact that, with him, everything is powerfully enhanced by his thinking of the absent and the future, whereby anxiety, fear, and hope really come into existence for the first time. But then these press much more heavily on him than can the present reality of pleasures or pains, to which the animal is confined. Thus the animal lacks reflection, that condenser of pleasures and pains which, therefore, cannot be accumulated, as happens in the case of man by means of his memory and foresight. On the contrary, with the animal, the suffering of the present moment always remains, even when this again recurs innumerable times, merely the suffering of the present moment as on the first occasion, and cannot be accumulated. Hence the enviable tranquility and placidity of animals. On the other hand, by means of reflection and everything connected therewith, there is developed in man from those same elements of pleasure and pain which he has in common with the animal, an enhancement of susceptibility to happiness and unhappiness which is capable of leading to momentary, and sometimes even fatal, ecstasy or else to the depths of despair and suicide. More closely considered, things seem to take the following course. In order to heighten his pleasure, man deliberately increases his needs, which were originally only a little more difficult to satisfy than those of the animal; hence luxury, delicacies, tobacco, opium, alcoholic liquors, pomp, display, and all that goes with this. Then in addition, in consequence of reflection, there is open to man alone a source of pleasure, and of pain as well, a source that gives him an excessive amount of trouble, in fact almost more than is given by all the others. I refer to ambition and the feeling of honor and shame, in plain words, what he thinks of other people's opinion of him. Now in a thousand different and often strange forms this becomes the goal of almost all his efforts that go beyond physical pleasure or pain. It is true that he certainly has over the animal the advantage of really intellectual pleasures which admit of many degrees from the most ingenuous trifling or conversation up to the highest achievements of the mind. But as a counterweight to this on the side of suffering, boredom appears in man, which is unknown to the animal, at any rate in the natural state, but which slightly attacks the most intelligent only if they are domesticated, whereas with man it becomes a real scourge. We see it in that host of miserable wretches who have always been concerned over filling their purses but never their heads, and for whom their very wealth now becomes a punishment by delivering them into the hands of tormenting boredom. To escape from this, they now rush about in all directions and travel here, there, and everywhere. No sooner do they arrive at a place than they anxiously inquire about its amusements and clubs, just as does a poor man about its sources of assistance; for, of course, want and boredom are the two poles of human life. Finally, I have to mention that, in the case of man, there is associated with sexual satisfaction an obstinate selection, peculiar to him alone, which rises sometimes to a more or less passionate love. [. . .] In this way, it becomes for him a source of much suffering and little pleasure.

Meanwhile, it is remarkable how, through the addition of thought, which the animal lacks, so lofty and vast a structure of human happiness and unhappiness is raised on the same narrow basis of joys and sorrows, which the animal also has. With reference to this, his feelings are exposed to such violent emotions, passions, and shocks that their stamp can be read in the permanent lines on his face; and yet in the end and in reality, it is only a question of the same things, which even the animal obtains, and indeed with incomparably less expenditure of emotion and distress. But through all this, the measure of pain increases in man much more than that of pleasure and is now in a special way very greatly enhanced by the fact that death is actually *known* to him. On the other hand, the animal runs away from death merely instinctively, without really knowing it and thus without ever actually coming face-to-face with it, as does man, who always has before him this prospect. And so, although only a few animals die a natural death, most of them get only just enough time to propagate their species and then, if not earlier, become the prey of some other animal. On the other hand, man alone in his species has managed to make the so-called natural death the rule, to which there are, however, important exceptions. Yet in spite of all this, the animals still have the advantage, for the reason I have given. Moreover, man reaches his really natural term of life just as rarely as do the animals, because his unnatural way of living, his struggles and passions, and the degeneration of the race resulting therefrom rarely enable him to succeed in this.

Animals are much more satisfied than we by mere existence; the plant is wholly satisfied, man according to the degree of his dullness. Consequently, the animal's life contains less suffering, but also less pleasure, than man's. This is due primarily to the fact that it remains free from *care and anxiety* together with their torment, on the one hand, but is also without real *hope*, on the other. And so it does not participate in that anticipation of a joyful future through ideas together with the delightful phantasmagoria, that source of most of our joys and pleasures, which accompanies those ideas and is given in addition by the imagination; consequently in this sense it is without hope. It is both these because its consciousness is restricted to what is intuitively perceived and so to the present moment. Thus only in reference to objects that already exist at this moment in intuitive perception does the animal have an extremely short fear and hope; whereas man's consciousness has an intellectual horizon that embraces the whole of life and even goes beyond this. But in consequence of this, animals, when compared with us, seem to be really wise in *one* respect, namely in their calm and undisturbed enjoyment of the present moment. The animal is the embodiment of the present; the obvious peace of mind which it thus shares frequently puts us to shame with our often restless and dissatisfied state that comes from thoughts and cares. And even those pleasures of hope and anticipation we have just been discussing are not to be had for nothing. Thus what a man enjoys in advance, through hoping and expecting a satisfaction, afterwards detracts from the actual enjoyment of this, since the thing itself then satisfies him by so much the less. The animal, on the other hand, remains free from such pleasure in advance as well as from that deduction of pleasure, and therefore enjoys the real and present thing itself, whole and undiminished. In the same way, evils press on the animal merely with their own actual weight, whereas for us they are often increased tenfold by fear and foresight. [. . .] It is just this complete absorption in the present moment, peculiar to animals, which contributes so much to the pleasure we derive from our domestic pets. They are the present moment personified and, to a certain extent, make us feel the value of every unburdened and unclouded hour, whereas with our thoughts we usually pass it over and leave it unheeded. But the above-mentioned capacity of animals to be more satisfied than we by mere existence is abused by egotistic and heartless man, and is often exploited to such an extent that he allows them absolutely nothing but bare existence. For example, the bird that is organized to roam through half the world is confined to a cubic foot of space where it slowly pines to death and cries; and the highly intelligent dog, man's truest and most faithful friend, put on a chain by him! Never do I see such a dog without feelings of the deepest sympathy for him and of profound indignation against his master. I think with satisfaction of a case, reported some years ago in *The Times*, where a lord kept a large dog on a chain. One day as he was walking through the yard, he took it into his head to go and pat the dog, whereupon the animal tore his arm open from top to bottom, and quite right too! What he meant by this was: You are not my master, but my devil, who makes a hell of my brief existence! May this happen to all who chain up dogs.

If the result of the foregoing remarks is that the enhanced power of knowledge renders the life of man more woebegone than that of the animal, we can reduce this to a universal law and thereby obtain a much wider view. In itself, knowledge is always painless. Pain concerns the *will* alone and consists in checking, hindering, or thwarting this; yet an additional requirement is that this checking be accompanied by knowledge. Thus just as light illuminates space only when objects exist to reflect it; just as a tone requires resonance and sound generally becomes audible at a distance only through waves of the vibrating air that break on hard bodies so that its effect is strikingly feeble on isolated mountain tops and a song in the open produces little effect; so also in the same way must the checking of the *will*, in order to be felt as pain, be accompanied by *knowledge* which in itself, however, is a stranger to all pain.

Thus *physical* pain is already conditioned by nerves and their connection with the brain; and so an injury to a limb is not felt if its nerves leading to the brain are severed, or when the brain itself loses its powers through chloroform. For the very same reason, we consider that, as soon as consciousness is extinguished when a person is dying, all subsequent convulsions are painless. It follows as a matter of course that *mental* pain is conditioned by knowledge; and that it increases with the degree of knowledge can easily be seen. [. . .] We can, therefore, figuratively express the whole relationship by saying that the will is the string, its thwarting or checking the vibration thereof, knowledge the sounding board, and pain the tone.

Now according to this, only that which is inorganic and also the plant are incapable of feeling pain, however often the will may be checked in both. On the other hand, every animal, even an infusorian, feels pain because knowledge, however imperfect, is the true characteristic of animal existence. As knowledge rises on the animal scale, so too does susceptibility to pain. It is, therefore, still extremely small in the case of the lowest animals; thus, for example, insects still go on eating when the back part of the body is nearly torn off and hangs by a mere thread of gut. But even in the highest animals, because of an absence of concepts and thought, pain is nothing like that which is suffered by man. Even the susceptibility to pain could reach its highest point only when, by virtue of our faculty of reason and its reflectiveness, there exists also the possibility of denying the will. For without that possibility, such susceptibility would have been purposeless cruelty.

In early youth we sit before the impending course of our life like children at the theater before the curtain is raised, who sit there in happy and excited expectation of the things that are to come. It is a blessing that we do not know what will actually come. For to the man who knows, the children may at times appear to be like innocent delinquents who are condemned not to death, it is true, but to life, and have not yet grasped the purport of their sentence. Nevertheless everyone wants to reach old age and thus to a state of life whereof it may be said: "It is bad today and every day it will get worse, until the worst of all happens."

If we picture to ourselves roughly as far as we can the sum total of misery, pain, and suffering of every kind on which the sun shines in its course, we shall admit that it would have been much better if it had been just as impossible for the sun to produce the phenomenon of life on earth as on the moon, and the surface of the earth, like that of the moon, had still been in a crystalline state.

We can also regard our life as a uselessly disturbing episode in the blissful repose of nothingness. At all events even the man who has fared tolerably well becomes more clearly aware, the longer he lives, that life on the whole is *a disappointment, nay a cheat,* in other words, bears the character of a great mystification or even a fraud. When two men who were friends in their youth meet again after the separation of a lifetime, the feeling uppermost in their minds when they see each other, in that it recalls old times, is one of complete *disappointment with the whole of life.* In former years under the rosy sunrise of their youth, life seemed to them so fair in prospect; it made so many promises and has kept so few. So definitely uppermost is this feeling when they meet that they do not even deem it necessary to express it in words, but both tacitly assume it and proceed to talk on that basis.

Whoever lives *two or three generations* feels like the spectator who, during the fair, sees the performances of all kinds of jugglers and, if he remains seated in the booth, sees them repeated two or three times. As the tricks were meant only for one performance, they no longer make any impression after the illusion and novelty have vanished.

We should be driven crazy if we contemplated the lavish and excessive arrangements, the countless flaming fixed stars in infinite space which have nothing to do but illuminate worlds, such being the scene of misery and desolation and, in the luckiest case, yielding nothing but boredom—at any rate to judge from the specimen with which we are familiar. No one is to be greatly *envied,* but many thousands are to be greatly *pitied.* Life is a task to be worked off; in this sense *defunctus* is a fine expression. Let us for a moment imagine that the act of procreation were not a necessity or accompanied by intense pleasure, but a matter of pure rational deliberation; could then the human race really continue to exist? Would not everyone rather feel so much sympathy for the coming generation that he would prefer to spare it the burden of existence, or at any rate would not like to assume in cold blood the responsibility of imposing on it such a burden? The world is just a *hell* and in it human beings are the tortured souls on the one hand, and the devils on the other.

I suppose I shall have to be told again that my philosophy is cheerless and comfortless simply because I tell the truth, whereas people want to hear that the Lord has made all things very well. Go to your churches and leave us philosophers in peace! At any rate, do not demand that they should cut their doctrines according to your pattern! This is done by knaves and philosophasters from whom you can order whatever doctrines you like. Brahma produces the world through a kind of original sin, but himself remains in it to atone for this until he has redeemed himself from it. This is quite a good idea! In Buddhism the world comes into being in consequence of an inexplicable disturbance (after a long period of calm) in the crystal clearness of the blessed and penitentially obtained state of Nirvana and hence through a kind of fatality which, however, is to be understood ultimately in a moral sense; although the matter has its exact analogue and corresponding picture in physics, in the inexplicable arising of a primordial nebula, whence a sun is formed. Accordingly, in consequence of moral lapses, it also gradually becomes physically worse and worse until it assumes its present sorry state. An excellent idea! To the Greeks the world and the gods were the work of an unfathomable necessity; this is fairly reasonable insofar as it satisfies us for the time being. [. . .] But that a God Jehovah creates this world of misery and affliction [. . .] and then applauds himself [. . .], this is something intolerable. [. . .] If Leibniz's demonstration were correct, that of all *possible* worlds this is nevertheless always the best, we should still not have a *Théodicée*, a defense of God's creation. For the Creator has created indeed not merely the world, but also the possibility itself; accordingly, he should have arranged this with a view to its admitting of a better world.

But generally, such a view of the world as the successful work of an all-wise, all-benevolent, and moreover almighty Being is too flagrantly contradicted by the misery and wretchedness that fill the world on the one hand, and by the obvious imperfection and even burlesque distortion of the most perfect of its phenomena on the other; I refer to the human phenomenon. Here is to be found a dissonance that can never be resolved. On the other hand, these very instances will agree with, and serve as a proof of, our argument if we look upon the world as the work of our own guilt and consequently as something that it were better never to have been. Whereas on the first assumption human beings become a bitter indictment against the Creator and provide material for sarcasm, they appear on the second as a denunciation of our own true nature and will, which is calculated to humble us. For they lead us to the view that we, as the offspring of dissolute fathers, have come into the world already burdened with guilt and that only because we have to be continually working off this debt does our existence prove to be so wretched and have death as its finale. Nothing is more certain than that, speaking generally, it is the great *sin of the world* which produces the many and great *sufferings of the world*; and here I refer not to the physically empirical connection, but to the metaphysical. According to this view, it is only the story of the Fall of Man that reconciles me to the Old Testament. In fact, in my eyes, it is the only metaphysical truth that appears in the book, although it is clothed in allegory. For to nothing does our existence bear so close a resemblance as to the consequence of a false step and guilty lust. I cannot refrain from recommending to the thoughtful reader a popular, but exceedingly profound, dissertation on this subject by Matthias Claudius which brings to light the essentially pessimistic spirit of Christianity and appears in the fourth part of the *Wandsbecker Bote* with the title "Cursed be the ground for thy sake."

To have always in hand a sure compass for guiding us in life and enabling us always to view this in the right light without ever going astray, nothing is more suitable than to accustom ourselves to regard this world as a place of penance and hence a penal colony, so to speak. [. . .] This view of the world also finds its theoretical and objective justification not merely in my philosophy, but in the wisdom of all ages, in Brahmanism, Buddhism, Empedocles, and Pythagoras. Cicero also mentions that it was taught by ancient sages and at the initiation into the Mysteries "That, on account of definite mistakes made in a previous life, we are born to pay the penalty." Nothing can be more conducive to patience in life and to a placid endurance of men and evils than a Buddhist reminder of this kind: "This is *Samsara*, the world of lust and craving and thus of birth, disease, old age, and death; it is a world that ought not to be. And this is here the population of *Samsara*. Therefore what better things can you expect?" I would like to prescribe that everyone repeat this four times a day, fully conscious of what he is saying.

But even in genuine Christianity which is properly understood, our existence is regarded as the consequence of a guilt, a false step. If we have acquired that habit, we shall adjust our expectations from life to suit the occasion and accordingly no longer regard as unexpected and abnormal its troubles, vexations, sufferings, worries, and misery, great and small. On the contrary, we shall find such things to be quite in order, well knowing that here everyone is punished for his existence and indeed each in his own way. For one of the evils of a penitentiary is also the society we meet there. What this is like will be known by anyone who is worthy of a better society without my telling him. A fine nature, as well as a genius, may sometimes feel in this world like a noble state-prisoner in the galleys among common criminals; and they, like him, will therefore attempt to isolate themselves. Generally speaking, however, the above-mentioned way of looking at things will enable us to regard without surprise and certainly without indignation the so-called imperfections, that is, the wretched and contemptible nature of most men both morally and intellectually, which is accordingly stamped on their faces. For we shall always remember where we are and consequently look on everyone primarily as a being who exists only as a result of his sinfulness and whose life is the atonement for the guilt of his birth. It is just this that Christianity calls the sinful nature of man. It is, therefore, the basis of the beings whom we meet in this world as our fellows. Moreover, in consequence of the constitution of the world, they are almost all, more or less, in a state of suffering and dissatisfaction which is not calculated to make them more sympathetic and amiable. Finally, there is the fact that, in almost all cases, their intellect is barely sufficient for the service of their will.

The correct standard for *judging any man* is to remember that he is really a being who should not exist at all, but who is atoning for his existence through many different forms of suffering and through death. What can we expect from such a being? We atone for our birth first by living and secondly by dying. This is also allegorized by *original sin.* [. . .] Accordingly, we have to regulate our claims on the society of this world. Whoever keeps firmly to this point of view might call the social impulse a pernicious tendency. In fact, the conviction that the world, and thus also man, is something that really ought not to be is calculated to fill us with forbearance towards one another; for what can we expect from beings in such a predicament? In fact, from this point of view, it might occur to us that the really proper address between one man and another should be, instead of *Sir, Monsieur,* and so on, *Leidensgefährte, socii malorum, compagnon de misères, my fellow sufferer.* However strange this may sound, it accords with the facts, puts the other man in the most correct light, and reminds us of that most necessary thing, tolerance, patience, forbearance, and love of one's neighbor, which everyone needs and each of us, therefore, owes to another.

The characteristic of the things of this world and especially of the world of men is not exactly *imperfection*, as has often been said, but rather *distortion*, in everything, in what is moral, intellectual, or physical. The excuse, sometimes made for many a vice, namely "that it is natural to man," is by no means adequate, but the proper rejoinder should be: "just because it is bad, it is *natural*; and just because it is *natural* it is bad." To understand this aright, we must have grasped the meaning of the doctrine of original sin. When judging a human individual, we should always keep to the point of view that the basis of such is something that ought not to be at all, something sinful, perverse, and absurd, that which has been understood as original sin, that on account of which he is doomed to die. This fundamentally bad nature is indeed characterized by the fact that no one can bear to be closely scrutinized. What can we expect from such a being? If, therefore, we start from this fact, we shall judge him more indulgently; we shall not be surprised when the devils lurking in him bestir themselves and peep out, and we shall be better able to appreciate any good point that has nevertheless been found in him, whether this be a consequence of his intellect or of anything else. In the second place, we should also be mindful of his position and remember that life is essentially a condition of want, distress, and often misery, where everyone has to fight and struggle for his existence and therefore cannot always put on a pleasant face. If, on the contrary, man were that which all optimistic religions and philosophies would like to make him, namely the work or even the incarnation of a God, in fact a being that in every sense ought to be and to be as he is, what a totally different effect would inevitably be produced by the first sight, the closer acquaintance, and the continued intercourse with every human being from that which is now produced!

Pardon's the word to all. [. . .] We should treat with indulgence every human folly, failing, and vice, bearing in mind that what we have before us are simply our own follies, failings, and vices. For they are just the failings of mankind to which we also belong; accordingly, we have in ourselves all its failings, and so those at which we are just now indignant, merely because they do not appear in us at this particular moment. Thus they are not on the surface, but lie deep down within us and will come up and show themselves on the first occasion, just as we see them in others; although one failing is conspicuous in one man and another in another, and the sum total of all bad qualities is undoubtedly very much greater in one man than in another. For the difference in individualities is incalculably great.

Two

On the Affirmation of the Will-to-Live

If the will-to-live exhibited itself merely as an impulse to self-preservation, that would be only an affirmation of the individual phenomenon for the span of time of its natural duration. The cares and troubles of such a life would not be great, and consequently existence would prove easy and cheerful. Since, on the contrary, the will wills life absolutely and for all time, it exhibits itself at the same time as sexual impulse, which has an endless series of generations in view. This impulse does away with that unconcern, cheerfulness, and innocence that would accompany a merely individual existence, since it brings into consciousness unrest, uneasiness, and melancholy, and into the course of life misfortunes, cares, and misery. On the other hand, if it is voluntarily suppressed, as we see in rare exceptions, then this is the turning of the will, which changes its course. It is then absorbed in, and does not go beyond, the individual; but this can happen only through his doing a painful violence to himself. If this has taken place, that unconcern and cheerfulness of the merely individual existence are restored to consciousness, and indeed raised to a higher power. On the other hand, tied up with the satisfaction of that strongest of all impulses and desires is the origin of a new existence, and hence the carrying out of life afresh with all its burdens, cares, wants, and pains, in *another* individual, it is true; yet if the two, who are different in the phenomenon, were such absolutely and in themselves, where then would eternal justice be found? Life presents itself as a problem, a task to be worked out, and in general therefore as a constant struggle against want and affliction. Accordingly everyone tries to get through with it and come off as well as he can; he disposes of life as he does of a compulsory service that he is in duty bound to carry out. But who has contracted this debt? His begetter, in the enjoyment of sensual pleasure. Therefore, because the one has enjoyed this pleasure, the other must live, suffer, and die. However, we know and look back to the fact that the difference of the homogeneous is conditioned by space and time, which I have called in this sense the *principium individuationis*; otherwise eternal justice would be irretrievably lost. Paternal love, by virtue of which the father is ready to do, to suffer, and to take a risk more for his child than for himself, and at the same time recognizes this as his obligation, is due to the very fact that the begetter recognizes himself once more in the begotten.

The life of a man, with its endless care, want, and suffering, is to be regarded as the explanation and paraphrase of the act of procreation, of the decided affirmation of the will-to-live. Further, it is also due to this that he owes nature the debt of death, and thinks of this debt with uneasiness. Is not this evidence of the fact that our existence involves guilt? But we certainly always exist on periodical payment of the toll, birth and death, and we enjoy successively all the sorrows and joys of life, so that none can escape us. This is just the fruit of the affirmation of the will-to-live. Thus the fear of death, which holds us firmly to life in spite of all its miseries, is really illusory; but just as illusory is the impulse that has enticed us into it. This enticement itself can be objectively perceived in the reciprocal longing glances of two lovers; they are the purest expression of the will-to-live in its affirmation. How gentle and tender it is here! It wills well-being, and quiet enjoyment, and mild pleasures for itself, for others, for all. This is the theme of Anacreon. Thus by allurement and flattery it works its way into life; but when it is in life, then misery introduces crime, and crime misery; horror and desolation fill the scene. This is the theme of Aeschylus.

But the act by which the will affirms itself and man comes into existence is one of which all in their heart of hearts are ashamed, and which therefore they carefully conceal; in fact, if they are caught in the act, they are as alarmed as if they had been detected in a crime. It is an action of which, on cool reflection, we think often with repugnance, and in an exalted mood with disgust. [. . .] A peculiar sadness and remorse follows close on it; yet these are felt most after the consummation of the act for the first time, and generally they are the more distinct, the nobler the character. Hence, even the pagan Pliny says: "Only man feels remorse after the first copulation; a course characteristic of life, that we feel remorse for our origin." On the other hand, in Goethe's *Faust*, what do devil and witches practice and sing on their Sabbath? Lewdness and obscene jokes. In the very same work (in the admirable Paralipomena to *Faust*), what does Satan incarnate preach before the assembled multitude? Lewdness and obscene talk, nothing more. But the human race continues to exist simply and solely by means of the constant practice of such an act as this. Now if optimism were right, if our existence were to be gratefully acknowledged as the gift of the highest goodness guided by wisdom, and accordingly, if it were in itself praiseworthy, commendable, and delightful, then certainly the act that perpetuates it would necessarily bear quite a different complexion. If, on the other hand, this existence is a kind of false step or wrong path, if it is the work of an originally blind will, the luckiest development of which is that it comes to itself in order to abolish itself, then the act perpetuating that existence must appear precisely as in fact it does.

With regard to the first fundamental truth of my teaching, the remark merits a place here that the above-mentioned shame over the business of procreation extends even to the parts that serve it, although, like all the other parts, they are given us by nature. Once again, this is a striking proof of the fact that not merely man's actions, but even his body, are to be regarded as the phenomenon, the objectification, of his *will*, and as its work. For he could not be ashamed of a thing that existed without his will.

The act of procreation is further related to the world as the solution is to the riddle. Thus the world is wide in space and old in time, and has an inexhaustible multiplicity of forms. Yet all this is only the phenomenon of the will-to-live; and the concentration, the focus of this will is the act of generation. Hence in this act the inner nature of the world most distinctly expresses itself. In this respect it is even worth noting that the act itself is also positively called "the will" in the very significant German phrase: *Er verlangte von ihr, sie sollte ihm zu Willen sein* (He expected her to be willing to serve him). Therefore that act, as the most distinct expression of the will, is the kernel, the compendium, the quintessence of the world; it is the solution to the riddle. Accordingly, it is understood by the "tree of knowledge"; for, after acquaintance with it, everyone begins to see life in its true light, as Byron (in *Don Juan*) also says: "The tree of knowledge has been pluck'd—all's known."

No less in keeping with this quality is the fact that it is the great "Unspeakable," the public secret which must never be distinctly mentioned anywhere, but is always and everywhere understood to be the main thing as a matter of course, and is therefore always present in the minds of all. For this reason, even the slightest allusion to it is instantly understood. The principal role played in the world by this act and by what is connected with it, because everywhere love-intrigues are pursued on the one hand, and assumed on the other, is quite in keeping with the importance of this *punctum saliens* of the world-egg. What is amusing is to be found only in the constant concealment of the main thing.

But see now how the young, innocent human intellect is startled at the enormity, when that great secret of the world first becomes known to it! The reason for this is that, on the long path that the will, originally without knowledge, had to traverse before it rose to intellect, especially to human, rational intellect, it became such a stranger to itself; and so it no longer knows its origin, that *poenitenda origo*, and from the standpoint of pure, hence innocent, knowledge is horrified thereat.

Now, as the focus of the will, that is to say, its concentration and highest expression, are the sexual impulse and its satisfaction, it is expressed very significantly and naively in the symbolical language of nature by the fact that individualized will, hence man and the animal, makes its entry into the world through the portal of the sexual organs.

The *affirmation of the will-to-live*, which accordingly has its center in the act of generation, is inevitable and bound to happen in the case of the animal. For the will that is the *natura naturans* first of all arrives at *reflection* in man. To arrive at reflection means not merely to know for the momentary need and necessity of the individual will, for its service in the urgent present moment—as is the case with the animal according to its completeness and its needs, which go hand in hand—but to have reached a greater breadth of knowledge, by virtue of a distinct recollection of the past, of an approximate anticipation of the future, and, in this way, of a comprehensive survey of the individual life, of one's own, of another, indeed of existence generally. Actually, the life of every animal species throughout the thousands of years of its existence is to a certain extent like a single moment; for it is mere consciousness of the *present* without that of the past and of the future, and consequently without that of death. In this sense it is to be regarded as a steady and enduring moment, a *Nunc stans*. Incidentally, we here see most distinctly that in general the form of life, or of the phenomenon of the will with consciousness, is primarily and immediately only the *present*. Past and future are added only in the case of man, and indeed only in the concept; they are known *in abstracto*, and are possibly illustrated by pictures of the imagination. Hence, after the will-to-live, i.e., the inner being of nature, has run through the whole series of animals in restless striving towards complete objectification and complete enjoyment—and this often happens at various intervals of successive animal series arising anew on the same planet—it ultimately arrives at *reflection* in the being endowed with the faculty of reason, namely man. Here the matter now begins to be grave and critical for him; the question forces itself on him whence is all this and for what purpose, and principally whether the trouble and misery of his life and effort are really repaid by the profit. Is the game worth the candle?

Accordingly, here is the point where, in the light of distinct knowledge, he decides for the affirmation or denial of the will-to-live, although he can as a rule bring the latter to consciousness only in a mythical cloak. Consequently, we have no ground for assuming that an even more highly developed objectification of the will is reached anywhere, for it has already reached its turning point here.

Three

On the Vanity and Suffering of Life

Awakened to life out of the night of unconsciousness, the will finds itself as an individual in an endless and boundless world, among innumerable individuals, all striving, suffering, and erring; and, as if through a troubled dream, it hurries back to the old unconsciousness. Yet till then its desires are unlimited, its claims inexhaustible, and every satisfied desire gives birth to a new one. No possible satisfaction in the world could suffice to still its craving, set a final goal to its demands, and fill the bottomless pit of its heart. In this connection, let us now consider what as a rule comes to man in satisfactions of any kind; it is often nothing more than the bare maintenance of this very existence, extorted daily with unremitting effort and constant care in conflict with misery and want, and with death in prospect. Everything in life proclaims that earthly happiness is destined to be frustrated, or recognized as an illusion. The grounds for this lie deep in the very nature of things. Accordingly, the lives of most people prove troubled and short. The comparatively happy are often only apparently so, or else, like those of long life, they are rare exceptions; the possibility of these still had to be left, as decoy-birds. Life presents itself as a continual deception, in small matters as well as in great. If it has promised, it does not keep its word, unless to show how little desirable the desired object was; hence we are deluded now by hope, now by what was hoped for. If it has given, it did so in order to take. The enchantment of distance shows us paradises that vanish like optical illusions, when we have allowed ourselves to be fooled by them. Accordingly, happiness lies always in the future, or else in the past, and the present may be compared to a small dark cloud driven by the wind over the sunny plain; in front of and behind the cloud everything is bright, only it itself always casts a shadow. Consequently, the present is always inadequate, but the future is uncertain, and the past irrecoverable. With its misfortunes, small, greater, and great, occurring hourly, daily, weekly, and yearly; with its deluded hopes and accidents bringing all calculations to naught, life bears so clearly the stamp of something which ought to disgust us that it is difficult to conceive how anyone could fail to recognize this, and be persuaded that life is here to be thankfully enjoyed, and that man exists in order to be happy. On the contrary, that continual deception and disillusionment, as well as the general nature of life, present themselves as intended and calculated to awaken the conviction that nothing whatever is worth our exertions, our efforts, and our struggles, that all good things are empty and fleeting, that the world on all sides is bankrupt, and that life is a business that does not cover the costs; so that our will may turn away from it.

The way in which this *vanity* of all objects of the will makes itself known and comprehensible to the intellect that is rooted in the individual is primarily *time*. It is the form by whose means that vanity of things appears as their transitoriness, since by virtue of this all our pleasures and enjoyments come to naught in our hands, and afterwards we ask in astonishment where they have remained. Hence that vanity itself is the only *objective* element of time, in other words, that which corresponds to it in the inner nature of things, and so that of which it is the expression. For this reason, time is the *a priori* necessary form of all our perceptions; everything must present itself in time, even we ourselves. Consequently, our life is primarily like a payment made to us in nothing but copper coins, for which we must then give a receipt; the coins are the days, and the receipt is death. For in the end time proclaims the judgment of nature on the worth of all beings that appear in it, since it destroys them. [. . .]

Thus old age and death, to which every life necessarily hurries, are a sentence of condemnation on the will-to-live which comes from the hands of nature herself. It states that this will is a striving that is bound to frustrate itself. "What you have willed," it says, "ends thus: will something better." Therefore the instruction afforded to everyone by his life consists on the whole in the fact that the objects of his desires constantly delude, totter, and fall; that in consequence they bring more misery than joy, until at last even the whole foundation on which they all stand collapses, since his life itself is destroyed. Thus he obtains the final confirmation that all his striving and willing was a perversity, a path of error:

> Then old age and experience, hand in hand,
> Lead him to death, and make him understand,
> After a search so painful and so long,
> That all his life he has been in the wrong.

But I wish to go into the matter in more detail, for it is these views in which I have met with most contradiction. First of all, I have to confirm by the following remarks the proof given in the text of the negative nature of all satisfaction, and hence of all pleasure and happiness, in opposition to the positive nature of pain.

We feel pain, but not painlessness; care, but not freedom from care; fear, but not safety and security. We feel the desire as we feel hunger and thirst; but as soon as it has been satisfied, it is like the mouthful of food which has been taken, and which ceases to exist for our feelings the moment it is swallowed. We painfully feel the loss of pleasures and enjoyments as soon as they fail to appear; but when pains cease, even after being present for a long time, their absence is not directly felt, but at most they are thought of intentionally by means of reflection. For only pain and want can be felt positively; and therefore they proclaim themselves; well-being, on the contrary, is merely negative. Therefore, we do not become conscious of the three greatest blessings of life as such, namely health, youth, and freedom, as long as we possess them, but only after we have lost them; for they too are negations. We notice that certain days of our life were happy only after they have made room for unhappy ones. In proportion as enjoyments and pleasures increase, susceptibility to them decreases; that to which we are accustomed is no longer felt as a pleasure. But in precisely this way is the susceptibility to suffering increased; for the cessation of that to which we are accustomed is felt painfully. Thus the measure of what is necessary increases through possession, and thereby the capacity to feel pain. The hours pass the more quickly the more pleasantly they are spent, and the more slowly the more pain-fully they are spent, since pain, not pleasure, is the positive thing, whose presence makes itself felt. In just the same way we become conscious of time when we are bored, not when we are amused. Both cases prove that our existence is happiest when we perceive it least; from this it follows that it would be better not to have it. Great and animated delight can be positively conceived only as the consequence of great misery that has preceded it; for nothing can be added to a state of permanent contentment except some amusement or even the satisfaction of vanity. Therefore, all poets are obliged to bring their heroes into anxious and painful situations, in order to be able to lib-erate them therefrom again. Accordingly, dramas and epics generally describe only fighting, suffering, tormented men and women, and every work of fiction is a peep show in which we observe the spasms and convulsions of the agonized human heart. Sir Walter Scott has naively set forth this aesthetic necessity in the "Conclusion" to his novel *Old Mortality*. Voltaire, so highly favored by nature and good fortune, also says, entirely in agreement with the truth I have demonstrated: "Happiness is only a dream, and pain is real. [. . .] I have experienced this for eighty years. I know of nothing better than to resign myself to this and to say that flies are born to be eaten by spiders, and men to be devoured by trouble and affliction."

Before we state so confidently that life is desirable or merits our gratitude, let us for once calmly compare the sum of the pleasures which are in any way possible, and which a man can enjoy in his life, with the sum of the sufferings which are in any way possible, and can come to him in his life. I do not think it will be difficult to strike the balance. In the long run, however, it is quite superfluous to dispute whether there is more good or evil in the world; for the mere existence of evil decides the matter, since evil can never be wiped off, and consequently can never be balanced, by the good that exists along with or after it. [. . .]

For that thousands had lived in happiness and joy would never do away with the anguish and death-agony of one individual; and just as little does my present well-being undo my previous sufferings. Therefore, were the evil in the world even a hundred times less than it is, its mere existence would still be sufficient to establish a truth that may be expressed in various ways, although always only somewhat indirectly, namely that we have not to be pleased but rather sorry about the existence of the world; that its nonexistence would be preferable to its existence; that it is something which at bottom ought not to be. [. . .]

If the world and life were an end in themselves, and accordingly were to require theoretically no justification, and practically no compensation or amends, but existed, perhaps as represented by Spinoza and present-day Spinozists, as the single manifestation of a God who, *animi causa*, or even to mirror himself, undertook such an evolution of himself, and consequently its existence needed neither to be justified by reasons nor redeemed by results—then the sufferings and troubles of life would not indeed have to be fully compensated by the pleasures and well-being in it. For, as I have said, this is impossible, because my present pain is never abolished by future pleasures, since the latter fill up their time just as the former fills its own. On the contrary, there would have to be no sufferings at all, and of necessity there would also not be death, or else it would have no terrors for us. Only thus would life pay for itself.

Now since our state or condition is rather something that it were better should not be, everything that surrounds us bears the traces of this—just as in hell everything smells of sulfur—since everything is always imperfect and deceptive, everything agreeable is mixed with something disagreeable, every enjoyment is always only half an enjoyment, every gratification introduces its own disturbance, every relief new worries and troubles, every expedient for our daily and hourly needs leaves us in the lurch at every moment and denies its service. The step on to which we tread so often gives way under us; in fact, misfortunes and accidents great and small are the element of our life, and in a word, we are like Phineus, all of whose food was contaminated and rendered unfit to eat by the Harpies. All that we lay hold on resists us, because it has a will of its own which must be overcome. Two remedies for this are tried; firstly prudence, foresight, cunning; it does not teach us fully, is not sufficient, and comes to naught. Secondly, stoical equanimity, seeking to disarm every misfortune by preparedness for all and contempt for everything; in practice, this becomes cynical renunciation which prefers to reject once and for all every means of help and every alleviation. It makes us dogs, like Diogenes in his tub. The truth is that we ought to be wretched, and are so. The chief source of the most serious evils affecting man is man himself; *homo homini lupus*: Man is a wolf for man. He who keeps this last fact clearly in view beholds the world as a hell, surpassing that of Dante by the fact that one man must be the devil of another. For this purpose, of course, one is more fitted than another, indeed an arch-fiend is more fitted than all the rest, and appears in the form of a conqueror; he sets several hundred thousand men, facing one another, and exclaims to them: "To suffer and die is your destiny; now shoot one another with musket and cannon!" and they do so. In general, however, the conduct of men towards one another is characterized as a rule by injustice, extreme unfairness, hardness, and even cruelty; an opposite course of conduct appears only by way of exception. The necessity for the State and for legislation rests on this fact, and not on your shifts and evasions. But in all cases not lying within the reach of the law, we see at once a lack of consideration for his like which is peculiar to man, and springs from his boundless egoism, and sometimes even from wickedness. How man deals with man is seen, for example, in Negro slavery, the ultimate object of which is sugar and coffee. However, we need not go so far; to enter at the age of five a cotton-spinning or other factory, and from then on to sit there every day first ten, then twelve, and finally fourteen hours, and perform the same mechanical work, is to purchase dearly the pleasure of drawing breath. But this is the fate of millions, and many more millions have an analogous fate.

We others, however, can be made perfectly miserable by trifling incidents, but perfectly happy by nothing in the world. Whatever we may say, the happiest moment of the happy man is that of his falling asleep, just as the unhappiest moment of the unhappy man is that of his awaking. An indirect but certain proof of the fact that people feel unhappy, and consequently are so, is also abundantly afforded by the terrible envy that dwells in all. In all the circumstances of life, on the occasion of every superiority or advantage, of whatever kind it be, this envy is roused and cannot contain its poison. Because people feel unhappy, they cannot bear the sight of one who is supposed to be happy. Whoever feels happy for the moment would at once like to make all around him happy and says: "May everyone here be happy in my joy."

If life in itself were a precious blessing, and decidedly preferable to nonexistence, the exit from it would not need to be guarded by such fearful watchmen as death and its terrors. But who would go on living life as it is, if death were less terrible? And who could bear even the mere thought of death, if life were a pleasure? But the former still always has the good point of being the end of life, and we console ourselves with death in regard to the sufferings of life, and with the sufferings of life in regard to death. The truth is that the two belong to each other inseparably, since they constitute a deviation from the right path, and a return to this is as difficult as it is desirable.

If the world were not something that, *practically* expressed, ought not to be, it would also not be *theoretically* a problem. On the contrary, its existence would either require no explanation at all, since it would be so entirely self-evident that astonishment at it and inquiry about it could not arise in any mind; or its purpose would present itself unmistakably. But instead of this it is indeed an insoluble problem, since even the most perfect philosophy will always contain an unexplained element, like an insoluble precipitate or the remainder that is always left behind by the irrational proportion of two quantities. Therefore, if anyone ventures to raise the question why there is not nothing at all rather than this world, then the world cannot be justified from itself; no ground, no final cause of its existence can be found in itself; it cannot be demonstrated that it exists for its own sake, in other words, for its own advantage. In pursuance of my teaching, this can, of course, be explained from the fact that the principle of the world's existence is expressly a groundless one, namely a blind will-to-live, which, as *thing-in-itself*, cannot be subject to the principle of sufficient reason or ground; for this principle is merely the form of phenomena, and through it alone every why is justified. But this is also in keeping with the nature and constitution of the world, for only a blind, not a seeing, will could put itself in the position in which we find ourselves. On the contrary, a seeing will would soon have made the calculation that the business does not cover the costs, since such a mighty effort and struggle with the exertion of all one's strength, under constant care, anxiety, and want, and with the inevitable destruction of every individual life, finds no compensation in the ephemeral existence itself, which is obtained by such effort, and comes to nothing in our hands. Therefore, the explanation of the world from the *nous* of Anaxagoras, in other words, from a will guided by *knowledge*, necessarily demands for its extenuation optimism, which is then set up and maintained in spite of the loudly crying evidence of a whole world full of misery. Life is then given out as a gift, whereas it is evident that anyone would have declined it with thanks, had he looked at it and tested it beforehand; just as Lessing admired the understanding of his son. Because this son had absolutely declined to come into the world, he had to be dragged forcibly into life by means of forceps; but hardly was he in it, when he again hurried away from it. On the other hand, it is well said that life should be, from one end to the other, only a lesson, to which, however, anyone could reply: "For this reason, I wish I had been left in the peace of the all-sufficient nothing, where I should have had no need either of lessons or of anything else." But if it were added that one day he was to give an account of every hour of his life, he would rather be justified in first himself asking for an account as to why he was taken away from that peace and quiet and put into a position so precarious, obscure, anxious, and painful. To this, then, false fundamental views lead. Far from bearing the character of a *gift*, human existence has entirely the character of a contracted *debt*. The calling in of this debt appears in the shape of the urgent needs, tormenting desires, and endless misery brought about through that existence. As a rule, the whole lifetime is used for paying off this debt, yet in this way only the interest is cleared off. Repayment of the capital takes place through death. And when was this debt contracted? At the begetting.

Accordingly, if man is regarded as a being whose existence is a punishment and an atonement, then he is already seen in a more correct light. The myth of the Fall of Man [. . .] is the only thing in the Old Testament to which I can concede a metaphysical, although only allegorical, truth; indeed it is this alone that reconciles me to the Old Testament. Thus our existence resembles nothing but the consequence of a false step and a guilty desire. New Testament Christianity, the ethical spirit of which is that of Brahmanism and Buddhism, and which is therefore very foreign to the otherwise optimistic spirit of the Old Testament, has also, extremely wisely, started from that very myth; in fact, without this, it would not have found one single point of connection with Judaism. If we wish to measure the degree of guilt with which our existence itself is burdened, let us look at the suffering connected with it. Every great pain, whether bodily or mental, states what we deserve; for it could not come to us if we did not deserve it. That Christianity also looks at our existence in this light is proved by a passage from Luther's *Commentary on Galatians*: "In our bodies and circumstances, however, we are all subject to the devil and are strangers in this world, of which he is prince and lord. Hence everything is under his rule, the bread we eat, the beverage we drink, the clothes we use, even the air and everything by which we live in the flesh." An outcry has been raised about the melancholy and cheerless nature of my philosophy; but this is to be found merely in the fact that, instead of inventing a future hell as the equivalent of sins, I have shown that where guilt is to be found, there is already in the world something akin to hell; but he who is inclined to deny this can easily experience it.

This world is the battleground of tormented and agonized beings who continue to exist only by each devouring the other. Therefore, every beast of prey in it is the living grave of thousands of others, and its self-maintenance is a chain of torturing deaths. Then in this world the capacity to feel pain increases with knowledge, and therefore reaches its highest degree in man, a degree that is the higher, the more intelligent the man. To this world the attempt has been made to adapt the system of *optimism*, and to demonstrate to us that it is the best of all possible worlds. The absurdity is glaring. However, an optimist tells me to open my eyes and look at the world and see how beautiful it is in the sunshine, with its mountains, valleys, rivers, plants, animals, and so on. But is the world, then, a peep show? These things are certainly beautiful to *behold*, but to *be* them is something quite different. A teleologist then comes along and speaks to me in glowing terms about the wise arrangement by virtue of which care is taken that the planets do not run their heads against one another; that land and sea are not mixed up into pulp, but are held apart in a delightful way; also that everything is neither rigid in continual frost nor roasted with heat; likewise that, in consequence of the obliquity of the ecliptic, there is not an eternal spring in which nothing could reach maturity, and so forth. But this and everything like it are indeed mere *conditiones sine quibus non*. If there is to be a world at all, if its planets are to exist at least as long as is needed for the ray of light from a remote fixed star to reach them, and are not, like Lessing's son, to depart again immediately after birth, then of course it could not be constructed so unskillfully that its very framework would threaten to collapse. But if we proceed to the results of the applauded work, if we consider the players who act on the stage so durably constructed, and then see how with sensibility pain makes its appearance, and increases in proportion as that sensibility develops into intelligence, and then how, keeping pace with this, desire and suffering come out ever more strongly, and increase, till at last human life affords no other material than that for tragedies and comedies, then whoever is not a hypocrite will hardly be disposed to break out into hallelujahs. The real but disguised origin of these latter has moreover been exposed, mercilessly but with triumphant truth, by David Hume in his *Natural History of Religion*. He also explains without reserve in the tenth and eleventh books of his *Dialogues Concerning Natural Religion*, with arguments very convincing yet quite different from mine, the miserable nature of this world and the untenableness of all optimism; here at the same time he attacks optimism at its source. [. . .]

Again, the founder of systematic *optimism* is Leibniz, whose services to philosophy I have no wish to deny, although I could never succeed in really thinking myself into the monadology, preestablished harmony, and *identitas indiscernibilium* (the principle of Leibniz according to which two indistinguishable things are identical). [. . .] I cannot assign to the *Théodicée*, that methodical and broad development of optimism, in such a capacity, any other merit than that it later gave rise to the immortal *Candide* of the great Voltaire. In this way, of course, Leibniz's oft-repeated and lame excuse for the evil of the world, namely that the bad sometimes produces the good, obtained proof that for him was unexpected. Even by the name of his hero, Voltaire indicated that it needed only sincerity to recognize the opposite of optimism. Actually, optimism cuts so strange a figure on this scene of sin, suffering, and death, that we should be forced to regard it as irony if we did not have an adequate explanation of its origin in its secret source (namely hypocritical flattery with an offensive confidence in its success), a source so delightfully disclosed by Hume, as previously mentioned.

But against the palpably sophistical proofs of Leibniz that this is the best of all possible worlds, we may even oppose seriously and honestly the proof that it is the *worst* of all possible worlds. For possible means not what we may picture in our imagination, but what can actually exist and last. Now this world is arranged as it had to be if it were to be capable of continuing with great difficulty to exist; if it were a little worse, it would be no longer capable of continuing to exist. Consequently, since a worse world could not continue to exist, it is absolutely impossible; and so this world itself is the worst of all possible worlds. For not only if the planets ran their heads against one another, but also if any one of the actually occurring perturbations of their course continued to increase, instead of being gradually balanced again by the others, the world would soon come to an end. Astronomers know on what accidental circumstances—in most cases on the irrational relation to one another of the periods of revolution—all this depends. They have carefully calculated that it will always go on well, and consequently that the world can also last and go on. Although Newton was of the opposite opinion, we will hope that the astronomers have not miscalculated, and consequently that the mechanical perpetual motion realized in such a planetary system will also not, like the rest, ultimately come to a standstill. Again, powerful forces of nature dwell under the firm crust of the planet. As soon as some accident affords these free play, they must necessarily destroy that crust with everything living on it. This has occurred at least three times on our planet, and will probably occur even more frequently. The earthquake of Lisbon, of Haiti, the destruction of Pompeii are only small, playful hints at the possibility. An insignificant alteration of the atmosphere, not even chemically demonstrable, causes cholera, yellow fever, black death, and so on, which carry off millions of people; a somewhat greater alteration would extinguish all life. A very moderate increase of heat would dry up all rivers and springs. The animals have received barely enough in the way of organs and strength to enable them with the greatest exertion to procure sustenance for their own lives and food for their offspring. Therefore, if an animal loses a limb, or even only the complete use of it, it is in most cases bound to perish. Powerful as are the weapons of understanding and reason possessed by the human race, nine-tenths of mankind live in constant conflict with want, always balancing themselves with difficulty and effort on the brink of destruction. Thus throughout, for the continuance of the whole as well as for that of every individual being, the conditions are sparingly and scantily given, and nothing beyond these. Therefore the individual life is a ceaseless struggle for existence itself, while at every step it is threatened with destruction. Just because this threat is so often carried out, provision had to be made, by the incredibly great surplus of seed, that the destruction of individuals should not bring about that of the races, since about these alone is nature seriously concerned. Consequently, the world is as bad as it can possibly be, if it is to exist at all. [. . .]

At bottom, optimism is the unwarranted self-praise of the real author of the world, namely of the will-to-live which complacently mirrors itself in its work. Accordingly, optimism is not only a false but also a pernicious doctrine, for it presents life as a desirable state and man's happiness as its aim and object. Starting from this, everyone then believes he has the most legitimate claim to happiness and enjoyment. If, as usually happens, these do not fall to his lot, he believes that he suffers an injustice, in fact that he misses the whole point of his existence; whereas it is far more correct to regard work, privation, misery, and suffering, crowned by death, as the aim and object of our life (as is done by Brahmanism and Buddhism, and also by genuine Christianity), since it is these that lead to the denial of the will-to-live. In the New Testament, the world is presented as a vale of tears, life as a process of purification, and the symbol of Christianity is an instrument of torture. Therefore, when Leibniz, Shaftesbury,

Bolingbroke, and Pope appeared with *optimism*, the general offense caused by it was due mainly to the fact that optimism is irreconcilable with Christianity. This is stated and explained by Voltaire in the preface to his excellent "Poem on the Lisbon Disaster," which also is expressly directed against optimism. [. . .]

If in conclusion, to confirm my view, I wished to record the sayings of great minds of all ages in this sense, which is opposed to optimism, there would be no end to the citations: for almost every one of them has expressed in strong terms his knowledge of the world's misery. Hence at the end of this chapter a few statements of this kind may find a place, not to confirm, but merely to embellish it.

First of all, let me mention here that, remote as the Greeks were from the Christian and lofty Asiatic worldview, and although they were decidedly at the standpoint of the affirmation of the will, they were nevertheless deeply affected by the wretchedness of existence. The invention of tragedy, which belongs to them, is already evidence of this. Another proof of it is given by the custom of the Thracians, first mentioned by Herodotus, and often referred to later, of welcoming the newborn child with lamentation, and recounting all the evils that face it, and, on the other hand, of burying the dead with mirth and merriment, because they have escaped from so many great sufferings. [. . .] It is to be attributed not to historical relationship, but to the moral identity of the matter, that the Mexicans welcomed the newborn child with the words: "My child, you are born to endure; therefore endure, suffer, and keep silence." And in pursuance of the same feeling, Swift (as Sir Walter Scott relates in his *Life of Swift*) early adopted the custom of celebrating his birthday not as a time of joy, but of sadness, and of reading on that day the passage from the Bible where Job laments and curses the day on which it was said in the house of his father that a man-child is born. Well known [. . .] is the passage in the *Apology of Socrates* where Plato represents this wisest of mortals as saying that, even if death deprived us of consciousness forever, it would be a wonderful gain, for a deep, dreamless sleep is to be preferred to any day, even of the happiest life.

Balthasar Gracián also brings before our eyes the misery of our existence in the darkest colors in the *Criticón*, [. . .] where he presents life in detail as a tragic farce. But no one has treated this subject so thoroughly and exhaustively as Leopardi in our own day. He is entirely imbued and penetrated with it; everywhere his theme is the mockery and wretchedness of this existence. He presents it on every page of his works, yet in such a multiplicity of forms and applications, with such a wealth of imagery, that he never wearies us, but, on the contrary, has a diverting and stimulating effect.

Four

Freedom of the Will

I was glad to recall to the reader all those glorious, poetical as well as philosophical, predecessors who stood for the truth which I also defend. However, it is not authorities but reasons that constitute the philosopher's weapon. Consequently, in defending my case I relied on reasons alone and yet hope to have supplied enough evidence to justify me fully in drawing the conclusion *a non posse ad non esse* (from impossibility to nonexistence) [   ]

The truth which I defend may be one of those to which the preconceived opinions of the shortsighted masses are opposed. Indeed, it may be offensive to the weak and the ignorant. But this must not keep me from presenting it without circumlocutions and without reserve, seeing that I am not talking here to the populace but to an enlightened Academy, which has posed its very timely question not for the sake of strengthening prejudice, but to honor the truth. Moreover, as long as it is a matter of establishing and confirming the truth, the honest seeker will always look to its grounds alone and not to its consequences. The time for that will come when the truth itself is established. Unconcerned about the consequences, we are only to examine our grounds, without first asking whether a recognized truth is or is not in harmony with the system of our other convictions. This is what Kant recommends, whose words I cannot refrain from repeating here:

This strengthens the maxim, already known and recommended by others, that in every scientific investigation we should unswervingly pursue our course with all possible accuracy and candor without attending to any extraneous difficulties it might involve, carrying out as far as we can our investigation by itself honestly and completely. Frequent observation has convinced me that once one has seen through such business, that which, when half-finished, appeared very dubious in view of extraneous theories is at last found to be in an unexpected way completely harmonious with that which had been discovered separately without the least regard for them, provided this dubiousness is left out of sight for a while and only the business at hand is attended to until it is finished. Writers would save themselves many errors and much labor lost (because spent on delusions) if they could only resolve to go to work with a little more ingenuousness (from *Critique of Practical Reason*).

Our metaphysical knowledge in general is still infinitely far from being so certain that one could afford to reject any thoroughly proper truth simply because its consequences do not fit in with that knowledge. It is rather the case that every attained and established truth is conquered territory in the realm of problems of knowledge in general. As such it is a firm point at which we may apply the lever which will move other loads and from which, in favorable cases, one may indeed soar all at once to a higher view of the whole than one had hitherto. For the concatenation of the truths in every area of knowledge is so great that one who has gained a completely firm possession of a single truth may possibly hope to conquer the whole from there. As in a difficult algebraic problem a single positively given magnitude is of inestimable value because it makes the solution possible, so in the most difficult of all human problems, which is metaphysics, such an inestimable datum is the certain knowledge, proved *a priori* and *a posteriori*, of the strict necessity with which acts follow from a given character and given motives. From this datum alone, using it as a starting point, we can arrive at the solution of the entire problem. Hence everything for which a firm, scientific verification cannot be produced must yield to such a well-founded truth, if it stands in its way, and not the other way around. And such a truth must by no means be subjected to accommodations and limitations in order to be harmonized with unproved and perhaps erroneous assertions.

Let me make still another general remark. A retrospect on our result occasions the observation that in respect to the two problems—already designated in the previous section of this essay as the deepest problems of modern philosophy (although not clearly apprehended by the ancients), namely, the problem of the freedom of the will and the problem of the relation between the ideal and the real—the healthy but untutored mind is not only incompetent, but even has a decided natural tendency to error. To free it of this error a highly developed philosophy is required. For in matters concerning cognition it is really natural for that mind to attribute altogether too much to the object. Therefore it took Locke and Kant to show how much of this arises from the subject. With respect to the will on the other hand, such a mind has the opposite tendency, to attribute too little to the object and too much to the subject. It makes the willing proceed exclusively from the subject, without taking proper account of the factor located in the object, that is, of the motives which really determine the entire individual character of actions. Only the general and essential aspect of actions, namely, their basic moral character, proceeds from the subject. However, such a perversity in speculative investigations, natural to the mind, should not surprise us, for originally the mind is designed only for practical and by no means for speculative purposes.

The result of our preceding exposition was to recognize the complete annulment of all freedom of human action and its thoroughgoing subjection to the strictest necessity. But it is precisely by this route that we are now led to the point where we shall be able to grasp the true moral freedom, which is of a higher sort.

For there is another fact of consciousness which until now I have left completely aside in order not to interfere with the process of my investigation. This is the wholly clear and certain feeling of the *responsibility* for what we do, of the accountability for our actions, which rests on the unshakable certainty that we ourselves are the doers of our deeds. By virtue of this consciousness it will never enter the head of even the one who is fully convinced of the necessity (set forth above) with which our actions take place to make this necessity excuse a transgression and to shift the blame from himself to the motives, arguing that when they entered in the act was inevitable. For he sees very clearly that this necessity has a subjective condition, and that objectively, that is, under the existing circumstances, hence under the influence of the motives which determined him, a quite different action, indeed, an action exactly opposite to the one he performed, was quite possible and could have happened, *if only he had been another*—this alone kept him from doing something else. To him, because he is this man and no other, because he has such and such a character, no different action was of course possible; but in itself, i.e., objectively, it *was* possible. So the responsibility of which he is conscious falls upon the act only provisionally and ostensibly, but basically it falls upon *his character*—for this he feels responsible. And it is for his character that the others also make him responsible; their verdict immediately abandons the act in order to establish the characteristics of the agent: "he is a bad man, a villain," or "he is a rascal," or "he is a small, false, despicable soul"—thus runs their verdict, and their reproaches fall back on his character. The act, together with motive, is considered in this connection only as a witness to the agent's character, but is nevertheless regarded as a sure symptom of the latter, through which it is irrevocably and forever established.

Aristotle says therefore quite correctly: "Hence it is only when a man has already done something that we bestow *encomiums* upon him. Yet the actual deeds are evidence of the doer's character: even if a man has not actually done a given good thing, we shall bestow *praise* on him, if we are sure that he is the sort of man who *would* do it." So hate, abhorrence, and contempt do not descend on the transitory act, but on the persisting characteristics of the agent, that is, on the character from which they issued. This explains why in all languages the epithets of moral badness, the abusive names which describe it, are predicates of men rather than of their actions. They are attached to the character, and the character must bear the guilt of which it has been convicted merely on the strength of its acts.

Where guilt lies, there responsibility must lie also, and since the latter is the only datum which entitles us to infer moral freedom, freedom must also have the same location, namely, in the character of man; the more so since we convinced ourselves sufficiently that it cannot be found immediately in individual actions, which take place with strict necessity when the character is assumed. But character [. . .] is inborn and unchangeable.

Let us now view somewhat more closely the freedom interpreted in this sense, the only sense for which the data are before us, in order, having inferred it from a fact of consciousness and found its location, to grasp it philosophically too, as far as that may be possible.

The result reached through earlier inquiry was that every action of a man is the product of two factors: his character along with a motive. This by no means signifies something which lies midway, a compromise as it were, between the motive and the character. No, it does full justice to both, as, in accordance with its total possibility, it rests on both at the same time in this way: the acting motive encounters this particular character, and this character is determinable by such a motive. The character is the empirically recognized, persistent, and unchangeable nature of an individual will. Since this character is just as necessary a factor of each action as is the motive, this fact explains the feeling that our acts proceed from ourselves, or explains that "I will" which accompanies all our actions and by virtue of which everyone must recognize them as *his* actions, for which he therefore feels morally responsible. But this is again that "I will, and will always only that which I will"—encountered above in the examination of the self-consciousness—which misleads the untutored understanding into maintaining stubbornly an absolute freedom of commission and omission, a *liberum arbitrium indifferentiae*. However, this is nothing more than the consciousness of the second factor of the action, which by itself would be quite incapable of bringing it about and which, on the other hand, is just as incapable of refraining from it after a motive appears. But only as it is thus put into action does it reveal its own nature to the cognitive faculty. This faculty, essentially directed outward, not inward, actually learns the nature of its own will only from its actions, empirically. What one calls conscience is really this closer and progressively more intimate acquaintance. For just this reason conscience makes itself heard directly only after the action. Prior to that it speaks, at most, only indirectly as it deliberates about a future occurrence by means of reflection and review of similar cases on which it has already declared itself.

This is the place for a reminder of the illustration already mentioned in the previous section. It was Kant's presentation of the relation between the empirical and the intelligible character and thereby of the possibility of uniting freedom with necessity. It is one of the most beautiful and profound ideas brought forth by that great mind, or indeed by men at any time. I need only to refer to it, because to repeat it here would be unnecessary and lengthy. But it is only with its help that it is possible to comprehend, insofar as human powers can, how the strict necessity of our actions nevertheless coexists with that freedom to which the feeling of responsibility testifies and by virtue of which we are the agents of our acts, these actions being morally ascribable to us.

That relation of the empirical to the intelligible character demonstrated by Kant rests entirely on that which constitutes the basic feature of his whole philosophy, namely, on the distinction between appearance and thing-in-itself. As for him the complete empirical reality of the world of experience coexists with its transcendental ideality, so the strict empirical necessity of action coexists with its transcendental freedom. For the empirical character, like the whole man, is a mere appearance as an object of experience, and hence bound to the forms of all appearance—time, space, and causality—and subject to their laws. On the other hand, the condition and the basis of this whole appearance—which as a thing-in-itself is independent of these forms and therefore is not subject to time distinctions but is persistent and unchangeable—is his intelligible character, i.e., his will as thing-in-itself. It is to the will in this capacity that freedom, and to be sure even absolute freedom, that is, independence of the law of causality (as a mere form of appearances), properly belongs.

This freedom, however, is transcendental, i.e., it does not occur in appearance. It is present only insofar as we abstract from the appearance and from all its forms in order to reach that which, since it is outside of all time, must be thought of as the inner being of man-in-himself. By virtue of this freedom all acts of man are of his own making, no matter how necessarily they proceed from the empirical character when it encounters the motives. This is so because the empirical character is only the appearance of the intelligible character, in our cognitive faculty as bound to time, space, and causality—i.e., the manner in which the essence-in-itself of our own self presents itself to this faculty. Accordingly, the will is of course free, but only in itself and outside of appearance. In appearance, on the contrary, it presents itself already with a definite character, with which all of its actions are in conformity and therefore, when further determined by the supervening motives, must turn out thus and not otherwise.

As can easily be seen, this road leads to the view that we must no longer seek the work of our freedom in our individual actions, as the general opinion does, but in the whole being and essence (*existentia et essentia*) of the man himself. This must be thought of as his free act, which only presents itself to the cognitive faculty as linked to time, space, and causality in a multiplicity and variety of actions. But precisely because of the original unity of that which manifests itself in them, all actions must have exactly the same character and therefore appear as strictly necessitated in each case by the motives by which they are called forth and determined in detail. Accordingly, for the world of experience the *operari sequitur esse* is firmly established without exception. Everything acts according to its nature, and its acts as they respond to causes make this nature known. Every man acts according to what he is, and the action, which is accordingly necessary in each case, is determined solely by the motives in the individual case.

The freedom which therefore cannot be encountered in the *operari* must lie in the *esse*. It has been a fundamental error of all ages, an unwarranted inversion, to attribute necessity to the *esse* and freedom to the *operari*. The converse is true: freedom lies in the *esse* alone, but the *operari* follows necessarily from it and the motives. *From what we do we know what we are*. On this, and not on the presumed *liberum arbitrium indifferentiae*, rests the consciousness of responsibility and the moral tendency of life. Everything depends on what one is; what he does will follow therefrom of itself, as a necessary corollary. The consciousness of self-determination and originality which undeniably accompanies all our acts, and by virtue of which they are *our* acts, is therefore not deceptive, in spite of their dependence on motives. But its true content reaches further than the acts and begins higher up. In truth it includes our being and essence itself, from which all acts proceed necessarily when motives arise. In this sense that consciousness of self-determination and originality, as well as the consciousness of responsibility accompanying our actions, can be compared to a hand which points to an object more remote than the one nearer by to which it seems to be pointing.

In a word: man does at all times only what he wills, and yet he does this necessarily. But this is due to the fact that he already *is* what he wills. For from that which he *is*, there follows of necessity everything that he, at any time, *does*. If we consider his behavior objectively, i.e., from the outside, we shall be bound to recognize that, like the behavior of every natural being, it must be subject to the law of causality in all its severity. Subjectively, however, everyone feels that he always does only what he wills. But this merely means that his activity is a pure expression of his very own being. Every natural being, even the lowest, would feel the same, if it could feel.

Consequently, my exposition does not eliminate freedom. It merely moves it out, namely, out of the area of simple actions, where it demonstrably cannot be found, up to a region which lies higher, but is not so easily accessible to our knowledge. In other words, freedom is transcendental. [. . .]

In the very beginning I introduced a division of freedom into physical, intellectual, and moral freedom. The first and the last have been discussed, and now I still have to examine the second. This is to be done merely for the sake of completeness, hence very briefly.

The intellect, or the cognitive faculty, is the medium of motives. Through this medium they act on the will, which is the real essence of man. Only insofar as this medium of motives is in a normal state, performs its function correctly, and hence puts before the choosing will the motives undistorted, as they are in the real external world, can this will decide according to its nature, that is, according to the man's individual character. In such a case it can express itself unconstrained, in accordance with its own essence. The man is then *intellectually* free, that is, his actions are the pure result of the reaction of his will to motives which are present to him in the external world as they are to others. Accordingly, actions must be charged up to him, both morally and legally.

This intellectual freedom is eliminated either when the medium of the motives—the cognitive faculty—is permanently or temporarily disarranged, or when in an individual case external circumstances falsify the comprehension of the motives. The former happens in madness, delirium, paroxysm, and somnolence, the latter in the case of definite and innocent error, for instance, when a man fills a glass with poison instead of medicine, or when he mistakes a servant entering at night for a burglar and shoots him, etc. For in both cases the motives are falsified and because of this the will cannot decide as it would decide had the intellect correctly reported to it the actual circumstances. Crimes committed under such circumstances are therefore not legally punishable. For the laws proceed from the correct assumption that the will is not morally free—in which case one could not guide it—but is subject to constraint by motives. Accordingly, by threat of punishment the laws want to confront all motives to crime with stronger countermotives. A criminal code is nothing but a list of countermotives to criminal actions. But if the intellect, through which these countermotives have to act, was incapable of grasping them and holding them up to the will, then their action was impossible: they did not exist for that will. It is as when one finds out that one of the wires required to move a machine is broken. Consequently, in such cases the guilt is transferred to the intellect. Intellect, however, is not subject to punishment; laws, as well as morality, have to do only with the will. It alone is the authentic man, while the intellect is merely its organ, its antennae to the outside, i.e., the medium for the action of motives upon it.

Just as little are such acts to be morally imputed. For they are not a feature of a man's character. Either he did something different from what he believed himself to be doing, or he was incapable of thinking of that which should have kept him from doing it, i.e., he was incapable of admitting countermotives. This is analogous to what may happen in investigating the chemical composition of a substance. A substance is exposed to the influence of several reagents in order to find out to which it has the strongest affinity. If after the completion of the experiment one should find that accidentally one of the reagents could not act at all, the experiment is invalid. Intellectual freedom, which in the above instance we regarded as completely eliminated, sometimes may be merely diminished, or eliminated only to some extent. This happens especially in passion and in intoxication. Passion is the sudden, violent excitation of the will by means of an idea which penetrates from the outside and becomes a motive. This idea possesses such a vivacity that it obscures all others which could work against it as countermotives and keeps them from entering clearly into consciousness. While the latter are for the most part only of an abstract nature, i.e., mere thoughts, the former idea is something perceptibly actual. Consequently, the countermotives do not get a chance to shoot, so to speak, and hence we do not have what in English is called fair play; the act has occurred before they could oppose it. It is as if in a duel one participant fired before the signal was given.

Accordingly, in this case too, the legal and the moral responsibility, depending on the circumstances, is more or less, but always in part, eliminated. In England, a murder committed in great precipitancy and without the slightest deliberation, or in the most violent, suddenly provoked anger, is called manslaughter and is only punished lightly, indeed, sometimes not at all.

Intoxication is a condition which disposes towards passions by heightening the liveliness of perceptual ideas, but, on the other hand, weakening the power to think *in abstracto*, while at the same time increasing the energy of the will. Instead of being responsible for acts we are responsible for the intoxication itself. Hence intoxication is not legally excused, even though in this case intellectual freedom is partly eliminated.

Aristotle speaks, although very briefly and insufficiently, of this intelectual freedom, of the "voluntary and involuntary with respect to reason." [. . .] This freedom is referred to when forensic medicine and criminal justice ask whether a criminal was in a state of freedom and hence accountable. In general, then, all those crimes are to be regarded as committed in the absence of intellectual freedom in which the man either did not know what he was doing or was simply not capable of considering that which should have kept him from doing it, namely, the consequences of the act. Accordingly, in such cases he is not to be punished.

Those who think that no criminal should be punished, simply because moral freedom does not exist and because, as a consequence, all actions of a given man are inevitable, start out from a false view of punishment, namely, that it is a visitation inflicted upon the crime for its own sake, a repayment of evil with evil on moral grounds. This, however, in spite of the fact that Kant taught it, would be absurd, useless, and completely unjustified. For how could a man be empowered to set himself up as an absolute moral judge of another, and as such to torment him because of his sins! Rather, the aim of the law, i.e., of the threat of punishment, is to act as a countermotive to crimes not yet committed. If in a given case the law fails in this effect, still it must be carried out, for otherwise it would also fail in all future cases. The criminal on his part suffers punishment in this case really as a consequence of his moral nature, which in combination with the circumstances (the motives) and his intellect (which falsely promised him the hope of escaping punishment) inevitably brought about the act. In this case injustice could be done to him only if his moral character were not of his own making, not his act as intelligible being, but the work of another.

The same relation of the act to its consequences holds when the consequences of his vicious behavior take place not in accordance with human but with natural laws, e.g., when wretched dissipations bring about terrible diseases, or when a man in attempting a burglary comes to grief accidentally, as in the case of a man who upon breaking into a pigpen at night in order to abduct its usual occupant encountered instead, approaching him with open arms, a bear, whose keeper had found shelter for the night in that inn.

Five

Principle of Sufficient Reason of Knowing

Yet even thinking and reflection in the narrower sense do not consist in the mere presence of abstract concepts in our consciousness, but rather in a combining or separating of two or more concepts under various restrictions and modifications, which are specified by logic in the theory of judgments. Thus such a concept relationship clearly conceived and expressed is called a *judgment*. Now, with regard to these judgments, here the principle of sufficient reason once again holds good, yet in a form very different from the one discussed previously, namely as the principle of sufficient reason of knowing, *principium rationis sufficientis cognoscendi*. As such it asserts that, if a judgment is to express a piece of *knowledge*, it must have a sufficient ground or reason (*Grund*); by virtue of this quality, it then receives the predicate *true*. *Truth* is therefore the reference of a judgment to something different therefrom. This something is called the ground or reason of the judgment and, as we shall see, itself admits of a considerable variety of classes. But as it is always something on which the judgment is supported or rests, the German word *Grund* (ground) is suitably chosen. In Latin and all languages derived therefrom, the words *ground of knowledge* (*Erkenntnissgrund*) are identical with the word *reason* (*Vernunft*). Hence the two are called *ratio, la ragione, la razón, la raison, the reason*. From this it is evident that, in knowledge of the grounds of judgments, one recognized the principal function of reason (*Vernunft*), its business *par excellence*. These grounds whereon a judgment can be based may now be divided into four kinds, and the truth then gained through the judgment is different according to each of the four kinds. These are stated in the four following sections.

LOGICAL TRUTH

A judgment can have as its reason or ground another judgment; its truth is then *logical* or *formal*. Whether it also has material truth remains undecided and depends on whether the judgment supporting it has material truth, or even whether the series of judgments, on which this judgment is based, leads back to one that has material truth. Such an establishment of one judgment by another results always from a comparison therewith. Now this comparison is made either directly in the mere conversion or contraposition of the judgment, or by the addition of a third judgment, wherefrom the mutual relation of the last two judgments the truth of the judgment to be established becomes evident. This operation is the complete *syllogism*. It is brought about both by the subsumption and the opposition of concepts. The syllogism, as the establishment of one judgment through another by means of a third, is always concerned only with judgments which are merely combinations of concepts, and concepts are the exclusive object of the faculty of reason. Therefore arguing, concluding, or inferring has rightly been regarded as the proper and particular business of the faculty of reason (*Vernunft*). The whole science of syllogisms is nothing but the sum total of rules for applying the principle of sufficient reason mutually to judgments; and so it is the canon of *logical truth*.

Those judgments whose truth is evident from the four well-known laws of thought can also be regarded as established by another judgment; for those four laws are themselves judgments from which the truth of the other judgments follows. For example, the judgment "A Triangle is a space enclosed by three lines" has as its ultimate ground the principle of identity, in other words, the idea expressed by that principle. The judgment "No body is without extension" has as its ultimate ground the principle of contradiction. The judgment "Every judgment is either true or not true" has as its ultimate ground the principle of the excluded middle. Finally, the judgment "No one can admit anything to be true without knowing why" has as its ultimate ground the principle of sufficient reason of knowing. In the ordinary use of our faculty of reason we assume as true the judgments that follow from the four laws of thought, without first reducing them to those laws as their premises, for indeed most people have never even heard of those abstract laws. This does not make those judgments anymore independent of these laws as their premises, just as when anyone says "This body will fall if its support is removed," such judgment is possible without his ever having been aware of the principle "All bodies tend towards the center of the earth," and yet the former judgment is dependent on the latter as its premise. I therefore cannot approve that hitherto in logic an *intrinsic truth* was attributed to all judgments based exclusively on the laws of thought, in other words, that they were declared to be directly *true*, and this *intrinsic logical truth* was distinguished from *extrinsic logical truth*, which would be reliance on another judgment as their ground. Every truth is the reference of a judgment to something *outside* it, and *intrinsic truth* is a contradiction.

EMPIRICAL TRUTH

A representation of the first class, thus an intuitive perception brought about by means of the senses, and consequently experience, can be the ground of a judgment which then has *material* truth; and indeed insofar as the judgment is founded *directly* on experience, this is *empirical* truth.

"A judgment has *material truth*" implies generally that its concepts are mutually connected, separated, or limited, as is required by the intuitive representations through which it is established. To know this is the immediate business of the *power of judgment* which, as I have said, is the mediator between the intuitive and abstract or discursive faculties of knowledge, and thus between understanding and faculty of reason.

TRANSCENDENTAL TRUTH

The *forms* of intuitive empirical knowledge, to be found in the understanding and pure sensibility, can, as conditions of the possibility of all experience, be the ground of a judgment, which is then synthetical *a priori*. But as such a judgment has material truth, this is transcendental, since the judgment rests not merely on experience but on the conditions of the entire possibility of experience which lie within us. For the judgment is determined precisely by that which determines experience itself, that is, either by the forms of space and time intuitively perceived by us *a priori*, or by the law of causality known to us *a priori*. Examples of such judgments are propositions such as: Two straight lines do not enclose a space. Nothing happens without a cause. $3 \times 7 = 21$. Matter can neither come into existence nor pass away. The whole of pure mathematics, as well as my table of the *Praedicabilia a priori* in the second volume of the *World as Will and Representation*, and also most of the propositions in Kant's *Metaphysical Foundations of Natural Science*, can be quoted as evidence of this kind of truth.

METALOGICAL TRUTH

Finally, the formal conditions of all thought which lie within our faculty of reason can also be the ground of a judgment, and then its truth is such that I think it is best defined when I call it *metalogical truth*. But this expression has nothing to do with the *Metalogicon*, written in the twelfth century by John of Salisbury; for in his *prologus*, he explains: "Because I support and defend logic, my book is called *Metalogicon*," and makes no further use of the word. There are, however, only four such judgments of metalogical truth which were found long ago by induction and called the laws of all thought; although complete agreement about their expression and number has never yet been reached, there is, however, complete unanimity about what they are supposed to indicate. They are:

1. A subject is equal to the sum of its predicates, or a = a.
2. No predicate can be simultaneously attributed and denied to a subject, or a = −a = 0.
3. Of every two contradictorily opposite predicates one must belong to every subject.
4. Truth is the reference of a judgment to something outside it as its sufficient ground or reason.

Through a reflection, which I might call a self-examination of the faculty of reason, we know that these judgments are the expression of the conditions of all thought and therefore have these as their ground. Thus by making vain attempts to think in opposition to these laws, the faculty of reason recognizes them as the conditions of the possibility of all thought. We then find that it is just as impossible to think in opposition to them as it is to move our limbs in a direction contrary to their joints. If the subject could know itself, we should know those laws *immediately*, and not first through experiments on objects, i.e., representations. In this respect it is just the same with the grounds of judgments of transcendental truth; they too do not come directly into our consciousness, but first *in concreto* by means of objects, i.e., representations. For example, if we attempt to think of a change without a preceding cause, or even of an arising or passing away of matter, we become aware of the impossibility of the business, indeed of an objective impossibility, although it has its roots in our intellect; otherwise we could not bring it to consciousness in a subjective way. Generally a great similarity and connection between transcendental and metalogical truths is noticeable, which shows that both have a common root. Here we see the principle of sufficient reason mainly as metalogical truth, after it had appeared in the previous section as transcendental truth. Later it will again appear as transcendental truth in another form. Precisely on this account I am attempting in this essay to establish the principle of sufficient reason as a judgment having a fourfold ground or reason. By this I do not mean four different grounds or reasons leading by chance to the same judgment, but one ground or reason presenting itself in a fourfold aspect, which I call figuratively a fourfold root. The other three metalogical truths are so similar that, when considering them, we attempt almost of necessity to seek for them a common expression, as I have done in the ninth chapter of the second volume of my chief work. On the other hand, they are very different from the principle of sufficient reason. If we wished to seek among the transcendental truths an analogue for those other three metalogical truths, the one to be chosen would be: Substance, I mean Matter, is permanent.

Six

The World as Will

In the first book, we considered the representation only as such, and hence only according to the general form. It is true that, so far as the abstract representation, the concept, is concerned, we also obtained a knowledge of it according to its content, insofar as it has all content and meaning only through its relation to the representation of perception, without which it would be worthless and empty. Therefore, directing our attention entirely to the representation of perception, we shall endeavor to arrive at a knowledge of its content, its more precise determinations, and the forms it presents to us. It will be of special interest for us to obtain information about its real significance, that significance, otherwise merely felt, by virtue of which these pictures or images do not march past us strange and meaningless, as they would otherwise inevitably do, but speak to us directly, are understood, and acquire an interest that engrosses our whole nature.

We direct our attention to mathematics, natural science, and philosophy, each of which holds out the hope that it will furnish a part of the information desired. In the first place, we find philosophy to be a monster with many heads, each of which speaks a different language. Of course, they are not all at variance with one another on the point here mentioned, the significance of the representation of perception. For, with the exception of the Skeptics and Idealists, the others in the main speak fairly consistently of an *object* forming the *basis* of the representation. This object indeed is different in its whole being and nature from the representation, but yet is in all respects as like it as one egg is like another. But this does not help us, for we do not at all know how to distinguish that object from the representation. We find that the two are one and the same, for every object always and eternally presupposes a subject, and thus remains representation. We then recognize also that being-object belongs to the most universal form of the representation, which is precisely the division into object and subject. Further, the principle of sufficient reason, to which we here refer, is also for us only the form of the representation, namely the regular and orderly combination of one representation with another, and not the combination of the whole finite or infinite series of representations with something which is not representation at all, and is therefore not capable of being in any way represented. We spoke above of the Skeptics and Idealists, when discussing the controversy about the reality of the external world.

Now, if we look to mathematics for the desired more detailed knowledge of the representation of perception, which we have come to know only quite generally according to the mere form, then this science will tell us about these representations only insofar as they occupy time and space, in other words, only insofar as they are quantities. It will state with extreme accuracy the how-many and the how-large; but as this is always only relative, that is to say, a comparison of one representation with another, and even that only from the one-sided aspect of quantity, this too will not be the information for which principally we are looking.

Finally, if we look at the wide province of natural science, which is divided into many fields, we can first of all distinguish two main divisions. It is either a description of forms and shapes, which I call *morphology*; or an explanation of changes, which I call *etiology*.

The former considers the permanent forms, the latter the changing matter, according to the laws of its transition from one form into another. Morphology is what we call natural history in its whole range, though not in the literal sense of the word. As botany and zoology especially, it teaches us about the various, permanent, organic, and thus definitely determined forms in spite of the incessant change of individuals; and these forms constitute a great part of the content of the perceptive representation. In natural history they are classified, separated, united, and arranged according to natural and artificial systems, and brought under concepts that render possible a survey and knowledge of them all. There is further demonstrated an infinitely fine and shaded analogy in the whole and in the parts of these forms which runs through them all (*unité de plan*), by virtue of which they are like the many different variations on an unspecified theme. The passage of matter into those forms, in other words the origin of individuals, is not a main part of the consideration, for every individual springs from its like through generation, which everywhere is equally mysterious, and has so far baffled clear knowledge. But the little that is known of this finds its place in physiology, which belongs to etiological natural science. Mineralogy, especially where it becomes geology, though it belongs mainly to morphology, also inclines to this etiological science. Etiology proper includes all the branches of natural science in which the main concern everywhere is knowledge of cause and effect. These sciences teach how, according to an invariable rule, one state of matter is necessarily followed by another definite state; how one definite change necessarily conditions and brings about another definite change; this demonstration is called *explanation*. Here we find principally mechanics, physics, chemistry, and physiology.

But if we devote ourselves to its teaching, we soon become aware that the information we are chiefly looking for no more comes to us from etiology than it does from morphology. The latter presents us with innumerable and infinitely varied forms that are nevertheless related by an unmistakable family likeness. For us they are representations that in this way remain eternally strange to us, and, when considered merely in this way, they stand before us like hieroglyphics that are not understood. On the other hand, etiology teaches us that, according to the law of cause and effect, this definite condition of matter produces that other condition, and with this it has explained it, and has done its part. At bottom, however, it does nothing more than show the orderly arrangement according to which the states or conditions appear in space and time, and teach for all cases what phenomenon must necessarily appear at this time and in this place. It therefore determines for them their position in time and space according to a law whose definite content has been taught by experience, yet whose universal form and necessity are known to us independently of experience. But in this way we do not obtain the slightest information about the inner nature of any one of these phenomena. This is called a *natural force*, and lies outside the province of etiological explanation, which calls the unalterable constancy with which the manifestation of such a force appears whenever its known conditions are present, a *law of nature*. But this law of nature, these conditions, this appearance in a definite place at a definite time, are all that it knows, or ever can know. The force itself that is manifested, the inner nature of the phenomena that appear in accordance with those laws, remain for it an eternal secret, something entirely strange and unknown, in the case of the simplest as well as of the most complicated phenomenon. For although etiology has so far achieved its aim most completely in mechanics, and least so in physiology, the force by virtue of which a stone falls to the ground, or one body repels another, is, in its inner nature, just as strange and mysterious as that which produces the movements and growth of an animal. Mechanics presupposes matter, weight, impenetrability, communicability of motion through impact, rigidity, and so on as unfathomable; it calls them forces of nature, and their necessary and regular appearance under certain conditions a law of nature. Only then does its explanation begin, and that consists in stating truly and with mathematical precision how, where, and when each force manifests itself, and referring to one of those forces every phenomenon that comes before it. Physics, chemistry, and physiology do the same in their province, only they presuppose much more and achieve less. Consequently, even the most perfect etiological explanation of the whole of nature would never be more in reality than a record of inexplicable forces, and a reliable statement of the rule by which their phenomena appear, succeed, and make way for one another in time and space. But the inner nature of the forces that thus appear was always bound to be left unexplained by etiology, which had to stop at the phenomenon and its arrangement, since the law followed by etiology does not go beyond this. In this respect it could be compared to a section of a piece of marble showing many different veins side by side, but not letting us know the course of these veins from the interior of the marble to the surface. Or, if I may be permitted a facetious comparison, because it is more striking, the philosophical investigator must always feel in regard to the complete etiology of the whole of nature like a man who, without knowing how, is brought into a company quite unknown to him, each member of which in turn presents to him another as his friend and cousin, and thus makes them sufficiently acquainted. The man himself, however, while assuring each person introduced of his pleasure at meeting him, always has on his lips the question: "But how the deuce do I stand to the whole company?"

Hence, about those phenomena known by us only as our representations, etiology can never give us the desired information that leads us beyond them. For after all its explanations, they still stand quite strange before us, as mere representations whose significance we do not understand. The causal connection merely gives the rule and relative order of their appearance in space and time, but affords us no further knowledge of that which so appears. Moreover, the law of causality itself has validity only for representations, for objects of a definite class, and has meaning only when they are assumed. Hence, like these objects themselves, it always exists only in relation to the subject, and so conditionally. Thus it is just as well known when we start from the subject, i.e., *a priori*, as when we start from the object, i.e., *a posteriori*, as Kant has taught us.

But what now prompts us to make inquiries is that we are not satisfied with knowing that we have representations, that they are such and such, and that they are connected according to this or that law, whose general expression is always the principle of sufficient reason. We want to know the significance of those representations; we ask whether this world is nothing more than representation. In that case, it would inevitably pass by us like an empty dream, or a ghostly vision not worth our consideration. Or we ask whether it is something else, something in addition, and if so what that something is. This much is certain, namely that this something about which we are inquiring must be by its whole nature completely and fundamentally different from the representation; and so the forms and laws of the representation must be wholly foreign to it. We cannot, then, reach it from the representation under the guidance of those laws that merely combine objects, representations, with one another; these are the forms of the principle of sufficient reason.

Here we already see that we can never get at the inner nature of things *from without*. However much we may investigate, we obtain nothing but images and names. We are like a man who goes round a castle, looking in vain for an entrance, and sometimes sketching the facades. Yet this is the path that all philosophers before me have followed.

In fact, the meaning that I am looking for of the world that stands before me simply as my representation, or the transition from it as mere representation of the knowing subject to whatever it may be besides this, could never be found if the investigator himself were nothing more than the purely knowing subject (a winged cherub without a body). But he himself is rooted in that world; and thus he finds himself in it as an *individual*; in other words, his knowledge, which is the conditional supporter of the whole world as representation, is nevertheless given entirely through the medium of a body, and the affections of this body are, as we have shown, the starting point for the understanding in its perception of this world. For the purely knowing subject as such, this body is a representation like any other, an object among objects. Its movements and actions are so far known to him in just the same way as the changes of all other objects of perception; and they would be equally strange and incomprehensible to him if their meaning were not unraveled for him in an entirely different way. Otherwise, he would see his conduct follow on presented motives with the constancy of a law of nature, just as the changes of other objects follow upon causes, stimuli, and motives. But he would be no nearer to understanding the influence of the motives than he is to understanding the connection with its cause of any other effect that appears before him. He would then also call the inner, to him incomprehensible, nature of those manifestations and actions of his body a force, a quality, or a character, just as he pleased, but he would have no further insight into it. All this, however, is not the case; on the contrary, the answer to the riddle is given to the subject of knowledge appearing as individual, and this answer is given in the word *Will*. This and this alone gives him the key to his own phenomenon, reveals to him the significance and shows him the inner mechanism of his being, his actions, his movements. To the subject of knowing, who appears as an individual only through his identity with the body, this body is given in two entirely different ways. It is given in intelligent perception as representation, as an object among objects, liable to the laws of these objects. But it is also given in quite a different way, namely as what is known immediately to everyone, and is denoted by the word *will*. Every true act of his will is also at once and inevitably a movement of his body; he cannot actually will the act without at the same time being aware that it appears as a movement of the body. The act of will and the action of the body are not two different states objectively known, connected by the bond of causality; they do not stand in the relation of cause and effect, but are one and the same thing, though given in two entirely different ways, first quite directly, and then in perception for the understanding. The action of the body is nothing but the act of will objectified, i.e., translated into perception. [. . .] Therefore, in a certain sense, it can also be said that the will is knowledge *a priori* of the body, and that the body is knowledge *a posteriori* of the will. Resolutions of the will relating to the future are mere deliberations of reason about what will be willed at some time, not real acts of will. Only the carrying out stamps the resolve; till then, it is always a mere intention that can be altered; it exists only in reason, in the abstract. Only in reflection are willing and acting different; in reality they are *one*. Every true, genuine, immediate act of the will is also at once and directly a manifest act of the body; and correspondingly, on the other hand, every impression on the body is also at once and directly an impression on the will. As such, it is called pain when it is contrary to the will, and gratification or pleasure when in accordance with the will. The gradations of the two are very different. However, we are quite wrong in calling pain and pleasure representations, for they are not these at all, but immediate affections of the will in its phenomenon, the body; an enforced, instantaneous willing or not-willing of the impression undergone by the body. There are only a certain few impressions on the body which do not rouse the will, and through these alone is the body an immediate object of knowledge; for, as perception in the understanding, the body is an indirect object like all other objects. These impressions are therefore to be regarded directly as mere representations, and hence to be excepted from what has just been said. Here are meant the affections of the purely objective senses of sight, hearing, and touch, although only insofar as their organs are affected in the specific natural way that is specially characteristic of them. This is such an exceedingly feeble stimulation of the enhanced and specifically modified sensibility of these parts that it does not affect the will, but, undisturbed by any excitement of the will, only furnishes for the understanding data from which perception arises. But every stronger or heterogeneous affection of these sense-organs is painful, in other words, is against the will; hence they too belong to its objectivity. Weakness of the nerves shows itself in the fact that the impressions which should have merely that degree of intensity that is sufficient to make them data for the understanding, reach the higher degree at which they stir the will, that is to say, excite pain or pleasure, though more often pain. This pain, however, is in part dull and inarticulate; thus it not merely causes us to feel painfully particular tones and intense light, but also gives rise generally to a morbid and hypochondriacal disposition without being distinctly recognized. The identity of the body and the will further shows itself, among other things, in the fact that every vehement and excessive movement of the will, in other words, every emotion, agitates the body and its inner workings directly and immediately, and disturbs the course of its vital functions. [. . .]

Finally, the knowledge I have of my will, although an immediate knowledge, cannot be separated from that of my body. I know my will not as a whole, not as a unity, not completely according to its nature, but only in its individual acts, and hence in time, which is the form of my body's appearing, as it is of every body. Therefore, the body is the condition of knowledge of my will. Accordingly, I cannot really imagine this will without my body. In the essay *On the Fourfold Root of the Principle of Sufficient Reason* the will, or rather the subject of willing, is treated as a special class of representations or objects. But even there we saw this object coinciding with the subject, in other words, ceasing to be object. We then called this coincidence the miracle *par excellence*; to a certain extent the whole of the present work is an explanation of this. Insofar as I know my will really as object, I know it as body; but then I am again at the first class of representations laid down in that essay, that is, again at real objects. As we go on, we shall see more and more that the first class of representations finds its explanation, its solution, only in the fourth class enumerated in that essay, which could no longer be properly opposed to the subject as object; and that, accordingly, we must learn to understand the inner nature of the law of causality valid in the first class, and of what happens according to this law, from the law of motivation governing the fourth class.

The identity of the will and of the body, provisionally explained, can be demonstrated only as is done here, and that for the first time, and as will be done more and more in the further course of our discussion. In other words, it can be raised from immediate consciousness, from knowledge in the concrete, to rational knowledge of reason, or be carried over into knowledge in the abstract. On the other hand, by its nature it can never be demonstrated, that is to say, deduced as indirect knowledge from some other more direct knowledge, for the very reason that it is itself the most direct knowledge. If we do not apprehend it and stick to it as such, in vain shall we expect to obtain it again in some indirect way as derived knowledge. It is a knowledge of quite a peculiar nature, whose truth cannot therefore really be brought under one of the four headings by which I have divided all truth in the essay *On the Fourfold Root of the Principle of Sufficient Reason*, § 29, namely, logical, empirical, transcendental, and metalogical. For it is not, like all these, the reference of an abstract representation to another representation, or to the necessary form of intuitive or of abstract representing, but it is the reference of a judgment to the relation that a representation of perception, namely the body, has to that which is not a representation at all, but is *toto genere* different therefrom, namely will. I should therefore like to distinguish this truth from every other, and call it *philosophical truth par excellence*. We can turn the expression of this truth in different ways and say: My body and my will are *one*; or, What as representation of perception I call my body, I call my will insofar as I am conscious of it in an entirely different way comparable with no other; or, My body is the *objectivity* of my will; or, Apart from the fact that my body is my representation, it is still my will, and so on.

Whereas in the first book we were reluctantly forced to declare our own body to be mere representation of the knowing subject, like all the other objects of this world of perception, it has now become clear to us that something in the consciousness of everyone distinguishes the representation of his own body from all others that are in other respects quite like it. This is that the body occurs in consciousness in quite another way, *toto genere* different, that is denoted by the word *will*. It is just this double knowledge of our own body which gives us information about that body itself, about its action and movement following on motives, as well as about its suffering through outside impressions, in a word, about what it is, not as representation, but as something over and above this, and hence what it is *in itself*. We do not have such immediate information about the nature, action, and suffering of any other real objects.

The knowing subject is an individual precisely by reason of this special relation to the one body which, considered apart from this, is for him only a representation like all other representations. But the relation by virtue of which the knowing subject is an *individual* subsists for that very reason only between him and one particular representation among all his representations. He is therefore conscious of this particular representation not merely as such, but at the same time in a quite different way, namely as a will. But if he abstracts from that special relation, from that twofold and completely heterogeneous knowledge of one and the same thing, then that one thing, the body, is a representation like all others. Therefore, in order to understand where he is in this matter, the knowing individual must either assume that the distinctive feature of that one representation is to be found merely in the fact that his knowledge stands in this double reference only to that one representation; that only into this one object of perception is an insight in two ways at the same time open to him; and that this is to be explained not by a difference of this object from all others, but only by a difference between the relation of his knowledge to this one object and its relation to all others. Or he must assume that this one object is essentially different from all others; that it alone among all objects is at the same time will and representation, the rest, on the other hand, being mere representation, i.e., mere phantoms. Thus he must assume that his body is the only real individual in the world, i.e., the only phenomenon of will, and the only immediate object of the subject. That the other objects, considered as mere *representations*, are like his body, in other words, like this body fill space (itself perhaps existing only as representation), and also, like this body, operate in space—this, I say, is demonstrably certain from the law of causality, which is *a priori* certain for representations, and admits of no effect without a cause. But apart from the fact that we can infer from the effect only a cause in general, not a similar cause, we are still always in the realm of the mere representation, for which alone the law of causality is valid, and beyond which it can never lead us. But whether the objects known to the individual only as representations are yet, like his own body, phenomena of a will, is, as stated in the previous book, the proper meaning of the question as to the reality of the external world. To deny this is the meaning of *theoretical egoism*, which in this way regards as phantoms all phenomena outside its own will, just as practical egoism does in a practical respect; thus in it a man regards and treats only his own person as a real person, and all others as mere phantoms. Theoretical egoism, of course, can never be refuted by proofs, yet in philosophy it has never been positively used otherwise than as a skeptical sophism, i.e., for the sake of appearance. As a serious conviction, on the other hand, it could be found only in a madhouse; as such it would then need not so much a refutation as a cure. Therefore we do not go into it any further, but regard it as the last stronghold of skepticism, which is always polemical. Thus our knowledge, bound always to individuality and having its limitation in this very fact, necessarily means that everyone can *be* only one thing, whereas he can *know* everything else, and it is this very limitation that really creates the need for philosophy. Therefore we, who for this very reason are endeavoring to extend the limits of our knowledge through philosophy, shall regard this skeptical argument of theoretical egoism, which here confronts us, as a small frontier fortress. Admittedly the fortress is impregnable, but the garrison can never sally forth from it, and therefore we can pass it by and leave it in our rear without danger.

The double knowledge which we have of the nature and action of our own body, and which is given in two completely different ways, has now been clearly brought out. Accordingly, we shall use it further as a key to the inner being of every phenomenon in nature. We shall judge all objects which are not our own body, and therefore are given to our consciousness not in the double way, but only as representations, according to the analogy of this body. We shall therefore assume that as, on the one hand, they are representation, just like our body, and are in this respect homogeneous with it, so on the other hand, if we set aside their existence as the subject's representation, what still remains over must be, according to its inner nature, the same as what in ourselves we call *will*. For what other kind of existence or reality could we attribute to the rest of the material world? From what source could we take the elements out of which we construct such a world? Besides the will and the representation, there is absolutely nothing known or conceivable for us. If we wish to attribute the greatest known reality to the material world, which immediately exists only in our representation, then we give it that reality which our own body has for each of us, for to each of us this is the most real of things. But if now we analyze the reality of this body and its actions, then, beyond the fact that it is our representation, we find nothing in it but the will; with this even its reality is exhausted. Therefore we can nowhere find another kind of reality to attribute to the material world. If, therefore, the material world is to be something more than our mere representation, we must say that, besides being the representation, and hence in itself and of its inmost nature, it is what we find immediately in ourselves as will. I say "of its inmost nature," but we have first of all to get to know more intimately this inner nature of the will, so that we may know how to distinguish from it what belongs not to it itself, but to its phenomenon, which has many grades. Such, for example, is the circumstance of its being accompanied by knowledge, and the determination by motives which is conditioned by this knowledge. As we proceed, we shall see that this belongs not to the inner nature of the will, but merely to its most distinct phenomenon as animal and human being. Therefore, if I say that the force which attracts a stone to the earth is of its nature, in itself, and apart from all representation, will, then no one will attach to this proposition the absurd meaning that the stone moves itself according to a known motive, because it is thus that the will appears in man. Thus we cannot in any way agree with Francis Bacon when he thinks that all mechanical and physical movements of bodies ensue only after a preceding perception in these bodies, although a glimmering of truth gave birth even to this false proposition. This is also the case with Kepler's statement, in his essay *De Planeta Martis*, that the planets must have knowledge in order to keep to their elliptical courses so accurately, and to regulate the velocity of their motion, so that the triangles of the plane of their course always remain proportional to the time in which they pass through their bases. But we will now prove, establish, and develop to its full extent, clearly and in more detail, what has hitherto been explained provisionally and generally.

As the being-in-itself of our own body, as that which this body is besides being object of perception, namely representation, the *will*, as we have said, proclaims itself first of all in the voluntary movements of this body, insofar as these movements are nothing but the visibility of the individual acts of the will. These movements appear directly and simultaneously with those acts of will; they are one and the same thing with them, and are distinguished from them only by the form of perceptibility into which they have passed, that is to say, in which they have become representation.

But these acts of the will always have a ground or reason outside themselves in motives. Yet these motives never determine more than what I will at *this* time, in *this* place, in *these* circumstances, not *that* I will in general, or *what* I will in general, in other words, the maxim characterizing the whole of my willing. Therefore the whole inner nature of my willing cannot be explained from the motives, but they determine merely its manifestation at a given point of time; they are merely the occasion on which my will shows itself. This will itself, on the other hand, lies outside the province of the law of motivation;

only the phenomenon of the will at each point of time is determined by this law. Only on the presupposition of my empirical character is the motive a sufficient ground of explanation of my conduct. But if I abstract from my character, and then ask why in general I will this and not that, no answer is possible, because only the *appearance* or *phenomenon* of the will is subject to the principle of sufficient reason, not the will itself, which in this respect may be called *groundless*. [. . .] We need only to draw attention to the fact that one phenomenon being established by another, as in this case the deed by the motive, does not in the least conflict with the essence-in-itself of the deed being will. The will itself has no ground; the principle of sufficient reason in all its aspects is merely the form of knowledge, and hence its validity extends only to the representation, to the phenomenon, to the visibility of the will, not to the will itself that becomes visible.

Now, if every action of my body is an appearance or phenomenon of an act of will in which my will itself in general and as a whole, and hence my character, again expresses itself under given motives, then phenomenon or appearance of the will must also be the indispensable condition and presupposition of every action. For the will's appearance cannot depend on something which does not exist directly and only through it, and would therefore be merely accidental for it, whereby the will's appearance itself would be only accidental. But that condition is the whole body itself. Therefore this body itself must be phenomenon of the will, and must be related to my will as a whole, that is to say, to my intelligible character, the phenomenon of which in time is my empirical character, in the same way as the particular action of the body is to the particular act of the will. Therefore the whole body must be nothing but my will become visible, must be my will itself, insofar as this is object of perception, representation of the first class. It has already been advanced in confirmation of this that every impression on my body also affects my will at once and immediately, and in this respect is called pain or pleasure, or in a lower degree, pleasant or unpleasant sensation. Conversely, it has also been advanced that every violent movement of the will, and hence every emotion and passion, convulses the body, and disturbs the course of its functions. Indeed an etiological, though very incomplete, account can be given of the origin of my body, and a somewhat better account of its development and preservation. Indeed this is physiology; but this explains its theme only in exactly the same way as motives explain action. Therefore the establishment of the individual action through the motive, and the necessary sequence of the action from the motive, do not conflict with the fact that action, in general and by its nature, is only phenomenon or appearance of a will that is in itself groundless. Just as little does the physiological explanation of the functions of the body detract from the philosophical truth that the whole existence of this body and the sum total of its functions are only the objectification of that will which appears in this body's outward actions in accordance with motives. If, however, physiology tries to refer even these outward actions, the immediate voluntary movements, to causes in the organism, for example, to explain the movement of a muscle from an affluxion of humors ("like the contraction of a cord that is wet"); [. . .] supposing that it really did come to a thorough explanation of this kind, this would never do away with the immediately certain truth that every voluntary movement (*functiones animales*) is phenomenon of an act of will. Now, just as little can the physiological explanation of vegetative life (*functiones naturales, vitales*), however far it may be developed, ever do away with the truth that this whole animal life, thus developing itself, is phenomenon of the will. Generally then, as already stated, no etiological explanation can ever state more than the necessarily determined position in time and space of a particular phenomenon and its necessary appearance there according to a fixed rule. On the other hand, the inner nature of everything that appears in this way remains forever unfathomable, and is presupposed by every etiological explanation; it is merely expressed by the name force, or law of nature, or, when we speak of actions, the name character or will. Thus, although every particular action, under the presupposition of the definite character, necessarily ensues with the presented motive, and although growth, the process of nourishment, and all the changes in the animal body take place according to necessarily acting causes (stimuli), the whole series of actions, and consequently every individual act and likewise its condition, namely the whole body itself which performs it, and therefore also the process through which and in which the body exists, are nothing but the phenomenal appearance of the will, its becoming visible, the *objectivity of the will*. On this rests the perfect suitability of the human and animal body to the human and animal will in general, resembling, but far surpassing, the suitability of a purposely made instrument to the will of its maker, and on this account appearing as fitness or appropriateness, i.e., the teleological accountability of the body. Therefore the parts of the body must correspond completely to the chief demands and desires by which the will manifests itself; they must be the visible expression of these desires. Teeth, gullet, and intestinal canal are objectified hunger; the genitals are objectified sexual impulse; grasping hands and nimble feet correspond to the more indirect strivings of the will which they represent. Just as the general human form corresponds to the general human will, so to the individually modified will, namely the character of the individual, there corresponds the individual bodily structure, which is therefore as a whole and in all its parts characteristic and full of expression. It is very remarkable that even Parmenides expressed this in the following verses, quoted by Aristotle (*Metaphysics*): "Just as everyone possesses the complex of flexible limbs, so does there dwell in men the mind in conformity with this. For everyone mind and complex of limbs are always the same; for intelligence is the criterion."

From all these considerations the reader has now gained in the abstract, and hence in clear and certain terms, a knowledge which everyone possesses directly in the concrete, namely as feeling. This is the knowledge that the inner nature of his own phenomenon, which manifests itself to him as representation both through his actions and through the permanent substratum of these his body, is his *will*. This will constitutes what is most immediate in his consciousness, but as such it has not wholly entered into the form of the representation, in which object and subject stand over against each other; on the contrary, it makes itself known in an immediate way in which subject and object are not quite clearly distinguished, yet it becomes known to the individual himself not as a whole, but only in its particular acts. The reader who with me has gained this conviction will find that of itself it will become the key to the knowledge of the innermost being of the whole of nature, since he now transfers it to all those phenomena that are given to him, not like his own phenomenon both in direct and in indirect knowledge, but in the latter solely, and hence merely in a one-sided way, as *representation* alone. He will recognize that same will not only in those phenomena that are quite similar to his own, in men and animals, as their innermost nature, but continued reflection will lead him to recognize the force that shoots and vegetates in the plant, indeed the force by which the crystal is formed, the force that turns the magnet to the North Pole, the force whose shock he encounters from the contact of metals of different kinds, the force that appears in the elective affinities of matter as repulsion and attraction, separation and union, and finally even gravitation, which acts so powerfully in all matter, pulling the stone to the earth and the earth to the sun; all these he will recognize as different only in the phenomenon, but the same according to their inner nature. He will recognize them all as that which is immediately known to him so intimately and better than everything else, and where it appears most distinctly is the *will*. It is only this application of reflection which no longer lets us stop at the phenomenon, but leads us on to the *thing-in-itself*. Phenomenon means representation and nothing more. All representation, be it of whatever kind it may, all *object*, is *phenomenon*. But only the *will* is *thing-in-itself*; as such it is not representation at all, but *toto genere* different therefrom. It is that of which all representation, all object, is the phenomenon, the visibility, the *objectivity*. It is the innermost essence, the kernel, of every particular thing and also of the whole. It appears in every blindly acting force of nature, and also in the deliberate conduct of man, and the great difference between the two concerns only the degree of the manifestation, not the inner nature of what is manifested.

Seven

Knowledge of the Idea

As we have said, the transition that is possible, but to be regarded only as an exception, from the common knowledge of particular things to knowledge of the Idea takes place suddenly, since knowledge tears itself free from the service of the will precisely by the subject's ceasing to be merely individual, and being now a pure will-less subject of knowledge. Such a subject of knowledge no longer follows relations in accordance with the principle of sufficient reason; on the contrary, it rests in fixed contemplation of the object presented to it out of its connection with any other, and rises into this.

To be made clear, this needs a detailed discussion, and the reader must suspend his surprise at it for a while, until it has vanished automatically after he has grasped the whole thought to be expressed in this work.

Raised up by the power of the mind, we relinquish the ordinary way of considering things, and cease to follow under the guidance of the forms of the principle of sufficient reason merely their relations to one another, whose final goal is always the relation to our own will. Thus we no longer consider the where, the when, the why, and the whither in things, but simply and solely the *what*. Further, we do not let abstract thought, the concepts of reason, take possession of our consciousness, but, instead of all this, devote the whole power

79

of our mind to perception, sink ourselves completely therein, and let our whole consciousness be filled by the calm contemplation of the natural object actually present, whether it be a landscape, a tree, a rock, a crag, a building, or anything else. We *lose* ourselves entirely in this object, to use a pregnant expression; in other words, we forget our individuality, our will, and continue to exist only as pure subject, as clear mirror of the object, so that it is as though the object alone existed without anyone to perceive it, and thus we are no longer able to separate the perceiver from the perception, but the two have become one, since the entire consciousness is filled and occupied by a single image of perception. If, therefore, the object has to such an extent passed out of all relation to something outside it, and the subject has passed out of all relation to the will, what is thus known is no longer the individual thing as such, but the *Idea*, the eternal form, the immediate objectivity of the will at this grade. Thus at the same time, the person who is involved in this perception is no longer an individual, for in such perception the individual has lost himself; he is *pure* will-less, painless, timeless *subject of knowledge*. This, which for the moment is so remarkable (which I well know confirms the saying, attributed to Thomas Paine, that "from the sublime to the ridiculous is but a step"), will gradually become clearer and less surprising through what follows. It was this that was in Spinoza's mind when he wrote in his *Ethics*: "The mind is eternal insofar as it conceives things from the standpoint of eternity." Now, in such contemplation, the particular thing at one stroke becomes the *Idea* of its species, and the perceiving individual becomes the *pure subject of knowing*. The individual, as such, knows only particular things; the pure subject of knowledge knows only Ideas. For the individual is the subject of knowledge in its relation to a definite particular phenomenon of will and in subjection thereto. This particular phenomenon of will is, as such, subordinate to the principle of sufficient reason in all its forms;

therefore all knowledge which relates itself to this, also follows the principle of sufficient reason, and no other knowledge than this is fit to be of any use to the will; it always has only relations to the object. The knowing individual as such and the particular thing known by him are always in a particular place, at a particular time, and are links in the chain of causes and effects. The pure subject of knowledge and its correlative, the Idea, have passed out of all these forms of the principle of sufficient reason. Time, place, the individual who knows, and the individual who is known, have no meaning for them. First of all, a knowing individual raises himself in the manner described to the pure subject of knowing, and at the same time raises the contemplated object to the Idea; the *world as representation* then stands out whole and pure, and the complete objectification of the will takes place, for only the Idea is the *adequate objectivity* of the will. In itself, the Idea includes object and subject in like manner, for these are its sole form. In it, however, both are of entirely equal weight; and as the object also is here nothing but the representation of the subject, so the subject, by passing entirely into the perceived object, has also become that object itself, since the entire consciousness is nothing more than its most distinct image.

This consciousness really constitutes the whole *world as representation*, since we picture to ourselves the whole of the Ideas, or grades of the will's objectivity, passing through it successively. The particular things of all particular times and spaces are nothing but the Ideas multiplied through the principle of sufficient reason (the form of knowledge of the individuals as such), and thus obscured in their pure objectivity. When the Idea appears, subject and object can no longer be distinguished in it, because the Idea, the adequate objectivity of the will, the real world as representation, arises only when subject and object reciprocally fill and penetrate each other completely. In just the same way the knowing and the known individual, as things-in-themselves, are likewise not different. For if we look entirely away from that true *world as representation*, there is nothing left but the *world as will*. The will is the "in-itself" of the Idea that completely objectifies it; it is also the "in-itself" of the particular thing and of the individual who knows it, and these two objectify it incompletely. As will, outside the representation and all its forms, it is one and the same in the contemplated object and in the individual who soars aloft in this contemplation, who becomes conscious of himself as pure subject. Therefore in themselves these two are not different; for in themselves they are the will that here knows itself. Plurality and difference exist only as the way in which this knowledge comes to the will, that is to say, only in the phenomenon, by virtue of its form, the principle of sufficient reason. Without the object, without the representation, I am not knowing subject, but mere, blind will; in just the same way, without me as subject of knowledge, the thing known is not object, but mere will, blind impulse. In itself, that is to say outside the representation, this will is one and the same with mine; only in the world as representation, the form of which is always at least subject and object, are we separated out as known and knowing individual. As soon as knowledge, the world as representation, is abolished, nothing in general is left but mere will, blind impulse. That it should obtain objectivity, should become representation, immediately supposes subject as well as object; but that this objectivity should be pure, complete, adequate objectivity of the will, supposes the object as Idea, free from the forms of the principle of sufficient reason, and the subject as pure subject of knowledge, free from individuality and from servitude to the will.

Now whoever has, in the manner stated, become so absorbed and lost in the perception of nature that he exists only as purely knowing subject, becomes in this way immediately aware that, as such, he is the condition, and hence the supporter, of the world and of all objective existence, for this now shows itself as dependent on his existence. He therefore draws nature into himself, so that he feels it to be only an accident of his own being. In this sense Byron says:

> Are not the mountains, waves, and skies, a part
> Of me and of my soul, as I of them?

But how could the person who feels this regard himself as absolutely perishable in contrast to imperishable nature? Rather will he be moved by the consciousness of what the Upanishads of the Vedas express: "I am all this creation collectively, and besides me there exists no other being."

In order to reach a deeper insight into the nature of the world, it is absolutely necessary for us to learn to distinguish the will as thing-in-itself from its adequate objectivity, and then to distinguish the different grades at which this objectivity appears more distinctly and fully, i.e., the Ideas themselves, from the mere phenomenon of the Ideas in the forms of the principle of sufficient reason, the restricted method of knowledge of individuals. We shall then agree with Plato, when he attributes actual being to the Ideas alone, and only an apparent, dreamlike existence to the things in space and time, to this world that is real for the individual. We shall then see how one and the same Idea reveals itself in so many phenomena, and presents its nature to knowing individuals only piecemeal, one side after another. Then we shall also distinguish the Idea itself from the way in which its phenomenon comes into the observation of the individual, and shall recognize the former as essential, and the latter as inessential. We intend to consider this by way of example on the smallest scale, and then on the largest. When clouds move, the figures they form are not essential, but indifferent to them. But that as elastic vapor they are pressed together, driven off, spread out, and torn apart by the force of the wind, this is their nature, this is the essence of the forces that are objectified in them, this is the Idea. The figures in each case are only for the individual observer. To the brook which rolls downwards over the stones, the eddies, waves, and foam-forms exhibited by it are indifferent and inessential; but that it follows gravity, and behaves as an inelastic, perfectly mobile, formless, and transparent fluid, this is its essential nature, this, *if known through perception*, is the Idea. Those foam-forms exist only for us so long as we know as individuals. The ice on the windowpane is formed into crystals according to the laws of crystallization, which reveal the essence of the natural force here appearing, which exhibit the Idea. But the trees and flowers formed by the ice on the windowpane are inessential, and exist only for us. What appears in clouds, brook, and crystal is the feeblest echo of that will which appears more completely in the plant, still more completely in the animal, and most completely in man. But only the *essential* in all these grades of the will's objectification constitutes the *Idea*; on the other hand, its unfolding or development, because drawn apart in the forms of the principle of sufficient reason into a multiplicity of many-sided phenomena, is inessential to the Idea; it lies merely in the individual's mode of cognition, and has reality only for that individual. Now the same thing necessarily holds good of the unfolding of that Idea which is the most complete objectivity of the will. Consequently, the history of the human race, the throng of events, the change of times, the many varying forms of human life in different countries and centuries, all this is only the accidental form of the phenomenon of the Idea. All this does not belong to the Idea itself, in which alone lies the adequate objectivity of the will, but only to the phenomenon. The phenomenon comes into the knowledge of the individual, and is just as foreign, inessential, and indifferent to the Idea itself as the figures they depict are to the clouds, the shape of its eddies and foam-forms to the brook, and the trees and flowers to the ice.

To the man who has properly grasped this, and is able to distinguish the will from the Idea, and the Idea from its phenomenon, the events of the world will have significance only insofar as they are the letters from which the Idea of man can be read, and not in and by themselves. He will not believe with the general public that time may produce something actually new and significant; that through it or in it something positively real may attain to existence, or indeed that time itself as a whole has beginning and end, plan and development, and in some way has for its final goal the highest perfection (according to their conceptions) of the latest generation that lives for thirty years. Therefore just as little will he, with Homer, set up a whole Olympus full of gods to guide the events of time, as he will, with Ossian, regard the figures of the clouds as individual beings. For, as we have said, both have just as much significance with regard to the Idea appearing in them. In the many different forms and aspects of human life, and in the interminable change of events, he will consider only the Idea as the abiding and essential, in which the will-to-live has its most perfect objectivity, and which shows its different sides in the qualities, passions, errors, and excellences of the human race, in selfishness, hatred, love, fear, boldness, frivolity, stupidity, slyness, wit, genius, and so on. All of these, running and congealing together into a thousand different forms and shapes (individuals), continually produce the history of the great and the small worlds, where in itself it is immaterial whether they are set in motion by nuts or by crowns. Finally, he will find that in the world it is the same as in the dramas of Gozzi, in all of which the same persons always appear with the same purpose and the same fate. The motives and incidents certainly are different in each piece, but the spirit of the incidents is the same. The persons of one piece know nothing of the events of another, in which, of course, they themselves performed. Therefore, after all the experiences of the earlier pieces, Pantaloon has become no more agile or generous, Tartaglia no more conscientious, Brighella no more courageous, and Columbine no more modest.

Suppose we were permitted for once to have a clear glance into the realm of possibility and over all the chains of causes and effects, then the earth-spirit would appear and show us in a picture the most eminent individuals, world-enlighteners, and heroes, destroyed by chance before they were ripe for their work. We should then be shown the great events that would have altered the history of the world, and brought about periods of the highest culture and enlightenment, but which the blindest chance, the most insignificant accident, prevented at their beginning. Finally, we should see the splendid powers of great individuals who would have enriched whole world-epochs, but who, misled through error or passion, or compelled by necessity, squandered them uselessly on unworthy or unprofitable objects, or even dissipated them in play. If we saw all this, we should shudder and lament at the thought of the lost treasures of whole periods of the world. But the earth-spirit would smile and say: "The source from which the individuals and their powers flow is inexhaustible, and is as boundless as are time and space; for, just like these forms of every phenomenon, they too are only phenomenon, visibility of the will. No finite measure can exhaust that infinite source; therefore undiminished infinity is still always open for the return of any event or work that was nipped in the bud. In this world of the phenomenon, true loss is as little possible as is true gain. The will alone is; it is the thing-in-itself, the source of all those phenomena. Its self-knowledge, and its affirmation or denial that is then decided on, is the only event in-itself."

History follows the thread of events; it is pragmatic insofar as it deduces them according to the law of motivation, a law that determines the appearing will where that will is illuminated by knowledge. At the lower grades of its objectivity, where it still acts without knowledge, natural science as etiology considers the laws of the changes of its phenomena, and as morphology considers what is permanent in them. This almost endless theme is facilitated by the aid of concepts that comprehend the general, in order to deduce from it the particular. Finally, mathematics considers the mere forms, that is, time and space, in which the Ideas appear drawn apart into plurality for the knowledge of the subject as individual. All these, the common name of which is science, therefore follow the principle of sufficient reason in its different forms, and their theme remains the phenomenon, its laws, connection, and the relations resulting from these. But now, what kind of knowledge is it that considers what continues to exist outside and independently of all relations, but which alone is really essential to the world, the true content of its phenomena, that which is subject to no change, and is therefore known with equal truth for all time, in a word, the *Ideas* that are the immediate and adequate objectivity of the thing-in-itself, of the will? It is *art*, the work of genius. It repeats the eternal Ideas apprehended through pure contemplation, the essential and abiding element in all the phenomena of the world. According to the material in which it repeats, it is sculpture, painting, poetry, or music. Its only source is knowledge of the Ideas; its sole aim is communication of this knowledge. Whilst science, following the restless and unstable stream of the fourfold forms of reasons or grounds and consequents, is with every end it attains again and again directed farther, and can never find an ultimate goal or complete satisfaction, any more than by running we can reach the point where the clouds touch the horizon; art, on the contrary, is everywhere at its goal. For it plucks the object of its contemplation from the stream of the world's course, and holds it isolated before it. This particular thing, which in that stream was an infinitesimal part, becomes for art a representative of the whole, an equivalent of the infinitely many in space and time. It therefore pauses at this particular thing; it stops the wheel of time; for it the relations vanish; its object is only the essential, the Idea. We can therefore define it accurately as *the way of considering things independently of the principle of sufficient reason*, in contrast to the way of considering them which proceeds in exact accordance with this principle, and is the way of science and experience. This latter method of consideration can be compared to an endless line running horizontally, and the former to a vertical line cutting the horizontal at any point. The method of consideration that follows the principle of sufficient reason is the rational method, and it alone is valid and useful in practical life and in science. The method of consideration that looks away from the content of this principle is the method of genius, which is valid and useful in art alone. The first is Aristotle's method; the second is, on the whole, Plato's. The first is like the mighty storm, rushing along without beginning or aim, bending, agitating, and carrying everything away with it; the second is like the silent sunbeam, cutting through the path of the storm, and quite unmoved by it. The first is like the innumerable violently agitated drops of the waterfall, constantly changing and never for a moment at rest; the second is like the rainbow silently resting on this raging torrent. Only through the pure contemplation described above, which becomes absorbed entirely in the object, are the Ideas comprehended; and the nature of *genius* consists precisely in the preeminent ability for such contemplation. Now as this demands a complete forgetting of our own person and of its relations and connections, the *gift of genius* is nothing but the most complete *objectivity*, i.e., the objective tendency of the mind, as opposed to the subjective directed to our own person, i.e., to the will. Accordingly, genius is the capacity to remain in a state of pure perception, to lose oneself in perception, to remove from the service of the will the knowledge which originally existed only for this service. In other words, genius is the ability to leave entirely out of sight our own interest, our willing, and our aims, and consequently to discard entirely our own personality for a time, in order to remain *pure knowing subject*, the clear eye of the world; and this not merely for moments, but with the necessary continuity and conscious thought to enable us to repeat by deliberate art what has been apprehended, and "what in wavering apparition gleams fix in its place with thoughts that stand forever!" (Goethe's *Faust*). For genius to appear in an individual, it is as if a measure of the power of knowledge must have fallen to his lot far exceeding that required for the service of an individual will; and this superfluity of knowledge having become free, now becomes the subject purified of will, the clear mirror of the inner nature of the world. This explains the animation, amounting to disquietude, in men of genius, since the present can seldom satisfy them, because it does not fill their consciousness. This gives them that restless zealous nature, that constant search for new objects worthy of contemplation, and also that longing, hardly ever satisfied, for men of like nature and stature to whom they may open their hearts. The common mortal, on the other hand, entirely filled and satisfied by the common present, is absorbed in it, and, finding everywhere his like, has that special ease and comfort in daily life which are denied to the man of genius. Imagination has been rightly recognized as an essential element of genius; indeed, it has sometimes been regarded as identical with genius, but this is not correct. The objects of genius as such are the eternal Ideas, the persistent, essential forms of the world and of all its phenomena; but knowledge of the Idea is necessarily knowledge through perception, and is not abstract. Thus the knowledge of the genius would be restricted to the Ideas of objects actually present to his own person, and would be dependent on the concatenation of circumstances that brought them to him, did not imagination extend his horizon far beyond the reality of his personal experience and enable him to construct all the rest out of the little that has come into his own actual apperception, and thus to let almost all the possible scenes of life pass by within himself. Moreover, the actual objects are almost always only very imperfect copies of the Idea that manifests itself in them. Therefore the man of genius requires imagination, in order to see in things not what nature has actually formed, but what she endeavored to form, yet did not bring about, because of the conflict of her forms with one another which was referred to previously. We shall return to this later, when considering sculpture. Thus imagination extends the mental horizon of the genius beyond the objects that actually present themselves to his person, as regards both quality and quantity. For this reason, unusual strength of imagination is a companion, indeed a condition, of genius. But the converse is not the case, for strength of imagination is not evidence of genius; on the contrary, even men with little or no touch of genius may have much imagination. For we can consider an actual object in two opposite ways, purely objectively, the way of genius grasping the Idea of the object, or in the common way, merely in its relations to other objects according to the principle of sufficient reason, and in its relations to our own will. In a similar manner, we can also perceive an imaginary object in these two ways. Considered in the first way, it is a means to knowledge of the Idea, the communication of which is the work of art. In the second case, the imaginary object is used to build castles in the air, congenial to selfishness and to one's own whim, which for the moment delude and delight; thus only the relations of the phantasms so connected are really ever known. The man who indulges in this game is a dreamer; he will easily mingle with reality the pictures that delight his solitude, and will thus become unfit for real life. Perhaps he will write down the delusions of his imagination, and these will give us the ordinary novels of all kinds which entertain those like him and the public at large, since the readers fancy themselves in the position of the hero, and then find the description very "nice" (*gemütlich*).

As we have said, the common, ordinary man, that manufactured article of nature which she daily produces in thousands, is not capable, at any rate continuously, of a consideration of things wholly disinterested in every sense, such as is contemplation proper. He can direct his attention to things only insofar as they have some relation to his will, although that relation may be only very indirect. As in this reference that always demands only knowledge of the relations, the abstract concept of the thing is sufficient and often even more appropriate, the ordinary man does not linger long over the mere perception, does not fix his eye on an object for long, but, in everything that presents itself to him, quickly looks merely for the concept under which it is to be brought, just as the lazy man looks for a chair, which then no longer interests him. Therefore he is very soon finished with everything, with works of art, with beautiful natural objects, and with that contemplation of life in all its scenes which is really of significance everywhere. He does not linger; he seeks only his way in life, or at most all that might at any time become his way. Thus he makes topographical notes in the widest sense, but on the consideration of life itself as such he wastes no time. On the other hand, the man of genius, whose power of knowledge is, through its excess, withdrawn for a part of his time from the service of his will, dwells on the consideration of life itself, strives to grasp the Idea of each thing, not its relations to other things. In doing this, he frequently neglects a consideration of his own path in life, and therefore often pursues this with insufficient skill. Whereas to the ordinary man his faculty of knowledge is a lamp that lights his path, to the man of genius it is the sun that reveals the world. This great difference in their way of looking at life soon becomes visible even in the outward appearance of them both. The glance of the man in whom genius lives and works readily distinguishes him; it is both vivid and firm and bears the character of thoughtfulness, of contemplation. We can see this in the portraits of the few men of genius which nature has produced here and there among countless millions. On the other hand, the real opposite of contemplation, namely spying or prying, can be readily seen in the glance of others, if indeed it is not dull and vacant, as is often the case. Consequently a face's "expression of genius" consists in the fact that a decided predominance of knowing over willing is visible in it, and hence that there is manifested in it a knowledge without any relation to a will, in other words, a *pure knowing*. On the other hand, in the case of faces that follow the rule, the expression of the will predominates, and we see that knowledge comes into activity only on the impulse of the will, and so is directed only to motives.

As the knowledge of the genius, or knowledge of the Idea, is that which does not follow the principle of sufficient reason, so, on the other hand, the knowledge that does follow this principle gives us prudence and rationality in life, and brings about the sciences. Thus individuals of genius will be affected with the defects entailed in the neglect of the latter kind of knowledge. Here, however, a limitation must be observed, that what I shall state in this regard concerns them only insofar as, and while, they are actually engaged with the kind of knowledge peculiar to the genius. Now this is by no means the case at every moment of their lives, for the great though spontaneous exertion required for the will-free comprehension of the Ideas necessarily relaxes again, and there are long intervals during which men of genius stand in very much the same position as ordinary persons, both as regards merits and defects. On this account, the action of genius has always been regarded as an inspiration, as indeed the name itself indicates, as the action of a superhuman being different from the individual himself, which takes possession of him only periodically. The disinclination of men of genius to direct their attention to the content of the principle of sufficient reason will show itself first in regard to the ground of being, as a disinclination for mathematics. The consideration of mathematics proceeds on the most universal forms of the phenomenon, space and time, which are themselves only modes or aspects of the principle of sufficient reason; and it is therefore the very opposite of that consideration that seeks only the content of the phenomenon, namely the Idea expressing itself in the phenomenon apart from all relations. Moreover, the logical procedure of mathematics will be repugnant to genius, for it obscures real insight and does not satisfy it; it presents a mere concatenation of conclusions according to the principle of the ground of knowing. Of all the mental powers, it makes the greatest claim on memory, so that one may have before oneself all the earlier propositions to which reference is made. Experience has also confirmed that men of great artistic genius have no aptitude for mathematics; no man was ever very distinguished in both at the same time. Alfieri relates that he was never able to understand even the fourth proposition of Euclid. Goethe was reproached enough with his want of mathematical knowledge by the ignorant opponents of his color theory. Here, where it was naturally not a question of calculation and measurement according to hypothetical data, but one of direct knowledge by understanding cause and effect, this reproach was so utterly absurd and out of place that they revealed their total lack of judgment just as much by such a reproach as by the rest of their Midas-utterances. The fact that even today, nearly half a century after the appearance of Goethe's color theory, the Newtonian fallacies still remain in undisturbed possession of the professorial chair even in Germany, and that people continue to talk quite seriously about the seven homogeneous rays of light and their differing refrangibility, will one day be numbered among the great intellectual peculiarities of mankind in general, and of the Germans in particular. From the same abovementioned cause may be explained the equally well-known fact that, conversely, distinguished mathematicians have little susceptibility to works of fine art. This is expressed with particular naivety in the well-known anecdote of that French mathematician who, after reading Racine's *Iphigenia*, shrugged his shoulders and asked: "What does all that prove?" Further, as keen comprehension of relations according to the laws of causality and motivation really constitutes prudence or sagacity, whereas the knowledge of genius is not directed to relations, a prudent man will not be a genius insofar as and while he is prudent, and a genius will not be prudent insofar as and while he is a genius. Finally, knowledge of perception generally, in the province of which the Idea entirely lies, is directly opposed to rational or abstract knowledge which is guided by the principle of the ground of knowing.

It is also well known that we seldom find great genius united with preeminent reasonableness; on the contrary, men of genius are often subject to violent emotions and irrational passions. But the cause of this is not weakness of the faculty of reason, but partly unusual energy of that whole phenomenon of will, the individual genius. This phenomenon manifests itself through vehemence of all his acts of will. The cause is also partly a preponderance of knowledge from perception through the senses and the understanding over abstract knowledge, in other words, a decided tendency to the perceptive. In such men the extremely energetic impression of the perceptive outshines the colorless concepts so much that conduct is no longer guided by the latter, but by the former, and on this very account becomes irrational. Accordingly, the impression of the present moment on them is very strong, and carries them away into thoughtless actions, into emotion and passion. Moreover, since their knowledge has generally been withdrawn in part from the service of the will, they will not in conversation think so much of the person with whom they are speaking as of the thing they are speaking about, which is vividly present in their minds. Therefore they will judge or narrate too objectively for their own interests; they will not conceal what it would be more prudent to keep concealed, and so on. Finally, they are inclined to soliloquize, and in general may exhibit several weaknesses that actually are closely akin to madness. It is often remarked that genius and madness have a side where they touch and even pass over into each other, and even poetic inspiration has been called a kind of madness, [. . .] and in the introduction to *Oberon* Wieland speaks of "amiable madness." Even Aristotle [. . .] is supposed to have said: "There has been no great mind without an admixture of madness." Plato expresses it in the myth of the dark cave by saying that those who outside the cave have seen the true sunlight and the things that actually are (the Ideas) cannot afterwards see within the cave anymore, because their eyes have grown unaccustomed to the darkness; they no longer recognize the shadow-forms correctly. They are therefore ridiculed for their mistakes by those others who have never left that cave and those shadow-forms. [. . .]

Eight

On the Inner Nature of Art

Not merely philosophy but also the fine arts work at bottom towards the solution of the problem of existence. For in every mind which once gives itself up to the purely objective contemplation of the world, a desire has been awakened, however concealed and unconscious, to comprehend the true nature of things, of life, and of existence. For this alone is of interest to the intellect as such, in other words, to the subject of knowing which has become free from the aims of the will and is therefore pure; just as for the subject, knowing as mere individual, only the aims and ends of the will have interest. For this reason the result of every purely objective, and so of every artistic, apprehension of things is an expression more of the true nature of life and of existence, more an answer to the question, "What is life?" Every genuine and successful work of art answers this question in its own way quite calmly and serenely. But all the arts speak only the naive and childlike language of *perception*, not the abstract and serious language of *reflection*; their answer is thus a fleeting image, not a permanent universal knowledge. Thus for *perception*, every work of art answers that question, every painting, every statue, every poem, every scene on the stage. Music also answers it, more profoundly indeed than do all the others, since in a language intelligible with absolute directness, yet not capable of translation into that of our faculty of reason, it expresses the innermost nature of all life and existence. Thus all the other arts together hold before the questioner an image or picture of perception and say: "Look here; this is life!" However correct their answer may be, it will yet always afford only a temporary, not a complete and final, satisfaction. For they always give only a fragment, an example instead of the rule, not the whole which can be given only in the universality of the *concept*. Therefore it is the task of philosophy to give for the concept, and hence for reflection and in the abstract, a reply to that question, which on that very account is permanent and satisfactory for all time. Moreover we see here on what the relationship between philosophy and the fine arts rests, and can conclude from this to what extent the capacity for the two, though very different in its tendency and in secondary matters, is yet radically the same.

Accordingly, every work of art really endeavors to show us life and things as they are in reality; but these cannot be grasped directly by everyone through the mist of objective and subjective contingencies. Art takes away this mist.

The works of poets, sculptors, and pictorial or graphic artists generally contain an acknowledged treasure of profound wisdom, just because the wisdom of the nature of things themselves speaks from them. They interpret the utterances of things merely by elucidation and purer repetition. Therefore everyone who reads the poem or contemplates the work of art must of course contribute from his own resources towards bringing that wisdom to light. Consequently, he grasps only so much of the work as his capacity and culture allow, just as every sailor in a deep sea lets down the sounding-lead as far as the length of its line will reach. Everyone has to stand before a picture as before a prince, waiting to see whether it will speak and what it will say to him; and, as with the prince, so he himself must not address it, for then he would hear only himself. It follows from all this that all wisdom is certainly contained in the works of the pictorial or graphic arts, yet only *virtualiter* or *implicite*. Philosophy, on the other hand, endeavors to furnish the same wisdom *actualiter* and *explicite*; in this sense philosophy is related to these arts as wine is to grapes. What it promises to supply would be, so to speak, a clear gain already realized, a firm and abiding possession, whereas that which comes from the achievements and works of art is only one that is always to be produced afresh. But for this it makes discouraging demands, hard to fulfill not merely for those who are to produce its works, but also for those who are to enjoy them. Therefore its public remains small, while that of the arts is large.

The above-mentioned cooperation of the beholder, required for the enjoyment of a work of art, rests partly on the fact that every work of art can act only through the medium of the imagination. It must therefore excite the imagination, which can never be left out of the question and remain inactive. This is a condition of aesthetic effect, and therefore a fundamental law of all the fine arts. But it follows from this that not everything can be given directly to the senses through the work of art, but only as much as is required to lead the imagination onto the right path. Something, and indeed the final thing, must always be left over for it to do. Even the author must always leave something over for the reader to think; for Voltaire has very rightly said: "The secret of being dull and tedious consists in our saying everything." But in addition to this, the very best in art is too spiritual to be given directly to the senses; it must be born in the beholder's imagination, though it must be begotten by the work of art. It is due to this that the sketches of great masters are often more effective than their finished paintings. Of course another advantage contributes to this, namely that they are completed at one stroke in the moment of conception, whereas the finished painting is brought about only through continued effort by means of clever deliberation and persistent premeditation, for the inspiration cannot last until the painting is completed. From the fundamental aesthetic law we are considering, it can also be explained why wax figures can never produce an aesthetic effect, and are therefore not real works of fine art, although it is precisely in them that the imitation of nature can reach the highest degree. For they leave nothing over for the imagination. Thus sculpture gives the mere form without the color; painting gives the color, but the mere appearance of the form; therefore both appeal to the imagination of the beholder. The wax figure, on the contrary, gives everything, form and color at the same time; from this arises the appearance of reality, and the imagination is left out of account. On the other hand, *poetry* appeals indeed to the imagination alone, and makes it active by means of mere words.

An arbitrary playing with the means of art without proper knowledge of the end is in every art the fundamental characteristic of bungling. Such bungling shows itself in the supports that carry nothing, in the purposeless volutes, prominences, and projections of bad architecture, in the meaningless runs and figures together with the aimless noise of bad music, in the jingling rhymes of verses with little or no meaning, and so on.

It follows from previous remarks on natural beauty and from my whole view of art that its object is to facilitate knowledge of the *Ideas* of the world (in the Platonic sense, the only one which I recognize for the word *Idea*). But the *Ideas* are essentially something of perception, and therefore, in its fuller determinations, something inexhaustible. The communication of such a thing can therefore take place only on the path of perception, which is that of art. Therefore whoever is imbued with the apprehension of an *Idea* is justified when he chooses art as the medium of his communication. The mere *concept*, on the other hand, is something completely determinable, hence something to be exhausted, something distinctly thought, which can be, according to its whole content, communicated coldly and dispassionately by words.

Now to wish to communicate such a thing through *a work of art* is a very useless indirect course; in fact, it belongs to that playing with the means of art without knowledge of the end which I have just censured. Therefore, a work of art, the conception of which has resulted from mere, distinct concepts, is always ungenuine. If, when considering a work of plastic art, or reading a poem, or listening to a piece of music (which aims at describing something definite), we see the distinct, limited, cold, dispassionate concept glimmer and finally appear through all the rich resources of art, the concept which was the kernel of this work, the whole conception of the work having therefore consisted only in clearly thinking this concept, and accordingly being completely exhausted by its communication, then we feel disgust and indignation, for we see ourselves deceived and cheated of our interest and attention. We are entirely satisfied by the impression of a work of art only when it leaves behind something that, in spite of all our reflection on it, we cannot bring down to the distinctness of a concept. The mark of that hybrid origin from mere concepts is that the author of a work of art should have been able, before setting about it, to state in distinct words what he intended to present; for then it would have been possible to attain his whole end through these words themselves. It is therefore an undertaking as unworthy as it is absurd when, as has often been attempted at the present day, one tries to reduce a poem of Shakespeare or Goethe to an abstract truth, the communication whereof would have been the aim of the poem. Naturally the artist should think when arranging his work, but only *that* idea which was *perceived* before it was thought has suggestive and stimulating force when it is communicated, and thereby becomes immortal and imperishable. Hence we will not refrain from remarking that the work done at one stroke, like the previously mentioned sketches of painters, perfected in the inspiration of the first conception and drawn unconsciously as it were; likewise the melody that comes entirely without reflection and wholly as if by inspiration; finally also the lyrical poem proper, the mere song, in which the deeply felt mood of the present and the impression of the surroundings flow forth as if involuntarily in words, whose meter and rhyme are realized automatically—that all these, I say, have the great merit of being the pure work of the rapture of the moment, of the inspiration, of the free impulse of genius, without any admixture of deliberation and reflection. They are therefore delightful and enjoyable through and through, without shell and kernel, and their effect is much more infallible than is that of the greatest works of art of slow and deliberate execution. In all these, e.g., in great historical paintings, long epic poems, great operas, and so on, reflection, intention, and deliberate selection play an important part. Understanding, technical skill, and routine must fill up here the gaps left by the conception and inspiration of genius, and all kinds of necessary subsidiary work must run through the really only genuine and brilliant parts as their cement. This explains why all such works, with the sole exception of the most perfect masterpieces of the very greatest masters (such as *Hamlet*, *Faust*, the opera *Don Giovanni*, for example), inevitably contain an admixture of something insipid and tedious that restricts the enjoyment of them to some extent. Proofs of this are Klopstock's *Messiah*, Tasso's *La Gerusalemme liberata*, even *Paradise Lost* and the *Aeneid*; and Horace makes the bold remark: "I am mortified whenever the great Homer sleeps." But that this is the case is a consequence of the limitation of human powers in general.

The mother of the useful arts is necessity; that of the fine arts superfluity and abundance. As their father, the former have understanding, the latter genius, which is itself a kind of superfluity, that of the power of knowledge beyond the measure required for the service of the will.

Nine

Metaphysics of the Beautiful and Aesthetics

As I have dealt in sufficient detail in my chief work *The World as Will and Representation* with the conception of the (Platonic) Ideas and with the correlative thereof, namely the pure subject of knowing, I should regard it as superfluous here to return to it once more, did I not bear in mind that this is a consideration which in this sense has never been undertaken prior to me. It is, therefore, better not to keep back anything which might at some time be welcome by way of their elucidation. In this connection, I naturally assume that the reader is acquainted with those earlier discussions. The real problem of the metaphysics of the beautiful may be very simply expressed by our asking how satisfaction with and pleasure in an object are possible without any reference thereof to our willing. Thus everyone feels that pleasure and satisfaction in a thing can really spring only from its relation to our will or, as we are fond of expressing it, to our aims, so that pleasure without a stirring of the will seems to be a contradiction. Yet the beautiful, as such, quite obviously gives rise to our delight and pleasure, without its having any reference to our personal aims and so to our will.

My solution has been that in the beautiful we always perceive the essential and original forms of animate and inanimate nature and thus Plato's Ideas thereof, and that this perception has as its condition their essential correlative, the *will-free subject of knowing*, in other words a pure intelligence without aims and intentions. On the occurrence of an aesthetic apprehension, the will thereby vanishes entirely from consciousness. But it alone is the source of all our sorrows and sufferings. This is the origin of that satisfaction and pleasure which accompany the apprehension of the beautiful. It therefore rests on the removal of the entire possibility of suffering. If it should be objected that the possibility of pleasure would then also be abolished, it should be remembered that, as I have often explained, happiness or satisfaction is of a *negative* nature, that is, simply the end of a suffering, whereas pain is that which is positive. And so with the disappearance of all willing from consciousness, there yet remains the state of pleasure, in other words, absence of all pain and here even absence of the possibility thereof. For the individual is transformed into a subject that merely knows and no longer wills; and yet he remains conscious of himself and of his activity precisely as such. As we know, the world as *will* is the first world (*ordine prior*), and the world as *representation*, the second (*ordine posterior*). The former is the world of craving and therefore of pain and a thousand different woes. The latter, however, is in itself essentially painless; moreover, it contains a spectacle worth seeing, altogether significant, and at least entertaining. Aesthetic pleasure consists in the enjoyment thereof. Complete satisfaction, the final quieting, the true desirable state, always present themselves only in the picture, *the work of art*, the poem, or music. [. . .] To become a pure subject of knowing means to be quit of oneself; the pure subject of knowing occurs in our forgetting ourselves in order to be absorbed entirely in the intuitively perceived objects, so that they alone are left in consciousness. But since in most cases people cannot do this, they are, as a rule, incapable of that purely objective apprehension of things which constitutes the gift of the artist.

However, let the individual will leave free for a while the power of representation which is assigned to it, and let it exempt this entirely from the service for which it has arisen and exists so that, for the time being, such power relinquishes concern for the will or for one's own person, this being its only natural theme and thus its regular business, but yet it does not cease to be energetically active and to apprehend clearly and with rapt attention what is intuitively perceptible. That power of representation then becomes at once perfectly *objective*, that is to say, the true mirror of objects or, more precisely, the medium of the objectification of the will that manifests itself in the objects in question. The inner nature of the will now stands out in the power of representation the more completely, the longer intuitive perception is kept up, until it has entirely exhausted that inner nature. Only thus does there arise with the pure subject the pure object, that is, the perfect manifestation of the will that appears in the intuitively perceived object, this manifestation being just the (Platonic) *Idea* thereof. But the apprehension of such an Idea requires that, while contemplating an object, I disregard its position in time and space and thus its individuality. For it is this *position* which is always determined by the law of causality and puts that object in some relation to me as an individual. Therefore only when that position is set aside does the object become the *Idea* and do I at the same time become the pure subject of knowing. Thus through the fact that every painting forever fixes the fleeting moment and tears it from time, it already gives us not the individual thing, but the *Idea*, that which endures and is permanent in all change. Now, for that required change in the subject and object, the condition is not only that the power of knowledge is withdrawn from its original servitude and left entirely to itself, but also that it nevertheless remains active with the whole of its energy, in spite of the fact that the natural spur of its activity, the impulse of the will, is now absent. Here lies the difficulty and in this the rarity of the thing; for all our thoughts and aspirations, all our seeing and hearing, are naturally always in the direct or indirect service of our countless greater and smaller personal aims. Accordingly it is the *will* that urges the power of knowledge to carry out its function and, without such impulse, that power at once grows weary. Moreover, the knowledge thereby awakened is perfectly adequate for practical life, even for the special branches of science which are directed always only to the *relations* of things, not to the real and true inner nature thereof; and so all their knowledge proceeds on the guiding line of the principle of sufficient reason [or ground], this element of relations. Thus wherever it is a question of knowledge of cause and effect, or of other grounds and consequents, and hence in all branches of natural science and mathematics, as also of history, inventions, and so forth, the knowledge sought must be a *purpose of the will*, and the more eagerly this aspires to it, the sooner will it be attained. Similarly, in the affairs of state, war, matters of finance or trade, intrigues of every kind, and so on, the will through the vehemence of its craving must first compel the intellect to exert all its strength in order to discover the exact clue to all the grounds and consequents in the case in question. In fact, it is astonishing how far the spur of the will can here drive a given intellect beyond the usual degree of its powers. And so for all outstanding achievements in such things, not merely a fine or brilliant mind is required, but also an energetic will which must first urge the intellect to laborious effort and restless activity, without which such achievements cannot be effected.

Now it is quite different as regards the apprehension of the objective original essence of things which constitutes their (Platonic) Idea and must be the basis of every achievement in the fine arts. Thus the will, which was there so necessary and indeed indispensable, must here be left wholly out of the question; for here only is that of any use which the intellect achieves entirely of itself and from its own resources and produces as a free-will offering. Here everything must go automatically; knowledge must be active without intention and so must be will-less. For only in the state of *pure knowing*, where a man's will and its aims together with his individuality are entirely removed from him, can that purely objective intuitive perception arise wherein the (Platonic) Ideas of things are apprehended. But it must always be such an apprehension which precedes the conception, i.e., the first and always intuitive knowledge. This subsequently constitutes the real material and kernel, as it were the soul, of a genuine work of art, a poem, and even a real philosophical argument. The unpremeditated, unintentional, and indeed partly unconscious and instinctive element that has at all times been observed in the works of *genius* is just a consequence of the fact that the original artistic knowledge is one that is entirely separate from, and independent of, the will, a will-free, will-less knowledge. And just because the will is the man himself, we attribute such knowledge to a being different from him, to genius. A knowledge of this kind has not, as I have often explained, the principle of sufficient reason [or ground] for its guiding line and is thus the antithesis of a knowledge of the first kind. By virtue of his objectivity, the genius with *reflectiveness* perceives all that others do not see. This gives him as a poet the ability to describe nature so clearly, palpably, and vividly, or as a painter, to portray it.

On the other hand, with the *execution* of the work, where the purpose is to communicate and present what is known, the *will* can, and indeed must, again be active, just because there exists a *purpose*. Accordingly, the principle of sufficient reason [or ground] here rules once more, whereby the means of art are suitably directed to the ends thereof. Thus the painter is concerned with the correctness of his drawing and the treatment of his colors; the poet with the arrangement of his plan and then with expression and meter.

But since the intellect has sprung from the will, it therefore presents itself objectively as brain and thus as a part of the body which is the objectification of the will. Accordingly, as the intellect is originally destined to serve the will, the activity natural to it is of the kind previously described, where it remains true to that natural form of its knowledge which is expressed by the principle of sufficient reason [or ground], and where it is brought into activity and maintained therein by the will, the primary and original element in man. Knowledge of the second kind, on the other hand, is an abnormal activity, unnatural to the intellect; accordingly, it is conditioned by a decidedly abnormal and thus very rare excess of intellect and of its objective phenomenon, the brain, over the rest of the organism and beyond the measure required by the aims of the will. Just because this excess of intellect is abnormal, the phenomena springing therefrom sometimes remind one of madness.

Here knowledge then breaks with and deserts its origin, the will. The intellect which has arisen merely to serve the will and, in the case of almost all men, remains in such service, their lives being absorbed in such use and in the results thereof, is used abnormally, as it were abused, in all the *free* arts and sciences; and in this use are set the progress and honor of the human race. In another way, it can even turn itself against the will, in that it abolishes this in the phenomena of holiness.

However, that purely objective apprehension of the world and of things which, as primary and original knowledge, underlies every artistic, poetical, and purely philosophical conception is only a fleeting one, on subjective as well as objective grounds. For this is due in part to the fact that the requisite exertion and attention cannot be maintained, and also to the fact that the course of the world does not allow us at all to remain in it as passive and indifferent spectators, like the philosopher according to the definition of Pythagoras. On the contrary, everyone must act in life's great puppet-play and almost always feels the wire which also connects him thereto and sets him in motion.

Now as regards the *objective* element of such aesthetic intuitive perception, the (Platonic) *Idea*, this may be described as that which we should have before us if time, this formal and subjective condition of our knowledge, were withdrawn, like the glass from the kaleidoscope. For example, we see the development of the bud, blossom, and fruit and are astonished at the driving force that never wearies of again going through this cycle. Such astonishment would vanish if we could know that, in spite of all that change, we have before us the one and unalterable Idea of the plant. However, we are unable intuitively to perceive this Idea as a unity of bud, blossom, and fruit, but are obliged to know it by means of the form of *time*, whereby it is laid out for our intellect in those successive states.

If we consider that both poetry and the plastic arts take as their particular theme an *individual* in order to present this with the greatest care and accuracy in all the peculiarities of its individual nature down to the most insignificant; and if we then review the sciences that work by means of *concepts*, each of which represents countless individuals by determining and describing, once for all, the characteristic of their whole species; then on such a consideration the pursuit of art might seem to us insignificant, trifling, and almost childish. But the essence of art is that its one case applies to thousands, since what it implies through that careful and detailed presentation of the individual is the revelation of the (Platonic) *Idea* of that individual's species. For example, an event, a scene from human life, accurately and fully described and thus with an exact presentation of the individuals concerned therein, gives us a clear and profound knowledge of the Idea of humanity itself, looked at from some point of view. For just as the botanist plucks a single flower from the infinite wealth of the plant world and then dissects it in order to demonstrate the nature of the plant generally, so does the poet take from the endless maze and confusion of human life, incessantly hurrying everywhere, a single scene and often only a mood or feeling, in order then to show us what are the life and true nature of man. We therefore see that the greatest minds, Shakespeare and Goethe, Raphael and Rembrandt, do not regard it as beneath their dignity to present with the greatest accuracy, earnestness, and care an individual who is not even out-standing, and to give down to the smallest detail a graphic description of all his peculiarities. For only through intuitive perception is the particular and individual thing grasped; I have, therefore, defined poetry as the art of bringing the imagination into play by means of words.

If we want to feel directly and thus become conscious of the advantage which knowledge through intuitive perception, as that which is primary and fundamental, has over abstract knowledge and thus see how art reveals more to us than any science can, let us contemplate, either in nature or through the medium of art, a beautiful and mobile human countenance full of expression. What a much deeper insight into the essence of man, indeed of nature generally, is given by this than by all the words and abstractions they express! Incidentally, it may be observed here that what, for a beautiful landscape is the sudden glimpse of the sun breaking through the clouds, is for a beautiful countenance the appearance of its laughter. Therefore, "laugh, girls, laugh!"

However, what enables a *picture* to bring us more easily than does something actual and real to the apprehension of a (Platonic) Idea and so that whereby the picture stands nearer to the Idea than does reality, is generally the fact that the work of art is the object which has already passed through a subject. Thus it is for the mind what animal nourishment, namely the vegetable already assimilated, is for the body. More closely considered, however, the case rests on the fact that the work of plastic art does not, like reality, show us that which exists only once and never again, thus the combination of *this* matter with *this* form, such combination constituting just the concrete and really particular thing, but that it shows us *the form alone*, which would be the Idea itself if only it were given completely and from every point of view. Consequently, the picture at once leads us away from the individual to the mere form. This separation of the form from matter already brings it so much nearer to the Idea. But every picture is such a separation, whether it be a painting or a statue. This severance, this separation, of the form from matter belongs, therefore, to the character of the aesthetic work of art, just because the purpose thereof is to bring us to the knowledge of a (Platonic) *Idea*. It is, therefore, *essential* to the work of art to give the form alone without matter, and indeed to do this openly and avowedly. Here is to be found the real reason why wax figures make no aesthetic impression and are, therefore, not works of art (in the aesthetic sense); although, if they are well made, they produce a hundred times more illusion than can the best picture or statue. If, therefore, deceptive imitation of the actual thing were the purpose of art, wax figures would necessarily occupy the front rank. Thus they appear to give not merely the form, but also the matter as well; and so they produce the illusion of our having before us the thing itself. Therefore, instead of having the true work of art that leads us away from what exists only once and never again, i.e., the individual, to what always exists an infinite number of times, in an infinite number of individuals, i.e., the mere form or Idea, we have the wax figure giving us apparently the individual himself and hence that which exists only once and never again, yet without that which lends value to such a fleeting existence, that is, without life. Therefore the wax figure causes us to shudder since its effect is like that of a stiff corpse.

It might be imagined that it was only the statue that gave form without matter, whereas the painting gave matter as well, insofar as it imitated, by means of color, matter, and its properties. This, however, would be equivalent to understanding form in the purely geometrical sense, which is not what was meant here. For in the philosophical sense, form is the opposite of matter and thus embraces also color, smoothness, texture, in short every quality. The statue is certainly the only thing that gives the purely geometrical form alone, presenting it in marble, thus in a material that is clearly foreign to it; and so in this way, the statue plainly and obviously isolates the form. The painting, on the other hand, gives us no matter at all, but the mere appearance of the form, not in the geometrical but in the philosophical sense just stated. The painting does not even give this form, but the mere appearance thereof, namely its effect on only one sense, that of sight, and even this only from one point of view. Thus even the painting does not really produce the illusion of our having before us the thing itself, that is, form and matter; but even the deceptive truth of the picture is still always under certain admitted conditions of this method of presentation. For example, through the inevitable falling away of the parallax of our two eyes, the picture always shows us things only as a one-eyed person would see them. Therefore even the painting gives only *the form* since it presents merely the effect thereof and indeed quite one-sidedly, namely on the eye alone. [. . .]

Akin to the foregoing consideration is the following where, however, the form must again be understood in the geometrical sense. Black-and-white copper engravings and etchings correspond to a nobler and more elevated taste than do colored engravings and watercolors, although the latter make a greater appeal to those of less cultivated taste. This is obviously due to the fact that black-and-white drawings give the *form* alone, *in abstracto* so to speak, whose apprehension is (as we know) intellectual, that is, the business of the intuitively perceiving understanding. Color, on the other hand, is merely a matter of the sense-organ and in fact of quite a special adaptation therein (qualitative divisibility of the retina's activity). In this respect, we can also compare the colored copper engravings to rhymed verses and black-and-white ones to the merely metrical. [. . .]

The impressions we receive in our youth are so significant and in the dawn of life everything presents itself in such idealistic and radiant colors. This springs from the fact that the individual thing still makes us first acquainted with its species, which to us is still new; and thus every particular thing represents for us its species. Accordingly, we apprehend in it the (Platonic) *Idea* of that species to which as such beauty is essential. The word *schön* [meaning *beautiful*] is undoubtedly connected with the English *to show* and accordingly would mean *showy*, "what shows well," what looks well, and hence stands out clearly in intuitive perception; consequently the clear expression of significant (Platonic) Ideas.

The word *malerisch* [meaning *picturesque*] at bottom has the same meaning as *schön* [or *beautiful*]. For it is attributed to that which so presents itself that it clearly brings to light the (Platonic) Idea of its species. It is, therefore, suitable for the painter's presentation since he is concerned with presenting and bringing out the Ideas which constitute what is objective in the beautiful.

Beauty and grace of the human form are in combination the clearest visibility of the will at the highest stage of its objectification and for this reason are the supreme achievement of plastic art. Yet every natural thing is certainly beautiful, as I have said in *The World as Will and Representation*; and so too is every animal. If this is not obvious to us in the case of some animals, the reason is that we are not in a position to contemplate them purely objectively and thus to apprehend their Idea, but are drawn away therefrom by some unavoidable association of thoughts. In most cases, this is the result of a similarity that forces itself on us, for example, that between man and monkey. Thus we do not apprehend the Idea of this animal, but see only the caricature of a human being. The similarity between the toad and dirt and mud seems to act in just the same way. Nevertheless, this does not suffice here to explain the unbounded loathing and even dread and horror which some feel at the sight of these animals, just as do others at the sight of spiders.

On the contrary, this seems to be grounded in a much deeper metaphysical and mysterious connection. In support of this opinion is the fact that these very animals are usually taken for sympathetic cures (and evil spells) and thus for magical purposes. For example, fever is driven away by a spider enclosed in a nutshell which is worn round the patient's neck until it is dead; or in the case of grave and mortal danger, a toad is laid in the urine of the patient, in a well-closed vessel, and is buried in the cellar of the house at midday, precisely at the stroke of twelve. Yet the slow torture to death of such animals demands an expiation from eternal justice. Now again this affords an explanation of the assumption that, whoever practices magic, makes a compact with the devil.

Insofar as inorganic nature does not consist of water, it has a very sad and even depressing effect on us when it manifests itself without anything organic. Instances of this are the districts that present us with merely bare rocks, particularly the long rocky valley without any vegetation, not far from Toulon, through which passes the road to Marseilles. The African desert is an instance on a large and much more impressive scale. The gloom of that impression of the inorganic springs primarily from the fact that the inorganic mass obeys exclusively the law of gravitation; and thus everything here tends in that direction. On the other hand, the sight of vegetation delights us directly and in a high degree, but naturally the more so, the richer, more varied, more extended it is, and also the more it is left to itself. The primary reason for this is to be found in the fact that the law of gravitation seems in vegetation to be overcome since the plant world raises itself in a direction which is the very opposite to that of gravitation. The phenomenon of life thus immediately proclaims itself to be a new and higher order of things. We ourselves belong to this; it is akin to us and is the element of our existence; our hearts are uplifted by it. And so it is primarily that vertical direction upwards whereby the sight of the plant world directly delights us. Therefore a fine group of trees gains immensely if a couple of long, straight, and pointed fir trees rise from its middle. On the other hand, a tree lopped all round no longer affects us; indeed a leaning tree has less effect than has one that has grown perfectly straight. The branches of the weeping willow which hang down and thus yield to gravity have given it this name. Water eliminates the sad and depressing effect of its inorganic nature to a large extent through its great mobility, which gives it an appearance of life, and through its constant play with light; moreover, it is the primary and fundamental condition of all life. Again, what makes the sight of vegetable nature so delightful is the expression of peace, calm, and satisfaction which it has; whereas animal nature often presents itself in a state of unrest, want, misery, and even conflict. Therefore vegetable nature so readily succeeds in putting us into a state of pure knowing which delivers us from ourselves. It is remarkable to see how vegetable nature, even the most ordinary and insignificant, at once displays itself in beautiful and picturesque groups the moment it is withdrawn from the influence of human caprice. We see this in every spot which has escaped or has not yet been reached by cultivation, even though it bears only thistles, thorns, and the commonest wild-flowers. In cornfields and market gardens, on the other hand, the aesthetic element of the plant world sinks to a minimum.

It has long been recognized that every work intended for human purposes and thus every utensil and building must have a certain resemblance to the works of nature in order to be beautiful. But here we are mistaken in supposing that such resemblance must be direct and lie immediately in the forms, so that, for instance, columns should represent trees or even human limbs, vessels should be shaped like shellfish, snails, or the calices of flowers, and vegetable or animal forms should appear everywhere. On the contrary, this resemblance should not be direct, but only indirect; in other words, it should reside not in the forms, but in the character thereof which can be the same, in spite of their complete difference. Accordingly, buildings and utensils should not imitate nature, but be created in her spirit. Now this shows itself when each thing and each part answers its purpose so directly that such is at once proclaimed by it. All this happens when the purpose is attained on the shortest path and in the simplest way. This obvious appropriateness or fitness is thus the characteristic of the product of nature. Now in this, of course, the will works outwards from within and has made itself the complete master of matter; whereas in the human work, acting from without, the will attains its end and first expresses itself through the medium of intuitive perception and even of a conception of the purpose of the thing, but then by overcoming and subduing a matter that is foreign, in other words, originally expresses another will. Nevertheless, in this case the above-mentioned characteristic of the product of nature can still be retained. Ancient architecture shows this in the exact suitability of each part or member to its immediate purpose which it thus naively displays. It shows it also in the absence of everything useless and purposeless, in contrast to Gothic architecture, which owes its dark and mysterious appearance precisely to the many pointless embellishments and appendages, in that we attribute to these a purpose which to us is unknown. The same may be said of every degenerate style of architecture which affects originality and which, in all kinds of unnecessary devious ways and in arbitrary frivolities, toys with the means of art without understanding their purpose. The same applies to antique vases whose beauty springs from the fact that they express in so naive a way what they are intended to be and do; and it applies also to all the other utensils of the ancients. Here we feel that, if nature were to produce vases, amphorae, lamps, tables, chairs, helmets, shields, armor, and so on, they would look like that. On the other hand, look at the scandalous, richly gilded, porcelain vessels, women's apparel, and other things of the present day. By exchanging the style of antiquity, already introduced, for the vile rococo, men have given evidence of their contemptible spirit and have branded their brows for all time. For this is indeed no trifling matter, but stamps the spirit of these times. A proof of this is furnished by their literature and the mutilation of the German language through ignorant ink-slingers who, in their arbitrary arrogance, treat it as do vandals works of art, and who are allowed to do so with impunity.

The origin of the fundamental idea for a work of art has been very appropriately called its *conception*; for it is the most essential thing just as is procreation to the origin of man; and like this it requires not exactly time, but rather mood and opportunity. Thus the object in general, as that which is the male, practices a constant act of procreation on the subject, as that which is the female. Yet this act becomes fruitful only at odd happy moments and with favored subjects; but then there arises from it some new and original idea which, therefore, lives on. And as with physical procreation, fruitfulness depends much more on the female than on the male; if the former (the subject) is in the mood suitable for conceiving, almost every object now falling within its apperception will begin to speak to it, in other words, to create in it a vivid, penetrating, and original idea. Thus the sight of a trifling object or event has sometimes become the seed of a great and beautiful work; for instance, by suddenly looking at a tin vessel, Jakob Böhme was put into a state of illumination and introduced into the innermost depths of nature. Yet ultimately everything turns on our own strength; and just as no food or medicine can impart or replace vital force, so no book or study can furnish an individual and original mind.

An *improviser*, however, is a man "who knows something at any hour," since he carries round a complete and well-assorted store of commonplaces of all kinds; thus he promises prompt service for every request according to the circumstances of the case and the occasion. A man who undertakes to live on the favor of the Muses, I mean on his gifts as a poet, seems to me to be somewhat like a girl who lives by her charms. For base profit and gain both profane what should be the free gift of their innermost nature. Both suffer from exhaustion, and in most cases both will end ignominiously. And so do not degrade your muse to a whore, but

> I sing, as sings the bird
> Who in the branches lives.
> The song that from his throat is heard,
> Is reward that richly gives,

should be the poet's motto (Goethe: "Der Sänger"). For poetic gifts belong to the holidays, not to the workdays of life. If, then, they should feel somewhat cramped and checked by an occupation which the poet carries on at the same time, they may yet succeed. For the poet does not need to acquire great knowledge and learning, as is the case with the philosopher; in fact poetic gifts are in this way condensed, just as they are diluted by too much leisure and through being exercised professionally. The philosopher, on the other hand, for the reason stated, cannot very well carry on another occupation at the same time, for to make money with philosophy has other serious and well-known drawbacks. For this reason the ancients made it the mark of the sophist in contrast to the philosopher. Solomon too should be commended when he says: "Wisdom is good with an inheritance: and by it there is profit to them that see the sun."

We have the classics of antiquity, that is to say, minds whose writings pass through thousands of years in the undiminished luster and brilliance of youth; and this is due for the most part to the fact that with the ancients the writing of books was not a trade or profession. Only in this way is it possible to explain why the superior works of those classical authors are not accompanied by any that are inferior. For, unlike even the best of modern authors, they did not, after the spirit had evaporated, still bring to market the residue in order to make some money from it.

Music is the true universal language which is everywhere understood; and so it is constantly spoken in all countries and throughout the centuries most eagerly and earnestly, and a significant and suggestive melody very soon finds its way round the globe. On the other hand, a melody that is poor and says nothing soon dies away and is forgotten, which shows that the contents of a melody are very easy to understand. Nevertheless, it speaks not of things, but simply of weal and woe as being for the *will* the sole realities. It therefore says so much to the heart, whereas to the head it has nothing *direct* to say; and it is an improper use if this is required of it, as happens in all *descriptive* music. Such music should, therefore, be rejected once for all, even though Haydn and Beethoven have been misguided into using it. Mozart and Rossini have, to my knowledge, never done this. For to express passions is one thing and to paint objects another.

Even the grammar of this universal language has been given the most precise rules, although only since Rameau laid the foundation for it. On the other hand, to explain the lexicon, I mean the undoubted importance of the contents of this grammar in accordance with the foregoing, in other words, to make intelligible to our reason, if only in a general way, what it is that music says in melody and harmony and what it is talking about, this was never even seriously attempted until I undertook to do it; which only shows, as do so many other things, how little inclined men are generally to reflect and think and how thoughtlessly they live their lives. Their intention everywhere is merely to enjoy themselves, and indeed with the least possible expenditure of thought. Such is their nature. It therefore seems to be so ludicrous when they imagine they have to play at being philosophers, as may be seen in our professors of philosophy, their precious works, and the sincerity of their zeal for philosophy and truth.

Speaking generally and at the same time popularly, we may venture to state that on the whole music is the melody to which the world is the text. But we obtain the proper meaning thereof only through my interpretation of music. But the relation of the art of music to the definite exterior that is always imposed on it, such as text, action, march, dance, sacred or secular festival, and so on, is analogous to that of architecture as a fine art, in other words, as art intended for purely aesthetic purposes, to the actual buildings which it has to erect and with whose utilitarian purposes it must, therefore, try to connect the aims that are peculiar to it, such purposes being foreign to architecture itself as an art. For it achieves its aims under the conditions imposed by those utilitarian purposes and accordingly produces a temple, palace, arsenal, playhouse, and so on, in such a way that the building in itself is beautiful as well as suitable for its purpose and even proclaims this through its aesthetic character. Music, therefore, stands to the text, or to the other realities imposed on it, in an analogous subjection, although this is not so unavoidable. It must first of all adapt itself to the text, although it certainly does not require this and in fact without it moves much more freely. However, music must not only adapt every note to the length and meaning of the words of the text, but must also assume throughout a certain homogeneity with the text and likewise bear the character of the other arbitrary aims imposed on it and accordingly be church, opera, military, dance, or other music. But all this is just as foreign to the nature of music as are human utilitarian purposes to purely aesthetic architecture. Therefore both music and architecture have to adapt themselves to such utilitarian purposes and to subordinate their own aims to those that are foreign to them. For architecture this is almost always unavoidable, but not for music, which freely moves in the concerto, the sonata, and above all the symphony, its finest scene of action wherein it celebrates its saturnalia.

Further, the wrong path, on which our music happens to be, is analogous to that taken by Roman architecture under the later emperors, where the overloading with decorations and embellishments partly concealed, and to some extent perverted, the simple and essential proportions. Thus our music gives us much noise, many instruments, much art, but very few clear, penetrating, and touching ideas. Moreover, in the shallow compositions of today which are devoid of meaning and melody, we again find the same taste of the times which puts up with an obscure, indefinite, nebulous, unintelligible, and even senseless way of writing. [. . .]

Give me Rossini's music that speaks without words! In present-day compositions more account is taken of harmony than of melody. Yet I hold the opposite view and regard melody as the core of music to which harmony is related as the sauce to roast meat.

Grand opera is really not a product of the pure artistic sense, but rather of the somewhat barbaric notion of the enhancement of aesthetic pleasure by the accumulation of the means, the simultaneous use of totally different impressions, and the intensification of the effect through an increase of the operative masses and forces. Music, on the other hand, as the most powerful of all the arts, is by itself alone capable of completely occupying the mind that is susceptible to it. Indeed, to be properly interpreted and enjoyed, the highest productions of music demand the wholly undivided and undistracted attention of the mind so that it may surrender itself to, and become absorbed in, them in order thoroughly to understand its incredibly profound and intimate language. Instead of this, the mind during a piece of highly complicated opera music is at the same time acted on through the eye by means of the most variegated display and magnificence, the most fantastic pictures and images, and the most vivid impressions of light and color; moreover, it is occupied with the plot of the piece. Through all this it is diverted, distracted, deadened, and thus rendered as little susceptible as possible to the sacred, mysterious, and profound language of tones; and so such things are directly opposed to an attainment of the musical purpose. In addition to all this, we have the ballet, a performance which is often directed more to lasciviousness than to aesthetic pleasure. Moreover, through the narrow range of its means and the monotony arising therefrom, the spectacle soon becomes extremely tedious and so tends to exhaust one's patience. In particular, through the wearisome repetition, often lasting a quarter of an hour, of the same second-rate dance melody, the musical sense is wearied and blunted so that it is no longer left with any susceptibility for subsequent musical impressions of a more serious and exalted nature.

It is possible that, although a thoroughly musical mind does not desire it, notwithstanding that the pure language of tones is self-sufficient and needs no assistance, it may be associated with and adapted to words, or even to an action produced through intuitive perception so that our intuitively perceiving and reflecting intellect, which does not like to be completely idle, may yet obtain an easy and analogous occupation. In this way, even the attention is more firmly fixed on the music and follows it; at the same time, a picture or image of intuitive perception, a model or diagram so to speak, like an example to a universal concept, is adapted to what the tones say in their universal language of the heart, a language that is without picture or image; indeed such things will enhance the impression of the music. It should nevertheless be kept within the limits of the greatest simplicity, as otherwise it acts directly against the principal musical purpose.

The great accumulation of vocal and instrumental parts in the opera certainly acts in a musical way; yet the enhancement of the effect, from the mere quartet up to those orchestras with their hundred instruments, bears no relation at all to the increase in the means. For the chord cannot have more than three, or in one case four, notes and the mind can never apprehend more at the same time, no matter by how many parts of the most different octaves those three or four notes may all at once be given. From all this we can explain how a fine piece of music, played only in four parts, may sometimes move us more deeply than does the whole serious opera in the grand style whose quintessence is furnished by it, just as a drawing sometimes has more effect than has an oil painting. However, what mainly depresses the effect of the quartet is that it lacks the extent of the harmony, in other words the distance of two or more octaves between the bass and the lowest of the three upper parts, just as from the depths of the double bass this extent is at the disposal of the orchestra. But for this reason, the effect of the orchestra is immensely enhanced if a large organ, reaching down to the limit of audibility, constantly plays the ground bass to it, as is done in the Catholic church in Dresden. For only thus does the harmony produce its full effect. But generally speaking, simplicity, which usually attaches to truth, is a law that is essential to all art, all that is beautiful, all intellectual presentation or description; at any rate to depart from it is always dangerous.

Strictly speaking, therefore, we could call the opera an unmusical invention for the benefit of unmusical minds into which music must first be smuggled through a medium that is foreign to it, possibly as the accompaniment to a long, spun-out, vapid love story and its wishy-washy poetry. For the text of the opera cannot possibly endure a poetry that is condensed and full of spirit and ideas, because the composition is unable to keep up with this. But to try to make music entirely the slave of bad poetry is the wrong way, which is taken especially by Gluck, whose opera music, apart from the overtures, is, therefore, not enjoyable at all without the words. Indeed it can be said that opera has become the ruin of music. For not only must the music bend and submit in order to suit the development and irregular course of events of an absurd and insipid plot; not only is the mind diverted and distracted from the music by the childish and barbaric pomp of the scenery and costumes, the antics of the dancers, and the short skirts of the ballet girls; no, but even the singing itself often disturbs the harmony, insofar as the *vox humana*, which musically speaking is an instrument like any other, will not coordinate and fit in with the other parts, but tries to dominate absolutely. This is, of course, all right where it is soprano or alto, because in this capacity the melody belongs essentially and naturally to it. But in the bass and tenor arias the leading melody in most cases devolves on the high instruments; and then the singing stands out like an arrogant and conceited voice, in itself merely harmonic, which the melody tries to drown. Or else the accompaniment is transferred contrapuntally to the upper octaves, entirely contrary to the nature of the music, in order to impart the melody to the tenor and bass voices; yet the ear always follows the highest notes and thus the accompaniment. I am really of the opinion that solo arias with orchestral accompaniment are suitable only for the alto or soprano and that male voices should, therefore, be employed only in the duet with these or in pieces of many parts, unless they sing without any accompaniment or with a mere bass accompaniment. Melody is the natural prerogative of the highest voices and instruments and must remain so. Therefore when in the opera a soprano aria comes after a forced and artificial baritone or bass aria, we at once feel with satisfaction that the former alone accords with nature and art. The fact that great masters like Mozart and Rossini are able to mitigate and even to overcome that drawback does not dispose of it.

A much purer musical pleasure than that afforded by the opera is that of the sung *mass*. Its words, which in most cases are not distinctly heard, or its endlessly repeated alleluias, glorias, eleisons, amens, and so on, become a mere solfeggio in which the music, preserving only the general ecclesiastical character, moves freely and is not, as in the case of operatic singing, impaired in its own sphere by miseries of every kind. Here unchecked it therefore develops all its forces since, unlike Protestant morality, it does not always grovel on the ground with the oppressive Puritan or Methodist character of Protestant church music, but like a seraph soars freely with its great pinions. The mass and symphony alone give pure and unalloyed musical pleasure, whereas in the opera the music is tortured by the shallow drama and its pseudo-poetry and tries to get on as best it can with the foreign burden that has been imposed on it. Although not exactly commendable, the sneering contempt with which the great Rossini has sometimes treated the text is at any rate genuinely musical. But speaking generally, since grand opera, by lasting three hours, continues to blunt our musical susceptibility, whilst the snail's pace of an often very insipid action puts our patience to the test, it is in itself essentially of a wearisome and tedious nature. This defect can be overcome only by the extraordinary excellence of the particular performance; and so in this class only masterpieces can be enjoyed and everything mediocre is to be condemned. The attempt should be made to concentrate and contract opera in order to limit it, if possible, to one act and one hour. Fully aware of this, the authorities at the Teatro della Valle in Rome when I was there hit upon the bad expedient of arranging alternately the acts of an opera and a comedy. The maximum duration of an opera should be two hours, that of a drama, on the other hand, three because the requisite attention and mental exertion hold out longer, since it wearies us much less than does the incessant music, which in the end becomes nerve-racking. The last act of an opera is therefore, as a rule, a torment to the audience and an even greater one to the singers and musicians. Accordingly, we might imagine that here we are looking at a large audience who are assembled for the purpose of self-torture, and who pursue it to the end with patience and endurance, an end for which all have long since secretly sighed, with the exception of the deserters.

The overture should prepare us for the opera by announcing the character of the music and the course of the events. Yet this should not be done too explicitly and distinctly, but only in the way in which we foresee coming events in a dream.

A *vaudeville* is comparable to one who parades in clothes he has picked up in a secondhand shop. Every article has already been worn by someone else for whom it was made and whom it fitted; moreover, we see that the different articles do not belong to one another. It is analogous to a harlequin's jacket that has been patched together out of the rags and tatters that are cut from the coats of respectable people. It is a positive musical abomination that should be forbidden by the police.

It is worth noting that in music the value of the composition outweighs that of the performance, whereas in drama the very opposite applies. Thus an admirable composition, only moderately yet clearly and correctly played, gives much more pleasure than does the most excellent performance of a bad composition. On the other hand, a bad theatrical piece, performed by outstanding actors, has much more effect than does the most admirable piece that is played by mere amateurs.

The task of an actor is to portray human nature in all its most varied aspects, in a thousand extremely different characters, yet all these on the common basis of *his* individuality which is given once and for all and can never be entirely effaced. Now, for this reason, he himself must be a capable and complete specimen of human nature, and least of all one so defective or dwarfed that, according to Hamlet's expression, he seems to be made not by nature herself, but "by some of her journeymen." Nevertheless, an actor will the better portray each character the nearer it stands to his own individuality; and he will play best of all that character which corresponds to this. And so even the worst actor has a role that he can play admirably, for he is then like a living face among masks.

To be a good actor, it is necessary for a man (1) to have the gift of being able to turn himself inside out and to show his inner nature; (2) to have sufficient imagination in order to picture fictitious circumstances and events so vividly that they stir his inner nature; and (3) to have enough intelligence, experience, and culture to enable him to have a proper understanding of human characters and relations.

"Man's struggle with fate," which our dull, hollow, puffed-up, and sickly sweet modern aesthetes have for about fifty years unanimously stated to be the universal theme of tragedy, has for its assumption the freedom of the will, that folly of all the ignorant, and also the categorical imperative whose moral purposes or commands, in spite of fate, are now to be carried out. [. . .] But that pretended theme of the tragedy is a ridiculous notion just because it would be the struggle with an invisible opponent, a tilter or jouster in a magic hood of mist, against whom every blow would, therefore, hit the air and into whose arms we should be cast in trying to avoid him, as happened to

Laius and Oedipus. Moreover, fate is all-powerful; and thus to fight it would be the most ludicrous of all presumptions, so that Byron is perfectly right in *Don Juan* in saying:

> To strive too with our fate were such a strife
> As if the corn-sheaf should oppose the sickle.

Shakespeare in *Twelfth Night* also understood the matter thus:

> Fate, show thy force: ourselves we do not owe;
> What is decreed must be, and be this so!

With the ancients the concept of fate is that of a necessity which is hidden in the totality of things. Without any consideration either for our wishes and prayers or guilt and merit, this necessity guides human affairs and draws together on its secret bond even those things that are outwardly most independent of one another, in order to bring them whither it will so that their obviously fortuitous coincidence is in a higher sense necessary. Now just as, by virtue of in this necessity, everything is preordained (*fatum*), so too is a previous *knowledge* of it possible through oracles, seers, dreams, and so on.

Providence is Christianized fate and thus fate transformed into the purpose of a God which is directed to the greatest good of the world.

I regard as the aesthetic purpose of the *chorus* in the tragedy firstly that, along with the view of things which the chief characters have who are stirred by the storm of passions, that of calm and disinterested deliberation should be mentioned; and secondly, that the essential moral of the piece, which is successively disclosed *in concreto* by the action thereof, may at the same time also be expressed as a reflection on this *in abstracto* and consequently in brief. Acting in this way, the chorus is like the bass in music which, as a constant accompaniment, enables one to perceive the fundamental note of each single chord of the progression.

Just as the strata of the earth show us in their impressions the forms of living creatures from a world of the remotest past, impressions that preserve throughout countless thousands of years the trace of a brief existence, so in their *comedies* have the ancients left us a faithful and lasting impression of their gay life and activity. The impression is so clear and accurate that it seems as if they had done this with the object of bequeathing to the remotest posterity at least a lasting picture of a fine and noble existence whose transitory and fleeting nature they regretted. Now if we again fill with flesh and blood these frames and forms which have been handed down to us, by presenting Plautus and Terence on the stage, then that brisk and active life of the remote past again appears fresh and bright before us, just as ancient mosaic floors, when wetted, stand out once more in the brilliance of their old colors. [. . .]

The drama generally, as the most perfect mirror of human existence, has a threefold climax in its way of interpreting this and consequently in its purpose and pretension. At the first and most frequent stage, it stops at what is merely interesting; the characters call for our sympathy in the pursuit of their own aims that are similar to ours. The action proceeds through the intrigue, the characters, and chance; and wit and the jest are the spice of the whole. At the second stage, the drama becomes sentimental; sympathy is excited for the heroes and indirectly for ourselves. The action becomes pathetic and yet at the end it returns to peace and contentment. At the highest and most difficult stage, the *tragic* is contemplated. The severe suffering and misery of existence are brought home to us and here the vanity of all human effort is the final conclusion. We are profoundly shaken and, either directly or as an accompanying harmonic note, there is stirred in us a turning away of the will from life.

Naturally I have not taken into consideration the drama of political tendency which flirts with the momentary whims of the flattering and sugary populace, that favorite product of our present-day writers. Such pieces soon lie as dead as old calendars, often in the following year. Yet this does not worry those writers, for the appeal to their Muse contains only one prayer: "Give us this day our daily bread."

All beginning, it is said, is difficult; in the art of drama, however, the opposite applies and all ending is difficult. This is proved by the innumerable dramas which promise well in the first half, but then become obscure, halting, uncertain, especially in the notorious fourth act, and finally peter out in a forced or unsatisfactory ending, or in one that was long foreseen by everyone, or sometimes, as in *Emilia Galotti*, in one that is revolting and sends the audience home in a thoroughly bad mood. This difficulty of the ending is due in part to the fact that it is always easier to entangle affairs than to unravel them; but also to some extent to the fact that at the beginning we give the poet *carte blanche*, whereas at the end we make definite demands. Thus it is to be either perfectly happy or wholly tragic, whereas human affairs do not readily take so decided a turn. Then again it must work out naturally, correctly, and in an unforced manner; and yet this must not be foreseen by anyone. The same applies to the epic and the romance; in the drama only its more compact nature makes it more apparent in that this increases the difficulty.

The "nothing comes from nothing" (Lucretius) applies also to the fine arts. For their historical pictures good painters have as their models real human beings and take for their heads actual faces drawn from life which they then idealize either as regards their beauty or their character. Good novelists, I believe, do the same thing; they base their characters on actual human beings of their acquaintance who serve as their models and whom they now idealize and complete in accordance with their own intentions.

The task of the novelist is not to narrate great events, but to make interesting those that are trifling. A novel will be of a loftier and nobler nature, the more of inner and the less of outer life it portrays; and this relation will, as a characteristic sign, accompany all gradations of the novel from *Tristram Shandy* down to the crudest and most eventful knight or robber romance. *Tristram Shandy* has, in fact, practically no action at all; but how little there is in *La nouvelle Héloïse* and *Wilhelm Meister*! Even *Don Quixote* has relatively little; it is very insignificant and tends to be comical; and these four novels are at the top of their class. Consider further the wonderful novels of Jean Paul and see how much inner life they set in motion on the narrowest foundation of the outer. Even the novels of Sir Walter Scott have a considerable preponderance of inner over outer life and indeed the latter always appears only for the purpose of setting the former in motion; whereas in inferior novels it is there for its own sake. Art consists in our bringing the inner life into the most intense action with the least possible expenditure of the outer; for the inner is really the object of our interest.

I frankly admit that the great reputation of the *Divina Commedia* seems to me to be exaggerated. The extravagant absurdity of the fundamental idea is largely responsible for this, and as a result the most repulsive aspect of Christian mythology is in the *Inferno* at once brought vividly to our notice. Then again the obscurity of the style and allusions also contributes its share. [...] Nevertheless, the brevity of style, often bordering on the laconic, the energy of expression, but even more the incomparable power of Dante's imagination, are certainly very remarkable. By virtue thereof he imparts to the description of impossible things a palpable truth that is consequently akin to that of a dream. For as he cannot have had any experience of such things, it seems that he must have dreamt them in order to be able to paint them in such vivid, exact, and distinct colors. On the other hand, what are we to say when, at the end of the eleventh canto of the *Inferno*, Virgil describes the breaking of the day and the setting of the stars, but forgets that he is in hell and under the earth and that only at the end of this main part will he "come out from there to see the stars again" (Dante)? The same blunder is found once more at the end of the twentieth canto. Are we to assume that Virgil carries a watch and therefore knows what at the moment is going on in heaven? To me this seems to be a worse case of forgetfulness than the well-known one concerning Sancho Panza's ass, of which Cervantes was guilty.

Ten

The Artist and the Sublime

Now, according to our explanation, genius consists in the ability to know, independently of the principle of sufficient reason, not individual things which have their existence only in the relation, but the Ideas of such things, and in the ability to be, in face of these, the correlative of the Idea, and hence no longer individual, but pure subject of knowing. Yet this ability must be inherent in all men in a lesser and different degree, as otherwise they would be just as incapable of enjoying works of art as of producing them. Generally they would have no susceptibility at all to the beautiful and to the sublime; indeed, these words could have no meaning for them. We must therefore assume as existing in all men that power of recognizing in things their Ideas, of divesting themselves for a moment of their personality, unless indeed there are some who are not capable of any aesthetic pleasure at all. The man of genius excels them only in the far higher degree and more continuous duration of this kind of knowledge. These enable him to retain that thoughtful contemplation necessary for him to repeat what is thus known in a voluntary and intentional work, such repetition being the work of art. Through this he communicates to others the Idea he has grasped. Therefore this Idea remains unchanged and the same, and hence aesthetic pleasure is essentially one and the same, whether it be called forth by a work of art, or directly by the contemplation of nature and of life. The work of art is merely a means of facilitating that knowledge in which this pleasure consists. That the Idea comes to us more easily from the work of art than directly from nature and from reality arises solely from the fact that the artist, who knew only the Idea and not reality, clearly repeated in his work only the Idea, separated it out from reality, and omitted all disturbing contingencies. The artist lets us peer into the world through his eyes. That he has these eyes, that he knows the essential in things which lies outside all relations, is the gift of genius and is inborn; but that he is able to lend us this gift, to let us see with his eyes, is acquired, and is the technical side of art. Therefore, after the account I have given in the foregoing remarks of the inner essence of the aesthetic way of knowing in its most general outline, the following more detailed philosophical consideration of the beautiful and the sublime will explain both simultaneously, in nature and in art, without separating them further. We shall first consider what takes place in a man when he is affected by the beautiful and the sublime. Whether he draws this emotion directly from nature, from life, or partakes of it only through the medium of art makes no essential difference, but only an outward one.

In the aesthetic method of consideration we found *two inseparable constituent parts*: namely, knowledge of the object not as individual thing, but as Platonic *Idea*, in other words, as persistent form of this whole species of things; and the self-consciousness of the knower, not as individual, but as *pure, will-less subject of knowledge*. The condition under which the two constituent parts appear always united was the abandonment of the method of knowledge that is bound to the principle of sufficient reason, a knowledge that, on the contrary, is the only appropriate kind for serving the will and also for science. Moreover, we shall see that the *pleasure* produced by contemplation of the beautiful arises from those two constituent parts, sometimes more from the one than from the other, according to what the object of aesthetic contemplation may be.

All *willing* springs from lack, from deficiency, and thus from suffering. Fulfillment brings this to an end; yet for one wish that is fulfilled there remain at least ten that are denied. Further, desiring lasts a long time, demands and requests go on to infinity; fulfillment is short and meted out sparingly. But even the final satisfaction itself is only apparent; the wish fulfilled at once makes way for a new one; the former is a known delusion, the latter a delusion not as yet known. No attained object of willing can give a satisfaction that lasts and no longer declines; but it is always like the alms thrown to a beggar, which reprieves him today so that his misery may be prolonged till tomorrow. Therefore, so long as our consciousness is filled by our will, so long as we are given up to the throng of desires with its constant hopes and fears, so long as we are the subject of willing, we never obtain lasting happiness or peace. Essentially, it is all the same whether we pursue or flee, fear harm or aspire to enjoyment; care for the constantly demanding will, no matter in what form, continually fills and moves consciousness; but without peace and calm, true well-being is absolutely impossible. Thus the subject of willing is constantly lying on the revolving wheel of Ixion, is always drawing water in the sieve of the Danaids, and is the eternally thirsting Tantalus.

When, however, an external cause or inward disposition suddenly raises us out of the endless stream of willing, and snatches knowledge from the thralldom of the will, the attention is now no longer directed to the motives of willing, but comprehends things free from their relation to the will. Thus it considers things without interest, without subjectivity, purely objectively; it is entirely given up to them insofar as they are merely representations, and not motives. Then all at once the peace, always sought but always escaping us on that first path of willing, comes to us of its own accord, and all is well with us. It is the painless state, prized by Epicurus as the highest good and as the state of the gods; for that moment we are delivered from the miserable pressure of the will. We celebrate the Sabbath of the penal servitude of willing; the wheel of Ixion stands still.

But this is just the state that I described above as necessary for knowledge of the Idea, as pure contemplation, absorption in perception, being lost in the object, forgetting all individuality, abolishing the kind of knowledge which follows the principle of sufficient reason and comprehends only relations. It is the state where, simultaneously and inseparably, the perceived individual thing is raised to the Idea of its species, and the knowing individual to the pure subject of will-less knowing, and now the two, as such, no longer stand in the stream of time and of all other relations. It is then all the same whether we see the setting sun from a prison or from a palace.

Inward disposition, predominance of knowing over willing, can bring about this state in any environment. This is shown by those admirable Dutchmen who directed such purely objective perception to the most insignificant objects, and set up a lasting monument of their objectivity and spiritual peace in paintings of *still life*. The aesthetic beholder does not contemplate this without emotion, for it graphically describes to him the calm, tranquil, will-free frame of mind of the artist which was necessary for contemplating such insignificant things so objectively, considering them so attentively, and repeating this perception with such thought. Since the picture invites the beholder to participate in this state, his emotion is often enhanced by the contrast between it and his own restless state of mind, disturbed by vehement willing, in which he happens to be. In the same spirit landscape painters, especially Ruysdael, have often painted extremely insignificant landscape objects, and have thus produced the same effect even more delightfully.

So much is achieved simply and solely by the inner force of an artistic disposition; but that purely objective frame of mind is facilitated and favored from without by accommodating objects, by the abundance of natural beauty that invites contemplation, and even presses itself on us. Whenever it presents itself to our gaze all at once, it almost always succeeds in snatching us, although only for a few moments, from subjectivity, from the thralldom of the will, and transferring us into the state of pure knowledge. This is why the man tormented by passions, want, or care is so suddenly revived, cheered, and comforted by a single, free glance into nature. The storm of passions, the pressure of desire and fear, and all the miseries of willing are then at once calmed and appeased in a marvelous way. For at the moment when, torn from the will, we have given ourselves up to pure, will-less knowing, we have stepped into another world, so to speak, where everything that moves our will, and thus violently agitates us, no longer exists. This liberation of knowledge lifts us as wholly and completely above all this as do sleep and dreams. Happiness and unhappiness have vanished; we are no longer the individual; that is forgotten; we are only pure subject of knowledge. We are only that *one* eye of the world which looks out from all knowing creatures, but which in man alone can be wholly free from serving the will. In this way, all difference of individuality disappears so completely that it is all the same whether the perceiving eye belongs to a mighty monarch or to a stricken beggar; for beyond that boundary neither happiness nor misery is taken with us. There always lies so near to us a realm in which we have escaped entirely from all our affliction; but who has the strength to remain in it for long? As soon as any relation to our will, to our person, even of those objects of pure contemplation, again enters consciousness, the magic is at an end. We fall back into knowledge governed by the principle of sufficient reason; we now no longer know the Idea, but the individual thing, the link of a chain to which we also belong, and we are again abandoned to all our woe. Most men are almost always at this standpoint, because they entirely lack objectivity, i.e., genius. Therefore they do not like to be alone with nature; they need company, or at any rate a book, for their knowledge remains subject to the will. Therefore in objects they seek only some relation to their will, and with everything that has not such a relation there sounds within them, as it were like a ground bass, the constant, inconsolable lament, "It is of no use to me." Thus in solitude even the most beautiful surroundings have for them a desolate, dark, strange, and hostile appearance.

Finally, it is also that blessedness of will-less perception which spreads so wonderful a charm over the past and the distant, and by a self-deception presents them to us in so flattering a light. For by our conjuring up in our minds days long past spent in a distant place, it is only the objects recalled by our imagination, not the subject of will, that carried around its incurable sorrows with it just as much then as it does now. But these are forgotten, because since then they have frequently made way for others. Now, in what is remembered, objective perception is just as effective as it would be in what is present, if we allowed it to have influence over us, if, free from will, we surrendered ourselves to it. Hence it happens that, especially when we are more than usually disturbed by some want, the sudden recollection of past and distant scenes flits across our minds like a lost paradise. The imagination recalls merely what was objective, not what was individually subjective, and we imagine that that something objective stood before us then just as pure and undisturbed by any relation to the will as its image now stands in the imagination; but the relation of objects to our will caused us just as much affliction then as it does now. We can withdraw from all suffering just as well through present as through distant objects, whenever we raise ourselves to a purely objective contemplation of them, and are thus able to produce the illusion that only those objects are present, not we ourselves. Then, as pure subject of knowing, delivered from the miserable self, we become entirely one with those objects, and foreign as our want is to them, it is at such moments just as foreign to us. Then the world as representation alone remains; the world as will has disappeared.

In all these remarks, I have sought to make clear the nature and extent of the share which the subjective condition has in aesthetic pleasure, namely the deliverance of knowledge from the service of the will, the forgetting of oneself as individual, and the enhancement of consciousness to the pure, will-less, timeless subject of knowing that is independent of all relations. With this subjective side of aesthetic contemplation there always appears at the same time as necessary correlative its objective side, the intuitive apprehension of the Platonic Idea. But before we turn to a closer consideration of this and to the achievements of art in reference to it, it is better to stop for a while at the subjective side of aesthetic pleasure, in order to complete our consideration of this by discussing the impression of the *sublime*, which depends solely on it, and arises through a modification of it. After this, our investigation of aesthetic pleasure will be completed by a consideration of its objective side.

But first of all, the following remarks appertain to what has so far been said. Light is most pleasant and delightful; it has become the symbol of all that is good and salutary. In all religions it indicates eternal salvation, while darkness symbolizes damnation. Ormuzd dwells in the purest light, Ahriman in eternal night. Dante's Paradise looks somewhat like Vauxhall in London, since all the blessed spirits appear there as points of light that arrange themselves in regular figures. The absence of light immediately makes us sad, and its return makes us feel happy. Colors directly excite a keen delight, which reaches its highest degree when they are translucent. All this is due to the fact that light is the correlative and condition of the most perfect kind of knowledge through perception, of the only knowledge that in no way directly affects the will. For sight, unlike the affections of the other senses, is in itself, directly, and by its sensuous effect, quite incapable of pleasantness or unpleasantness of *sensation* in the organ; in other words, it has no direct connection with the will. Only perception arising in the understanding can have such a connection, which then lies in the relation of the object to the will. In the case of hearing, this is different; tones can excite pain immediately, and can also be directly agreeable sensuously without reference to harmony or melody. Touch, as being one with the feeling of the whole body, is still more subject to this direct influence on the will; and yet there is a touch devoid of pain and pleasure. Odors, however, are always pleasant or unpleasant, and tastes even more so. Thus the last two senses are most closely related to the will, and hence are always the most ignoble, and have been called by Kant the subjective senses. Therefore the pleasure from light is in fact the pleasure from the objective possibility of the purest and most perfect kind of knowledge from perception. As such it can be deduced from the fact that pure knowing, freed and delivered from all willing, is extremely gratifying, and, as such, has a large share in aesthetic enjoyment. Again, the incredible beauty that we associate with the reflection of objects in water can be deduced from this view of light. That lightest, quickest, and finest species of the effect of bodies on one another, that to which we owe also by far the most perfect and pure of our perceptions, namely the impression by means of reflected light rays, is here brought before our eyes quite distinctly, clearly, and completely, in cause and effect, and indeed on a large scale. Hence our aesthetic delight from it, which in the main is entirely rooted in the subjective ground of aesthetic pleasure, and is delight from pure knowledge and its ways.

All these considerations are intended to stress the subjective part of aesthetic pleasure, namely, that pleasure insofar as it is delight in the mere knowledge of perception as such, in contrast to the will. Now directly connected with all this is the following explanation of that frame of mind which has been called the feeling of the *sublime*.

It has already been observed that transition into the state of pure perception occurs most easily when the objects accommodate themselves to it, in other words, when by their manifold and at the same time definite and distinct form they easily become representatives of their Ideas, in which beauty, in the objective sense, consists. Above all, natural beauty has this quality, and even the most stolid and apathetic person obtains therefrom at least a fleeting, aesthetic pleasure. Indeed, it is remarkable how the plant world in particular invites one to aesthetic contemplation, and, as it were, obtrudes itself thereon. It might be said that such accommodation was connected with the fact that these organic beings themselves, unlike animal bodies, are not immediate object of knowledge. They therefore need the foreign intelligent individual in order to come from the world of blind willing into the world of the representation. Thus they yearn for this entrance, so to speak, in order to attain at any rate indirectly what directly is denied to them. For the rest, I leave entirely undecided this bold and venturesome idea that perhaps borders on the visionary, for only a very intimate and devoted contemplation of nature can excite or justify it. I am now all the more delighted and surprised, forty years after advancing this thought so timidly and hesitatingly, to discover that St. Augustine had already expressed it: "The trees offer to the senses for perception the many different forms by which the structure of this visible world is adorned, so that, because they are unable to *know*, they may appear, as it were, to want to *be known*."

Now, so long as it is this accommodation of nature, the significance and distinctness of its forms, from which the Ideas individualized in them readily speak to us; so long as it is this which moves us from knowledge of mere relations serving the will into aesthetic contemplation, and thus raises us to the will-free subject of knowing, so long is it merely the *beautiful* that affects us, and the feeling of beauty that is excited. But these very objects, whose significant forms invite us to a pure contemplation of them, may have a hostile relation to the human will in general, as manifested in its objectivity, the human body. They may be opposed to it; they may threaten it by their might that eliminates all resistance, or their immeasurable greatness may reduce it to naught. Nevertheless, the beholder may not direct his attention to this relation to his will which is so pressing and hostile, but, although he perceives and acknowledges it, he may consciously turn away from it, forcibly tear himself from his will and its relations, and, giving himself up entirely to knowledge, may quietly contemplate, as pure, will-less subject of knowing, those very objects so terrible to the will. He may comprehend only their Idea that is foreign to all relation, gladly linger over its contemplation, and consequently be elevated precisely in this way above himself, his person, his willing, and all willing. In that case, he is then filled with the feeling of the *sublime*; he is in the state of exaltation, and therefore the object that causes such a state is called *sublime*. Thus what distinguishes the feeling of the sublime from that of the beautiful is that, with the beautiful, pure knowledge has gained the upper hand without a struggle, since the beauty of the object, in other words that quality of it which facilitates knowledge of its Idea, has removed from consciousness, without resistance and hence imperceptibly, the will and knowledge of relations that slavishly serve this will. What is then left is pure subject of knowing, and not even a recollection of the will remains. On the other hand, with the sublime, that state of pure knowing is obtained first of all by a conscious and violent tearing away from the relations of the same object to the will which are recognized as unfavorable, by a free exaltation, accompanied by consciousness, beyond the will and the knowledge related to it. This exaltation must not only be won with consciousness, but also be maintained, and it is therefore accompanied by a constant recollection of the will, yet not of a single individual willing, such as fear or desire, but of human willing in general, insofar as it is expressed universally through its objectivity, the human body. If a single, real act of will were to enter consciousness through actual personal affliction and danger from the object, the individual will, thus actually affected, would at once gain the upper hand. The peace of contemplation would become impossible, the impression of the sublime would be lost, because it had yielded to anxiety, in which the effort of the individual to save himself supplanted every other thought. A few examples will contribute a great deal to making clear this theory of the aesthetically sublime, and removing any doubt about it. At the same time they will show the difference in the degrees of this feeling of the sublime. For in the main it is identical with the feeling of the beautiful, with pure will-less knowing, and with the knowledge, which necessarily appears therewith, of the Ideas out of all relation that is determined by the principle of sufficient reason. The feeling of the sublime is distinguished from that of the beautiful only by the addition, namely the exaltation beyond the known hostile relation of the contemplated object to the will in general. Thus there result several degrees of the sublime, in fact transitions from the beautiful to the sublime, according as this addition is strong, clamorous, urgent, and near, or only feeble, remote, and merely suggested. I regard it as more appropriate to the discussion to adduce first of all in examples these transitions, and generally the weaker degrees of the impression of the sublime, although those whose aesthetic susceptibility in general is not very great, and whose imagination is not vivid, will understand only the examples, given later, of the higher and more distinct degrees of that impression. They should therefore confine themselves to these, and should ignore the examples of the very weak degree of the abovementioned impression, which are to be spoken of first.

Just as man is simultaneously impetuous and dark impulse of willing (indicated by the pole of the genitals as its focal point), and eternal, free, serene subject of pure knowing (indicated by the pole of the brain), so, in keeping with this antithesis, the sun is simultaneously the source of *light*, the condition for the most perfect kind of knowledge, and therefore of the most delightful of things; and the source of *heat*, the first condition of all life, in other words, of every phenomenon of the will at its higher grades. Therefore what heat is for the will, light is for knowledge. For this reason, light is the largest diamond in the crown of beauty, and has the most decided influence on the knowledge of every beautiful object. Its presence generally is an indispensable condition; its favorable arrangement enhances even the beauty of the beautiful. But above all else, the beautiful in architecture is enhanced by the favor of light, and through it even the most insignificant thing becomes a beautiful object. Now, if in the depth of winter, when the whole of nature is frozen and stiff, we see the rays of the setting sun reflected by masses of stone, where they illuminate without warming, and are thus favorable only to the purest kind of knowledge, not to the will, then contemplation of the beautiful effect of light on these masses moves us into the state of pure knowing, as all beauty does. Yet here, through the faint recollection of the lack of warmth from those rays, in other words, of the absence of the principle of life, a certain transcending of the interest of the will is required. There is a slight challenge to abide in pure knowledge, to turn away from all willing, and precisely in this way we have a transition from the feeling of the beautiful to that of the sublime. It is the faintest trace of the sublime in the beautiful, and beauty itself appears here only in a slight degree. The following is an example almost as weak.

Let us transport ourselves to a very lonely region of boundless horizons, under a perfectly cloudless sky, trees and plants in the perfectly motionless air, no animals, no human beings, no moving masses of water, the profoundest silence. Such surroundings are as it were a summons to seriousness, to contemplation, with complete emancipation from all willing and its cravings; but it is just this that gives to such a scene of mere solitude and profound peace a touch of the sublime. For, since it affords no objects, either favorable or unfavorable, to the will that is always in need of strife and attainment, there is left only the state of pure contemplation, and whoever is incapable of this is abandoned with shameful ignominy to the emptiness of unoccupied will, to the torture and misery of boredom. To this extent it affords us a measure of our own intellectual worth, and for this generally the degree of our ability to endure solitude, or our love of it, is a good criterion. The surroundings just described, therefore, give us an instance of the sublime in a low degree, for in them with the state of pure knowing in its peace and all-sufficiency there is mingled, as a contrast, a recollection of the dependence and wretchedness of the will in need of constant activity. This is the species of the sublime for which the sight of the boundless prairies of the interior of North America is renowned.

Now let us imagine such a region denuded of plants and showing only bare rocks; the will is at once filled with alarm through the total absence of that which is organic and necessary for our subsistence. The desert takes on a fearful character; our mood becomes more tragic. The exaltation to pure knowledge comes about with a more decided emancipation from the interest of the will, and by our persisting in the state of pure knowledge, the feeling of the sublime distinctly appears.

The following environment can cause this in an even higher degree. Nature in turbulent and tempestuous motion; semidarkness through threatening black thunderclouds; immense, bare, overhanging cliffs shutting out the view by their interlacing; rushing, foaming masses of water; complete desert; the wail of the wind sweeping through the ravines. Our dependence, our struggle with hostile nature, our will that is broken in this, now appear clearly before our eyes. Yet as long as personal affliction does not gain the upper hand, but we remain in aesthetic contemplation, the pure subject of knowing gazes through this struggle of nature, through this picture of the broken will, and comprehends calmly, unshaken and unconcerned, the Ideas in those very objects that are threatening and terrible to the will. In this contrast is to be found the feeling of the sublime.

But the impression becomes even stronger when we have before our eyes the struggle of the agitated forces of nature on a large scale, when in these surroundings the roaring of a falling stream deprives us of the possibility of hearing our own voices. Or when we are abroad in the storm of tempestuous seas; mountainous waves rise and fall, are dashed violently against steep cliffs, and shoot their spray high into the air. The storm howls, the sea roars, the lightning flashes from black clouds, and thunderclaps drown the noise of storm and sea. Then in the unmoved beholder of this scene the twofold nature of his consciousness reaches the highest distinctness. Simultaneously, he feels himself as individual, as the feeble phenomenon of will, which the slightest touch of these forces can annihilate, helpless against powerful nature, dependent, abandoned to chance, a vanishing nothing in face of stupendous forces; and he also feels himself as the eternal, serene subject of knowing, who as the condition of every object is the supporter of this whole world, the fearful struggle of nature being only his mental picture or representation; he himself is free from, and foreign to, all willing and all needs, in the quiet comprehension of the Ideas.

This is the full impression of the sublime. Here it is caused by the sight of a power beyond all comparison superior to the individual, and threatening him with annihilation.

The impression of the sublime can arise in quite a different way by our imagining a mere magnitude in space and time, whose immensity reduces the individual to naught. By retaining Kant's terms and his correct division, we can call the first kind the dynamically sublime, and the second the mathematically sublime, although we differ from him entirely in the explanation of the inner nature of that impression, and can concede no share in this either to moral reflections or to hypostases from scholastic philosophy.

If we lose ourselves in contemplation of the infinite greatness of the universe in space and time, meditate on the past millennia and on those to come; or if the heavens at night actually bring innumerable worlds before our eyes, and so impress on our consciousness the immensity of the universe, we feel ourselves reduced to nothing; we feel ourselves as individuals, as living bodies, as transient phenomena of will, like drops in the ocean, dwindling and dissolving into nothing. But against such a ghost of our own nothingness, against such a lying impossibility, there arises the immediate consciousness that all these worlds exist only in our representation, only as modifications of the eternal subject of pure knowing. This we find ourselves to be, as soon as we forget individuality; it is the necessary, conditional supporter of all worlds and of all periods of time. The vastness of the world, which previously disturbed our peace of mind, now rests within us; our dependence on it is now annulled by its dependence on us. All this, however, does not come into reflection at once, but shows itself as a consciousness, merely felt, that in some sense or other (made clear only by philosophy) we are one with the world, and are therefore not oppressed but exalted by its immensity. It is the felt consciousness of what the Upanishads of the Vedas express repeatedly in so many different ways, but most admirably in the saying already quoted: "I am all this creation collectively, and besides me there exists no other being." It is an exaltation beyond our own individuality, a feeling of the sublime.

We receive this impression of the mathematically sublime in quite a direct way through a space which is small indeed as compared with the universe, but which, by becoming directly and wholly perceptible to us, affects us with its whole magnitude in all three dimensions, and is sufficient to render the size of our own body almost infinitely small. This can never be done by a space that is empty for perception, and therefore never by an open space, but only by one that is directly perceivable in all its dimensions through delimitation, and so by a very high and large dome, like that of Saint Peter's in Rome or of Saint Paul's in London. The feeling of the sublime arises here through our being aware of the vanishing nothingness of our own body in the presence of a greatness which itself, on the other hand, resides only in our representation, and of which we, as knowing subject, are the supporter. Therefore, here as everywhere, it arises through the contrast between the insignificance and dependence of ourselves as individuals, as phenomena of will, and the consciousness of ourselves as pure subject of knowing. Even the vault of the starry heavens, if contemplated without reflection, has only the same effect as that vault of stone, and acts not with its true, but only with its apparent, greatness. Many objects of our perception excite the impression of the sublime; by virtue both of their spatial magnitude and of their great antiquity, and therefore of their duration in time, we feel ourselves reduced to naught in their presence, and yet revel in the pleasure of beholding them. Of this kind are very high mountains, the Egyptian pyramids, and colossal ruins of great antiquity.

Our explanation of the sublime can indeed be extended to cover the ethical, namely what is described as the sublime character. Such a character springs from the fact that the will is not excited here by objects certainly well calculated to excite it, but that knowledge retains the upper hand. Such a character will accordingly consider men in a purely objective way, and not according to the relations they might have to his will. For example, he will observe their faults, and even their hatred and injustice to himself, without being thereby stirred to hatred on his own part. He will contemplate their happiness without feeling envy, recognize their good qualities without desiring closer association with them, perceive the beauty of women without hankering after them. His personal happiness or unhappiness will not violently affect him; he will be rather as Hamlet describes Horatio:

> For thou hast been
> As one, in suffering all, that suffers nothing;
> A man that fortune's buffets and rewards
> Hast ta'en with equal thanks.

For, in the course of his own life and in its misfortunes, he will look less at his own individual lot than at the lot of mankind as a whole, and accordingly will conduct himself in this respect rather as a knower than as a sufferer.

Eleven

On Education

In consequence of the nature of our intellect, *concepts* should arise through abstraction from *intuitive perceptions*, and hence the latter should exist before the former. If this course is actually taken, as is the case with the man who has for his teacher and book merely his own experience, then he knows quite well what intuitive perceptions there are which belong to, and are represented by, each of his concepts. He knows both exactly, and accordingly deals accurately with everything that happens to him. We can call this way the natural education.

On the other hand, with artificial education, the head is crammed full of concepts by being lectured and taught and through reading, before there is yet any extended acquaintance with the world of intuitive perception. Experience is then supposed subsequently to furnish the intuitive perceptions to all those concepts; but until then, the latter are falsely applied and accordingly people and things are judged from the wrong point of view, seen in the wrong light, and treated in the wrong way. In this manner, education produces distorted and biased minds, which is the reason why in our youth, after much learning and reading, we enter the world partly as simpletons and partly as cranks, and then behave nervously at one moment and rashly at another. For our minds are full of concepts which we now attempt to apply, but almost invariably introduce in an ill-judged and absurd way. This is the consequence of that "confusion of the earlier with the later or of ground with consequent" whereby we obtain first of all concepts and last of all intuitive perceptions, in direct opposition to the natural course of our mental development. For instead of developing in the child the capacity to discern, judge, and think for himself, teachers are merely concerned to cram his head full of the ready-made ideas of others. A long experience has then to correct all those judgments which have resulted from a false application of concepts. Seldom is this entirely successful; and thus very few scholars have the ordinary common sense that is frequently found among the quite illiterate.

According to what has been said, the chief point in education is that an *acquaintance with the world*, to obtain which can be described as the purpose of all education, may be *started at the right end*. But this depends, as I have shown, mainly on the fact that in each thing *intuitive perception* precedes the *concept*; further that the narrower concept precedes the wider; and that the whole instruction thus takes place in the order in which the concepts of things *presuppose* one another. But as soon as in this sequence something is skipped, there result defective concepts and from these come false ones and finally a distorted view of the world peculiar to the individual, which almost everyone entertains for some time and many all their lives. Whoever applies the test to himself will discover that a correct or clear understanding of many fairly simple things and circumstances dawned on him only at a very mature age and sometimes quite suddenly. Till then there had been here in his acquaintance with the world an obscure point which had arisen from his skipping the subject in the early period of his education, whether such had been artificial through instructors or merely natural through his own experience.

Accordingly, one should try to examine the really natural sequence of knowledge, so that children may be made acquainted with the things and circumstances of the world methodically and in accordance with that sequence, without getting into their heads absurd ideas which often cannot again be dislodged. Here one would first have to prevent children from using words with which they did not associate any clear concept. Even children frequently have the fatal tendency to be satisfied with words instead of trying to understand things, and a desire to learn by heart such words in order to get themselves out of a difficulty when the occasion arises. Such tendency afterwards remains when they grow up, and this is why the knowledge of many scholars is mere verbiage. But the main point should be always that intuitive perceptions precede concepts, and not vice versa, as is usually and unfortunately the case; as if a child were to come into the world feet first, or a verse be written down rhyme first! Thus while the child's mind is still quite poor in intuitive perceptions, concepts, and judgments, or rather prejudices, are impressed on it. He then applies this ready-made apparatus to intuitive perception and experience. Instead of this, the concepts and judgments should have crystallized out from intuitive perception and experience. Such perception is rich and varied and, therefore, cannot compete in brevity and rapidity with the abstract concept which is soon finished and done with everything; and so it will be a long time in correcting such preconceived notions, or perhaps it may never bring this to an end. For whichever of its aspects it shows to be contradictory to those preconceived notions, its declaration is rejected in advance as being one-sided, or is even denied; and people shut their eyes to it so that the preconceived notion may not come to any harm. And so it happens that many a man carries round throughout his life a burden of absurd notions, whims, crotchets, fancies, and prejudices that ultimately become fixed ideas. Indeed, he has never attempted to abstract for himself fundamental concepts from intuitive perception and experience, because he has taken over everything ready-made;

and it is just this that makes him and countless others so shallow and insipid. Therefore instead of this, the natural course of forming knowledge should be kept up in childhood. No concept must be introduced except by means of intuitive perception; at any rate it must not be substantiated without this. The child would then obtain few concepts, but they would be well grounded and accurate. He would then learn to measure things by his own standard instead of with someone else's. He would never conceive a thousand caprices and prejudices whose eradication is bound to require the best part of subsequent experience and the school of life; and his mind would once and for all be accustomed to the thoroughness and clearness of its own judgment and freedom from prejudice.

Children generally should not become acquainted with life in every respect from the copy before getting to know it from the original. Therefore instead of hastening to place only books in their hands, let us make them gradually acquainted with things and human circumstances. Above all, we should endeavor to introduce them to a clear grasp of real life and to enable them to draw their concepts always directly from the world of reality. They should form such concepts in accordance with reality and not get them from anywhere else, from books, fairy tales, or the talk of others, and subsequently apply them ready-made to real life. For in that case, their heads will be full of chimeras and to some extent they will falsely interpret reality, or vainly attempt to remodel it in accordance with such chimeras and thus go astray theoretically or even practically. For it is incredible how much harm is done by early implanted chimeras and by the prejudices arising therefrom. The later education which is given to us by the world and real life must then be used mainly for eradicating such prejudices. Even the answer given by Antisthenes according to Diogenes Laertius rests on this: "When asked what was the most necessary thing to take up, he replied 'to unlearn what is bad.'"

Just because early imbibed errors are often deeply engraved and indelible and the power of judgment is the last thing to reach maturity, we should keep children up to the age of sixteen free from all theories and doctrines where there may be great errors. Thus they should be kept from all philosophy, religion, and general views of all kinds and be allowed to pursue only those subjects where either no errors are possible, as in mathematics, or none is very dangerous, as in languages, natural science, history, and so on. Generally they should at every age study only those branches of knowledge which are accessible and thoroughly intelligible thereto. Childhood and youth are the time for collecting data and making a special and thorough acquaintance with individual and particular things. On the other hand, judgment generally must still remain suspended and ultimate explanations be deferred. As power of judgment presupposes maturity and experience, it should be left alone and care should be taken not to anticipate it by inculcating prejudices, whereby it is forever paralyzed.

On the other hand, since memory is strongest and most tenacious in youth, it should be specially taxed; yet this should be done with the most careful selection and scrupulous forethought. For what is well learnt in youth sticks for all time; and so this precious faculty should be used for the greatest possible gain. If we call to mind how deeply engraved in our memory are those whom we knew in the first twelve years of our life and how the events of those years and generally most of what we experienced, heard, and learnt at the time are also indelibly impressed on the memory, it is a perfectly natural idea to base education on that receptivity and tenacity of the youthful mind by strictly, methodically, and systematically guiding all impressions thereon in accordance with precept and rule. Now, since only a few years of youth are allotted to man and the capacity of the memory generally, and even more so that of the individual, is always limited, it is all-important to fill it with what is most essential and vital in any branch of knowledge to the exclusion of everything else. This selection should be made and its results fixed and settled after the most mature deliberation by the most capable minds and masters in every branch of learning. Such a selection would have to be based on a sifting of what is necessary and important for a man to know generally and what is important and necessary for him in any particular profession or branch of knowledge. Again, knowledge of the first kind would have to be classified into graduated courses or encyclopedias, adapted to the degree of general education that is intended for everyone in accordance with his external circumstances. It would begin with a course limited to the barest primary education and end with the comprehensive list of all the subjects taught by the philosophical faculty. Knowledge of the second kind, however, would be left to the selection of the real masters in each branch. The whole would provide a specially-worked-out canon of intellectual education which would naturally need to be revised every ten years. Thus by such arrangements, youth's power of memory would be used to the greatest possible advantage and would furnish excellent material for the power of judgment when this subsequently appeared.

Maturity of knowledge, that is, the perfection this can reach in every individual, consists in the fact that a precise connection has been brought about between all his abstract concepts and his intuitively perceiving faculty. Thus each of his concepts rests, directly or indirectly, on a basis of intuitive perception, and only through this does such a concept have any real value. Moreover, this *maturity* consists in his being able to bring under the correct and appropriate concept every intuitive perception that happens to him; it is the work of experience alone and consequently of time. For as we often acquire our knowledge of intuitive perception and our abstract knowledge separately, the former in the natural way and the latter through instruction and what others tell us whether good or bad, there is often in our youth little agreement and connection between our concepts that are fixed by mere words and our real knowledge that has been obtained through intuitive perception. Only gradually do the two approach and mutually correct each other; and maturity of knowledge exists only when they have completely grown together. Such maturity is quite independent of the other greater or less perfection of everyone's abilities which rests not on the connection between abstract and intuitive knowledge, but on the intensive degree of both.

For the practical man the most necessary study is the attainment of an exact and thorough knowledge of the *real ways of the world*. But it is also the most wearisome, since it continues until he is very old without his coming to the end of his study; whereas in the sciences he masters the most important facts when he is still young. In that knowledge the boy and the youth have to learn as novices the first and most difficult lessons; but even the mature man often has to make up for many lessons. This difficulty in itself is serious, but it is doubled by *novels* which describe a state of affairs and a course of human actions, such as, in fact, do not occur in real life. These are now accepted with the credulity of youth and are assimilated in the mind, whereby the place of mere negative ignorance is now taken by a whole tissue of false assumptions, as positive error, which afterwards confuses even the school of experience itself and causes the teachings thereof to appear in a false light. If previously the youth groped about in the dark, he is now misled by a will-o'-the-wisp; and even more often is this the case with a girl. Through novels a thoroughly false view of life is foisted on them and expectations have been aroused which can never be fulfilled. In many cases, this has the most pernicious influence on their whole life. In this respect, those who in their youth have had neither the time nor the opportunity to read novels, such as artisans, mechanics, and the like, have a decided advantage.

There are a few novels which are exceptions and do not merit the above reproach; in fact they have the opposite effect. For example, we have above all *Gil Blas* and the other works of Lesage (or rather their Spanish originals); then *The Vicar of Wakefield*; and to some extent the novels of Sir Walter Scott. *Don Quixote* may be regarded as a satirical presentation of that false path itself.

Twelve

On Noise

Kant wrote an essay on the *living forces*; but I would like to write a dirge and threnode thereon, for their excessively frequent use in knocking, hammering, and banging has been throughout my life a daily torment to me. There are certainly those, quite a number in fact, who smile at such things because they are not sensitive to noise. Yet they are the very people who are also not sensitive to arguments, ideas, poetry, and works of art, in short, to mental impressions of every kind; for this is due to the toughness and solid texture of their brain substance. On the other hand, in the biographies or other accounts of the personal statements of almost all great authors, such as Kant, Goethe, Lichtenberg, Jean Paul, I find complaints about the torture which thinkers have to endure from noise. If such complaints are not to be found in some authors, this is merely because the context did not lead up to them. I explain the matter as follows. A large diamond cut up into pieces is equal in value to just so many small ones; and an army dispersed and scattered, in other words disbanded into small bodies, is no longer capable of anything. In the same way a great mind is no more capable than an ordinary one the moment it is interrupted, disturbed, and diverted. For its superiority is conditioned by its concentrating all its powers, as does a concave mirror all its rays, on to one point and object; and it is precisely here that it is prevented by a noisy interruption. This is why eminent minds have always thoroughly disliked every kind of disturbance, interruption, and diversion, but above all the violent disturbance caused by din and noise. Others, on the contrary, are not particularly upset by such things. The most sensible and intelligent of all European nations has even laid down an eleventh commandment, the rule "Never interrupt!" Din is the most impertinent of all forms of interruption, for it interrupts, in fact disrupts, even our own thoughts. However, where there is nothing to interrupt, din will naturally not be particularly felt. At times, I am tormented and disturbed for a while by a moderate and constant noise before I am clearly conscious thereof, since I feel it merely as a constant increase in the difficulty of thinking, like a weight tied to my foot, until I become aware of what it is.

Passing now from the genus to the species, I have to denounce as the most inexcusable and scandalous noise the truly infernal cracking of whips in the narrow resounding streets of towns; for it robs life of all peace and pensiveness. Nothing gives me so clear an idea of the apathy, stupidity, and thoughtlessness of men as the toleration of this whip-cracking. This sudden sharp crack which paralyzes the brain, tears and rends the thread of reflection and murders all thoughts, must be painfully felt by anyone who carries in his head anything resembling an idea. All such cracks must, therefore, disturb hundreds in their mental activity, however humble its nature; but they shoot through a thinker's meditations as painfully and fatally as the executioner's ax cuts the head from the body. No sound cuts through the brain so sharply as does this cursed whip-cracking; one feels in one's brain the very sting of the lash and it affects the brain as does touch the *Mimosa pudica*, and lasts as long. With all due respect to the most sacred doctrine of utility, I really do not see why a fellow, fetching a cartload of sand or manure, should thereby acquire the privilege of nipping in the bud every idea that successively arises in ten thousand heads (in the course of half an hour's journey through a town). Hammering, the barking of dogs, and the screaming of children are terrible, but the real murderer of ideas is only the crack of a whip. It is meant to crush every good moment for meditation which anyone may at times have. If to urge on draught animals there existed no means other than this most abominable of all noises, there would be some excuse for it, but quite the contrary is the case. This cursed whip-cracking is not only unnecessary, but even useless. Thus the intended psychic effect on the horses is entirely blunted and fails to occur because, through constant abuse of the whip, they have grown accustomed thereto. The horses, accordingly, do not go any faster; and this is also seen especially in the case of cabmen who are on the lookout for a fare and incessantly crack their whips while driving at the slowest pace. The slightest touch of the whip has more effect. But assuming that it were absolutely necessary constantly to remind the horses of the whip's presence by sounding it, then a sound a hundred times quieter would suffice for the purpose. For it is well known that animals notice the slightest scarcely perceptible indications, both audible and visible, the most surprising examples being furnished by trained dogs and canaries. Accordingly, the matter proves to be a piece of pure wantonness and in fact an insolent disregard for those who work with their heads on the part of those members of the community who work with their hands. That such an infamy is tolerated in towns is a crude barbarity and an iniquity, the more so as it could very easily be stopped by a police order to the effect that every whipcord should have a knot at the end. There can be no harm in drawing the attention of the proletarians to the mental work of the classes above them, for they have a mortal dread of all such work. A fellow who rides through the narrow streets of a populous town with free post-horses or on a free cart-horse, or even accompanies animals on foot, and keeps on cracking with all his might a whip several yards long, deserves to be taken down at once and given five really good cuts with a stick. All the philanthropists in the world, and all the legislative assemblies which on good grounds abolish all corporal punishment, will not persuade me to the contrary. But something even worse can often enough be seen, namely a carter who, alone and without horses, walks through the streets and incessantly cracks his whip. This fellow has become so accustomed to the crack of a whip, thanks to inexcusable leniency and toleration. With the universal tenderness for the body and all its gratifications, is the thinking mind to be the only thing that never experiences the slightest consideration or protection, to say nothing of respect? Carters, porters, messengers, and the like are the beasts of burden of the human community; they should certainly be treated humanely with justice, fairness, consideration, and care, but they should not be allowed to thwart the higher endeavors of the human race by wantonly making a noise. I would like to know how many great and fine thoughts have already been cracked out of the world by these whips. If I had to give an order, there would soon be established in the heads of car men an indelible association of ideas between cracking a whip and getting a whipping. Let us hope that the more intelligent and refined nations will make a start in this direction and that, by way of example, the Germans will then be made to follow suit. Meanwhile, Thomas Hood says: "For a musical people, they are the most noisy I ever met with." That they are so, however, is not due to their being more inclined than others to make a noise, but to the apathy and insensibility (with the result of obtuseness) of those who have to listen to it. They are not thereby disturbed in their thinking or reading for the very reason that they do not think, but merely smoke, such being for them a substitute for thinking. The universal toleration of unnecessary noise, for example the extremely vulgar and ill-mannered slamming of doors, is simply a sign of mental bluntness and a general want of thought. In Germany it seems as though it were positively the intention that no one should come to his senses on account of noise; pointless drumming, for example.

Finally, as regards the literature that deals with the subject of this chapter, I can recommend only one work, but it is a fine one, namely a poetical epistle in *terze rime* by the famous painter Bronzino entitled "De' romori, a Messer Luca Martini." Here a detailed and amusing description is given in a tragicomic style of the torment that one has to endure from the many different noises of an Italian town.

Thirteen

On Women

The true praise of women is in my opinion better expressed by Étienne de Jouy's few words than by Schiller's well-considered poem, "Würde der Frauen," which produces its effect by means of antithesis and contrast. Jouy says: "Without women the beginning of our life would be cut off from help, the middle from pleasures, and the end from consolation." The same thing is expressed more pathetically by Byron in his *Sardanapalus*:

> The very first
> Of human life must spring from woman's breast,
> Your first small words are taught you from her lips,
> Your first tears quench'd by her, and your last sighs
> Too often breathed out in a woman's hearing
> When men have shrunk from the ignoble care
> Of watching the last hour of him who led them.

Both express the right point of view for the value of women.

The sight of the female form tells us that woman is not destined for great work, either intellectual or physical. She bears the guilt of life not by doing but by suffering; she pays the debt by the pains of childbirth, care for the child, submissiveness to her husband, to whom she should be a patient and cheerful companion. The most intense sufferings, joys, and manifestations of power do not fall to her lot; but her life should glide along more gently, mildly, and with less importance than man's, without being essentially happier or un-happier.

Women are qualified to be the nurses and governesses of our ear-liest childhood by the very fact that they are themselves childish, trifling, and shortsighted, in a word, are all their lives grown-up chil-dren: a kind of intermediate stage between the child and the man, who is a human being in the real sense. Just see how, for days on end, a girl will fondle and dance with a child and sing to it, and imagine what a man with the best will in the world could do in her place!

With girls, nature has had in view what in a dramaturgic sense is called a stage-effect or sensation. For she has endowed them for a few years with lavish beauty, charm, and fullness at the expense of the rest of their lives. This she has done so that, during those few years, they might capture a man's imagination to the extent that he is car-ried away into giving in some form an honorable undertaking to look after them for the rest of their lives. Mere rational deliberation would not appear to give a sufficiently adequate guarantee to induce him to take such a step. Accordingly, nature has endowed women, as she has every other creature, with the weapons and instruments needed for the security of their existence and for as long as they require them, a course wherein she has proceeded with her usual parsimony. For just as the female ant after copulation loses her wings which are now superfluous and, as regards breeding, even dangerous, so does the woman generally lose her beauty after one or two confinements, and probably for the same reason.

Accordingly, young girls in their hearts regard their domestic or business affairs as something secondary and indeed as a mere piece of fun. They consider love, conquests, and everything connected therewith, such as dress, cosmetics, dancing, and so on, to be their only serious vocation.

The nobler and more perfect a thing is, the later and more slowly does it come to maturity. A man does not arrive at a maturity of his rational faculty and mental powers much before his twenty-eighth year; woman attains it at the age of eighteen. But it is, in consequence, a very meager and limited faculty of reason. And so throughout their lives women remain children, always see only what is nearest to them, cling to the present, take the appearance of things for the reality, and prefer trivialities to the most important affairs. Thus it is the faculty of reason by virtue whereof man does not, like the animal, live merely in the present, but surveys and considers the past and future; and from all this spring his foresight, wariness, care, anxiety, and frequent uneasiness. In consequence of her weaker faculty of reason, woman shares less in the advantages and disadvantages that this entails. Rather is she an intellectual myope, since her intuitive understanding sees quite clearly what is near, but has a narrow range of vision into which the distant object does not enter. Thus everything that is absent, past, or future has a much feebler effect on women than on men, whence arises the tendency to extravagance which occurs much more frequently in women and occasionally borders on craziness. "Woman is by nature extravagant" (Menander). In their hearts, women imagine that men are born to earn money, whilst they are meant to get through it, if possible during the man's lifetime, but at any rate after his death. They are strengthened in this belief by the fact that the man hands over to them for housekeeping what he has earned. However many disadvantages all this may entail, there is yet one good point, namely that woman is more absorbed in the present than man and, therefore, enjoys this better if only it is bearable. The result of this is that cheerfulness which is peculiar to woman and makes her suited for the recreation, and if necessary the consolation, of the man who is burdened with cares.

In difficult and delicate matters, it is by no means a bad thing to consult women, after the manner of the ancient Germans. For their way of apprehending things is quite different from man's, more particularly as they like to go the shortest way to the goal and generally keep in view what lies nearest to them. But just because this lies under men's noses, it is generally overlooked by them, in which case it is then necessary for them to be brought back to it so that they may regain the near and simple view. Moreover, women are decidedly more matter-of-fact than men and thus do not see in things more than actually exists, whereas when the passions of men are aroused, they easily magnify what is present or add something imaginary.

From the same source may be traced the fact that women show more compassion and thus more loving-kindness and sympathy for the unfortunate than do men; on the other hand, they are inferior to men in the matter of justice, honesty, and conscientiousness. For in consequence of their weak faculty of reason, that which is present, intuitively perceptual, immediately real, exercises over them a power against which abstract ideas, established maxims, fixed resolves, and generally a consideration for the past and future, the absent and distant, are seldom able to do very much. Accordingly, they certainly have the first and fundamental thing for virtue; on the other hand, they lack the secondary, the often necessary instrument for it. In this respect, they might be compared to an organism which had liver, it is true, but no gallbladder. [. . .] In accordance with the foregoing, we find that injustice is the fundamental failing of the female character. It arises primarily from the above-mentioned want of reasonableness and reflection and is further supported by the fact that, as the weaker, they are by nature dependent not on force but cunning; hence their instinctive artfulness and ineradicable tendency to tell lies. For just as nature has armed the lion with claws and teeth, the elephant and boar with tusks, the bull with horns, and the cuttlefish with ink that blackens water, so for their defense and protection has she endowed women with the art of dissimulation. She has bestowed on them in the form of this gift all the force she has given to men in the form of physical strength and power of reason. Dissimulation is, therefore, inborn in women and is thus almost as characteristic of the stupid as of the clever woman; and so to make use of it on every occasion is as natural to her as it is to the above-mentioned animals to make immediate use of their weapons when they are attacked, and to a certain extent she feels that here she is exercising her right. Therefore an entirely truthful and unaffected woman is perhaps impossible. For the same reason, they so easily see through dissimulation in others that it is not advisable to try it on them. But from that fundamental failing and its attendant qualities arise falseness, faithlessness, treachery, ingratitude, and so on. Women are much more often guilty of perjury than men; and in general it might be questioned whether they should be allowed to take the oath. From time to time one repeatedly comes across the case where in a shop a lady who wants for nothing secretly pilfers and pockets things.

Young, strong, and handsome men are called by nature for the propagation of the human race so that it may not degenerate. Herein is nature's firm will and the passions of women are its expression. In age and force, that law comes before any other. Therefore woe to him who so arranges his rights and interests that they stand in its way; whatever he may say or do, they will be mercilessly crushed on the first important occasion. For the secret, unexpressed, indeed unconscious but innate, morality of women is as follows: "We are justified in deceiving those who imagine they have acquired a right over the species by the fact that they barely provide for us, the individuals. The constitution, and consequently the welfare, of the species are placed in our hands and entrusted to our care by means of the next generation coming from us; we will conscientiously carry this out."

Women, however, are by no means conscious of this supreme principle *in abstracto* but only *in concreto*; and for it they have no other expression than their course of action when the opportunity occurs. Here their conscience is generally less disturbed than we suppose, for in the darkest recesses of their hearts they feel that, through a breach of duty to the individual, they have so much better fulfilled that to the species, whose rights are infinitely greater.

Because, at bottom, women exist solely for the propagation of the race with which their destiny is identified, they live generally more in the species than in individuals. At heart, they take more seriously the affairs of the species than those of individuals. This gives to their whole nature and action a certain frivolity and generally an attitude which is fundamentally different from that of the man and gives rise to that discord and disharmony which are so frequent and almost normal in marriage.

Between men there is by nature merely indifference; but between women there is already by nature hostility. This is due to the fact that with men the "professional jealousy" is limited to their particular guild, whereas with women it embraces the whole sex, since they all have only one line of business. Even when they meet in the street, they look at one another like Guelphs and Ghibellines. Moreover on first acquaintance, two women meet each other obviously with more stiffness and dissimulation than do two men in a similar situation. Therefore the compliments between two women prove to be far more ridiculous than those between men. Again, whereas the man, as a rule, speaks with a certain consideration and humanity, even to one who is far beneath him in rank, it is intolerable to see how proudly and disdainfully, for the most part, a woman of rank and position behaves towards one in a lower position (who is not in her service) when she speaks to her. It may be due to the fact that all difference of rank is much more precarious with women than with men and can much more rapidly be altered and abolished. For whereas with men a hundred things turn the scale, with women only one thing decides, namely what man they have charmed. There is also the fact that, on account of the one-sidedness of their calling, they stand much nearer to one another than do men and for that reason endeavor to stress class distinctions.

Only the male intellect, clouded by the sexual impulse, could call the undersized, narrow-shouldered, broad-hipped, and short-legged sex the fair sex; for in this impulse is to be found its whole beauty. The female sex could be more aptly called the unaesthetic. They really and truly have no bent and receptivity either for music, poetry, or the plastic arts; but when they affect and profess to like such things, it is mere aping for the sake of their keen desire to please. This is why they are incapable of taking a *purely objective interest* in anything, and I think the following is the reason for this. In everything man aspires to a *direct* mastery over things, either by understanding or controlling them. But woman is always and everywhere driven to a merely *indirect* mastery by means of the man who alone has to be directly mastered by her. It therefore lies in the nature of women to regard everything merely as a means to win the man; and their interest in anything else is always only simulated, a mere roundabout way; in other words, it ends in coquetry and aping. Thus even Rousseau said: "Women in general do not like any art, are no judges of any, and have no genius." Everyone who has gone beyond appearances will also have noticed it. We need only observe the direction and nature of their attention at a concert, an opera, and a play, and see, for instance, the childlike ingenuousness with which they carry on their chatting during the finest passages of the greatest masterpieces. If the Greeks did not really admit women to the play, they were right; at least it would have been possible to hear something in their theaters. For our own times it would be proper to add to the "Let your women keep silence in the churches" a silence order for the theater, or to substitute it and put it in large letters on the curtain in the theater. We cannot expect anything else from women when we reflect that the most eminent minds of the whole sex have never been able to produce a single, really great, genuine, and original achievement in the fine arts, or to bring anywhere into the world a work of permanent value. This is most striking in regard to painting, for its technique is at any rate just as suited to them as it is to men and thus they pursue it with diligence; yet they cannot boast of a single great painting, just because they lack all objectivity of mind, the very thing that is most directly demanded of painting. Everywhere they remain in the subjective. In keeping with this is the fact that the average woman is not even susceptible to painting in the real sense; for "Nature makes no jumps (she proceeds very gradually from one species to another)." [. . .]

Isolated and partial exceptions do not alter the case but, generally speaking, women are and remain the most downright and incurable Philistines. And so with the positively absurd arrangement whereby they share the position and title of the man, they are constantly spurring him on in his ignoble ambition. Moreover, on account of the same quality, their predominance and the way they set the fashion are the ruin of modern society. In respect of the first, we should be guided by the saying of Napoleon I: "Women have no station in life," and for the rest, Chamfort quite rightly says: "They are made to deal with our weaknesses, our folly, but not with our faculty of reason. Between them and men there is only a superficial sympathy and very little sympathy of mind, soul, and character." They are the sex that takes second place in every respect. We should accordingly treat their weakness with forbearance; but to show them excessive reverence and respect is ridiculous and lowers us in their own eyes. When nature split the human race into two halves, she did not make the division precisely through the middle. In spite of all polarity, the difference between the positive and negative poles is not merely qualitative but also quantitative.

Thus did the ancients and oriental races regard woman; and her proper place was accordingly much more correctly recognized by them than by us with our old French gallantry and absurd veneration of women, this culminating point of Christian-Germanic stupidity. It has merely served to make women so arrogant and inconsiderate that we are sometimes reminded of the sacred apes at Benares who, conscious of their sanctity and invulnerability, think that they are at liberty to do anything and everything. Woman in the West, especially what is called the "lady," finds herself in a distorted position; for woman, rightly called by the ancients the "inferior sex," is by no means qualified to be the object of our respect and veneration, to carry her head higher than man and have equal rights with him. We see well enough the consequences of this distorted position. It would accordingly be very desirable even in Europe for this number two of the human race to be again assigned to her natural place and for this lady-nonsense to be stopped, which not only the whole of Asia ridicules, but Greece and Rome would also have laughed at. From a social, civil, and political point of view, the consequences of this would be of incalculable benefit. As a superfluous truism, the Salic law ought not to be necessary. The European lady proper is a being who should not exist at all; on the contrary, there should be housewives and girls who hope to become so and thus are brought up not to arrogance, but to domesticity and submissiveness. Just because there are ladies in Europe, the women of the lower classes, and thus the great majority of the sex, are much more unhappy than those in the East. Even Lord Byron says: "Thought of the state of women under the ancient Greeks—convenient enough. Present state, a remnant of the barbarism of the chivalry and feudal ages—artificial and unnatural. They ought to mind home—and be well fed and clothed—but not mixed in society. Well educated, too, in religion—but to read neither poetry nor politics—nothing but books of piety and cookery. Music, drawing, dancing, also a little gardening and plowing now and then. I have seen them mending the roads in Epirus with good success. Why not, as well as hay-making and milking?"

In our monogamous continent, to marry means to halve one's rights and double one's duties. Yet when the laws conceded to women equal rights with men, they should also have endowed them with a man's faculty of reason. On the other hand, the more the rights and honors which the laws confer on woman exceed her natural position, the more they reduce the number of women who actually share these privileges; and they deprive all the rest of as many natural rights as they have given in excess to those privileged women. For with the unnaturally favorable position which is given to woman by the monogamous institution and the marriage laws connected therewith, in that they generally regard the woman as the absolute equal of man, which she in no sense is, prudent and cautious men very often hesitate to make so great a sacrifice and to enter into so unequal an agreement. And so whereas among the polygamous races every woman is provided for, among the monogamous the number of married women is limited and many women are left without support. In the upper classes they vegetate as useless old maids, but in the lower they have to do hard and unsuitable work, or become prostitutes who lead a life as joyless as it is disreputable, but who in such circumstances become necessary for the satisfaction of the male sex. They thus appear as a publicly recognized class or profession whose special purpose is to protect from being seduced those women who are favored by fortune and have found or hope to find husbands. In London alone there are eighty thousand women of this class. What, then, are they but women who have become the most fearful losers through the monogamous institution, actual human sacrifices on the altar of monog-

amy? All such women who are so badly off are the inevitable offset to
the European lady with her pretensions and arrogance. Accordingly
for the female sex, considered as a whole, polygamy is a real benefit.
On the other hand, no valid reason can be given why a man should
not have a second wife when his first is suffering from chronic illness, is barren, or has gradually become too old. What gains so many
converts for the Mormons seems to be precisely the removal of this
unnatural monogamy. As regards the sexual relation, no continent is
so immoral as Europe in consequence of unnatural monogamy.

Moreover, giving woman unnatural rights has also imposed on
her unnatural duties whose breach, however, makes her unhappy.
Thus considerations of position or means render marriage inexpedient to many a man, unless perhaps there are brilliant conditions
attached thereto. He will then want to obtain a woman of his choice
under different conditions that will place on a firm footing her lot
and that of the children. Now even if these are ever so fair, reasonable, and suited to the case, and she consents by not insisting on the
disproportionate rights that marriage alone offers, she thus becomes,
to a certain extent, disreputable, because marriage is the basis of civil
society, and she must lead a sad life. For, human nature being what it
is, we attach a wholly exaggerated value to the opinion of others. If,
on the other hand, she does not consent, she runs the risk either of
having to be married to a man she detests or of drying up as an old
maid; for the time during which a man is willing to provide for her
is very limited. As regards this side of our monogamous institution,
Thomasius's profound essay *De concubinatu* is well worth reading.
From it we see that, among all cultured peoples and at all times down
to the Lutheran Reformation, concubinage was a permitted institution; in fact it was, to a certain extent, even legally recognized, with
no dishonor attaching to it. From this position it was overthrown
merely by the Lutheran Reformation, which recognized in its aboli-

tion a further means for justifying marriage of the clergy; whereupon the Catholic side could not be left behind. *Polygamy* is not a matter of *dispute* at all, but is to be taken as a fact that is met with everywhere; its mere *regulation* is the problem. For where are there actual monogamists? We all live in polygamy *at any rate* for a time, but in most cases always. Consequently, as every man needs many women, nothing is more just than that it should be open to him, indeed incumbent on him, to provide for many women. In this way, woman is also brought back to her correct and natural standpoint as a subordinate being and the *lady*, that monster of European civilization and Christian-Germanic stupidity with her ridiculous claims to respect and veneration, disappears from the world. There are then only *women*, but of course no longer any *unfortunate women*, of whom Europe is now full. The Mormons are right.

In Hindustan no woman is ever independent, but each is under the guardianship of a father, husband, brother, or son, in accordance with the Law of Manu. That widows burn themselves on the corpses of their husbands is of course shocking; but that they squander on their lovers the fortune which has been acquired by the husband through the incessant hard work of a lifetime, and in the belief that he was working for his children, is also shocking. "The fortunate and happy keep to the mean." As in animals, so in man, the original maternal love is purely instinctive and therefore ceases with the physical helplessness of the children. In its place, there should then appear one based on habit and reasoning; but often it fails to appear, especially when the mother has not loved the father. The father's love for his children is of a different kind and is more enduring. It rests on his again recognizing in them his own innermost self and is thus of metaphysical origin.

With almost all ancient and modern races on earth, even with the Hottentots, property is inherited merely by the male descendants;

only in Europe has a departure been made from this, yet not with the nobility. Property acquired by the long and constant hard work of men subsequently passes into the hands of women who in their folly get through it or otherwise squander it in a short time. This is an enormity, as great as it is frequent, which should be prevented by restricting woman's right of inheritance. It seems that the best arrangement would be for women, whether as widows or daughters, always to inherit only a life annuity secured by mortgage, not landed property or capital, unless there are no male descendants at all. Those who earn and acquire wealth and property are men, not women; and therefore women are not entitled to their absolute possession, nor are they capable of managing them. At any rate, women should never be free to dispose of inherited property in the real sense, namely capital, houses, and land. They always need a guardian; and so in no case whatever should they receive the guardianship of their children. The vanity of women, even if it may not be greater than that of men, is bad because it is centered entirely on material things, on their personal beauty, and then on finery, pomp, and display; and hence society is so very much their element. This makes them inclined to extravagance, especially with their weak powers of reasoning. The vanity of men, on the other hand, is often centered on nonmaterial virtues and merits, such as understanding, intellect, learning, courage, and the like. In the *Politics*, Aristotle explains what great disadvantages arose for the Spartans from the fact that too much was conceded to their women who had the right of inheritance, the dowry, and great freedom and independence, and how all this greatly contributed to the decline of Sparta. Was not the ever-growing influence of women in France from the time of Louis XIII responsible for the gradual corruption of the court and government which produced the first revolution, the consequences of this being all the subsequent upheavals? At all events, a false position of the female sex, such as has its most acute symptom in our lady-business, is a fundamental defect of the state of society. Proceeding from the heart of this, it is bound to spread its noxious influence to all parts.

That woman by nature is meant to obey may be recognized from the fact that every woman placed in the position of complete independence, which to her is unnatural, at once attaches herself to some man by whom she allows herself to be guided and ruled, because she needs a master. If she is young, he is a lover, and if old, a father confessor.

Fourteen

On Suicide

As far as I can see, it is only the monotheistic, and hence Jewish, religions whose followers regard suicide as a crime. This is the more surprising since neither in the Old Testament nor in the New is there to be found any prohibition or even merely a definite condemnation of suicide. Teachers of religion have, therefore, to base their objection to suicide on their own philosophical grounds; but their arguments are in such a bad way that they try to make up for what these lack in strength by the vigorous expressions of their abhorrence and thus by being abusive. We then of necessity hear that suicide is the greatest cowardice, that it is possible only in madness, and such like absurdities; or else the wholly meaningless phrase that suicide is "wrong," whereas there is obviously nothing in the world over which every man has such an indisputable *right* as his own person and life. As I have said, suicide is even accounted a crime and connected with this, especially in vulgar bigoted England, are an ignominious burial and the confiscation of legacies; for which reason a jury almost invariably brings in a verdict of insanity. First of all, we should allow moral feeling to decide the matter and compare the impression made on us by the news that an acquaintance of ours had committed a crime, such as murder, cruelty, fraud, or theft, with that made by the report of his voluntary death. Whereas the former report arouses lively indignation, the greatest resentment, and a demand for punishment or revenge, the latter will move us to sorrow and sympathy often mingled with a certain admiration for his courage rather than with the moral condemnation that accompanies a bad action. Who has not had acquaintances, friends, and relations who have voluntarily departed from the world? And should we all regard these with abhorrence as criminals? I say no, certainly not! I am rather of the opinion that the clergy should be challenged once and for all to tell us with what right they stigmatize as a *crime* an action that has been committed by many who were honored and beloved by us; for they do so from the pulpit and in their writings without being able to point to any biblical authority and in fact without having any valid philosophical arguments, and they refuse an honorable burial to those who voluntarily depart from the world. But here it should be stipulated that we want *reasons* and shall not accept in their place mere empty phrases or words of abuse. If criminal law condemns suicide, that is not an ecclesiastically valid reason and is, moreover, definitely ridiculous; for what punishment can frighten the man who seeks death? If we punish the *attempt* to commit suicide, then we are simply punishing the want of skill whereby it failed.

[. . .] In Massilia and on the island of Ceos, the cup of hemlock was even publicly handed to the man who could state convincing reasons for quitting life. And how many heroes and sages of antiquity have not ended their lives by a voluntary death! It is true that Aristotle says (in the *Nicomachean Ethics*) suicide is a wrong against the State, although not against one's own person. [. . .]

We find suicide extolled as a noble and heroic action even by the Stoics, as can be proved from hundreds of passages, the most vigorous of which are from Seneca. Further with the Hindus, it is well known that suicide often occurs as a religious action, particularly as widow-burning, self-destruction under the wheels of the Juggernaut Car, self-sacrifice to the crocodiles of the Ganges or the sacred temple tanks, and otherwise. It is precisely the same at the theater, that mirror of life; for example, in the celebrated Chinese play *L'Orphelin de la Chine* we see almost all the noble characters end in suicide without there being any suggestion or its occurring to the spectator that they had committed a crime. In fact, at bottom on our own stage it is not otherwise, for example, Palmira in *Mahomet*, Mortimer in *Maria Stuart*, Othello, Countess Terzky. [. . .] Is Hamlet's monologue the meditation of a crime? He merely states that, if we were sure of being absolutely annihilated by death, we would undoubtedly choose it in view of the state of the world. "Ay, there's the rub." But the reasons against suicide which are advanced by the clergy of the monotheistic, i.e., Jewish, religions and by the philosophers who accommodate themselves to them are feeble sophisms which can easily be refuted. [. . .] The most thorough refutation of them has been furnished by Hume in his essay "On Suicide," which first appeared after his death and was at once suppressed in England by the disgraceful bigotry and scandalous power of the parsons. And so only a few copies were sold secretly and at a high price, and for the preservation of this and another essay by that great man we are indebted to the Basel reprint. [. . .] But that a purely philosophical essay, coldly and rationally refuting the current reasons against suicide and coming from one of the leading thinkers and authors of England, had to be secretly smuggled through that country like a forbidden thing until it found refuge abroad, brings great discredit on the English nation. At the same time, it shows what kind of a conscience the Church has on this point. I have expounded in my chief work the only valid moral reason against suicide. It lies in the fact that suicide is opposed to the attainment of the highest moral goal since it substitutes for the real salvation from this world of woe and misery one that is merely apparent. But it is still a very long way from this aberration to a crime, such as the Christian clergy would like to stamp it.

In its innermost core, Christianity bears the truth that suffering (the cross) is the real purpose of life; and therefore as suicide opposes such purpose, Christianity rejects it, whereas antiquity, from a lower point of view, approved and even honored it. That reason against suicide is, however, ascetic and therefore applies only to an ethical standpoint much higher than that which European moral philosophers have ever occupied. But if we descend from that very high point, there is no longer any valid moral reason for condemning suicide. It seems, therefore, that the extraordinarily lively zeal of the clergy of the monotheistic religions against suicide, a zeal that is not supported either by the Bible or by valid grounds, must have a hidden foundation. Might it not be that the voluntary giving up of life is a poor compliment to him who said "(And God saw) every thing (that he had made, and behold, it) was very good"? So once again, it is the customary and orthodox optimism of these religions which denounces suicide in order not to be denounced by it.

On the whole, we shall find that, as soon as a point is reached where the terrors of life outweigh those of death, man puts an end to his life. The resistance of the latter is nevertheless considerable; they stand, so to speak, as guardians at the gate of exit. Perhaps there is no one alive who would not already have made an end of his life if such an end were something purely negative, a sudden cessation of existence. But it is something positive, namely the destruction of the body, and this frightens people back just because the body is the phenomenon of the will-to-live.

However, the struggle with those guardians is not, as a rule, *so* difficult as it may seem from a distance and indeed in consequence of the antagonism between mental and bodily sufferings. Thus if physically we suffer very severely or continuously, we become indifferent to all other troubles; only our recovery is uppermost in our thoughts. In the same way, severe mental suffering makes us indifferent to physical; we treat it with contempt. In fact, if physical suffering should predominate, this is a wholesome diversion, a pause in the mental suffering. It is precisely this that makes suicide easier, since the physical pain associated with this loses all importance in the eye of one who is tormented by an excessive amount of mental suffering. This becomes particularly noticeable in those who are driven to suicide through a purely morbid deep depression. It does not cost such men any self-restraint at all; they need not make a resolute rush at it, but, as soon as the warder appointed to look after them leaves them for two minutes, they quickly put an end to their life.

If in heavy horrible dreams anxiety reaches its highest degree, it causes us to wake up, whereby all those monstrous horrors of the night vanish. The same thing happens in the dream of life when the highest degree of anxiety forces us to break it off.

Suicide can also be regarded as an experiment, a question we put to nature and try to make her answer, namely what change the existence and knowledge of man undergo through death. But it is an awkward experiment, for it abolishes the identity of the consciousness that would have to listen to the answer.

Fifteen

On the Basis of Ethics

So far all our steps have been supported by the firm rock of experience. But at this point it fails us, and the solid earth sinks from under our feet, as we press forward in our search after a final theoretical satisfaction, there, where no experience can ever by any possibility penetrate; and happy shall we be, if perchance we gain one hint, one transient gleam, that may bring us a certain measure of content. What, however, shall not desert us is the honesty that has hitherto attended our procedure. We shall not make shift with dreams, and serve up fairy tales, after the fashion of the so-called post-Kantian philosophers; nor shall we, like them, seek, by a wordy exuberance, to impose upon the reader, and cast dust in his eyes. A little is all we promise; but that little will be presented in perfect sincerity.

The principle, which we discovered to be the final explanation of Ethics, now in turn itself requires explaining; so that our present problem has to deal with that natural Compassion, which in every man is innate and indestructible, and which has been shown to be the sole source of non-egoistic conduct, this kind alone being of real moral worth. Now, many modern thinkers treat the conceptions of good and bad as simple, that is, as neither needing, nor admitting, any elucidation, and then they go on, for the most part, to talk very mysteriously and devoutly of an "Idea of the Good," out of which they make a pedestal for their moral system, or at least a cloak for their poverty. Hence I am obliged in this connection to point out parenthetically that these conceptions are anything but simple, much less *a priori*; that they in fact express a relation, and are derived from the commonest daily experience. Whatever is in conformity with the desires of any individual will, is, relatively to it, termed good; for instance, good food, good roads, a good omen; the contrary is called bad, and, in the case of living beings, malicious. And so one, who by virtue of his character has no wish to oppose what others strive after, but rather, as far as he reasonably may, shows himself favorable and helpful to them; one, who, instead of injuring, assists his neighbors and promotes their interests, when he can, is named by the latter, in respect to themselves, a good man; the term good being applied to him in the sense of the above definition, and from their own point of view, which is thus relative, empirical, and centered in the passive subject. Now, if we examine the nature of such a man, not only as it affects others, but as it is in itself, we are enabled by the foregoing exposition to perceive that the virtues of justice and loving-kindness, which he practices, are due to a direct participation in weal and woe external to himself; and we have learnt that the source of such participation is Compassion. If, further, we pause to consider what is the essential part in this type of character, we shall certainly find it to lie in the fact that such a person draws less distinction between himself and others than is usually done.

In the eyes of the malicious individual this difference is so great that he takes direct delight in the spectacle of suffering—a delight which he accordingly seeks without thought of any other benefit to himself, nay, sometimes, even to his own hurt. From the egoist's point of view the same difference is still large enough to make him bring much trouble on his neighbors, in order to obtain a small personal advantage. Hence for both of these, between the ego, which is limited to their own persons, and the non-ego, which includes all the rest of the world, there is fixed a great gulf, a mighty abyss: "the world may perish, provided I be safe" is their maxim. For the good man, on the contrary, this distinction is by no means so pronounced; indeed, in the case of magnanimous deeds, it appears to become a vanishing quantity, because then the weal of another is advanced at the cost of the benefactor, the self of another placed on an equality with his own. And when it is a question of saving a number of fellow beings, total self-obliteration may be developed, the one giving his life for many.

The inquiry now presents itself, whether the latter way of looking at the relation subsisting between the ego and the non-ego, which forms the mainspring of a good man's conduct, is mistaken and due to an illusion; or whether the error does not rather attach to the opposite view, on which Egoism and Malice are based. No doubt the theory lying at the root of Egoism is, from the empirical standpoint, perfectly justified. From the testimony of experience, the distinction between one's own person and that of another appears to be absolute. I do not occupy the same space as my neighbor, and this difference, which separates me from him physically, separates me also from his weal and woe. But in the first place, it should be observed that the knowledge we have of our own selves is by no means exhaustive and transparent to its depths. By means of the intuition, which the brain constructs out of the data supplied by the senses, that is to say, in an indirect manner, we recognize our body as an object in space; through an inward perception, we are aware of the continuous series of our desires, of our volitions, which arise through the agency of external motives; and finally, we come to discern the manifold movements, now stronger, now weaker, of our will itself, to which all feelings from within are ultimately traceable. And that is all: for the perceiving faculty is not in its turn perceived. On the contrary, the real substratum of our whole phenomenal nature, our inmost essence in itself, that which wills and perceives, is not accessible to us. We see only the outward side of the ego; its inward part is veiled in darkness. Consequently, the knowledge we possess of ourselves is in no sort radical and complete, but rather very superficial. The larger and more important part of our being remains unknown, and forms a riddle to speculate about; or, as Kant puts it: "The ego knows itself only as a phenomenon; of its real essence, whatever that may be, it has no knowledge." Now, as regards that side of the self which falls within our ken, we are, undoubtedly, sharply distinguished, each from the other; but it does not follow therefrom that the same is true of the remainder, which, shrouded in impenetrable obscurity, is yet, in fact, the very substance of which we consist. There remains at least the possibility that the latter is in all men uniform and identical.

What is the explanation of all plurality, of all numerical diversity of existence? Time and Space. Indeed it is only through the latter that the former is possible: because the concept "many" inevitably connotes the idea either of succession (time) or of relative position (space). Now, since a homogeneous plurality is composed of individuals, I call Space and Time, as being the conditions of multiplicity, the *principium individuationis* (the principle of individuation). [. . .]

If in the disclosures which Kant's wonderful acumen gave to the world there is anything true beyond the shadow of a doubt, this is to be found in the Transcendental Aesthetics, that is to say, in his doctrine of the ideality of Space and Time. On such solid foundations is the structure built that no one has been able to raise even an apparent objection. It is Kant's triumph, and belongs to the very small number of metaphysical theories which may be regarded as really proved, and as actual conquests in that field of research. It teaches us that Space and Time are the forms of our own faculty of intuition, to which they consequently belong, and not to the objects thereby perceived; and further, that they can in no way be a condition of things in themselves, but rather attach only to their mode of appearing, such as is alone possible for us who have a consciousness of the external world determined by strictly physiological limits. Now, if to the Thing in itself, that is, to the Reality underlying the cosmos, as we perceive it, Time and Space are foreign, so also must multiplicity be. Consequently that which is objectivated in the countless phenomena of this world of the senses cannot but be a unity, a single indivisible entity, manifested in each and all of them. And conversely, the web of plurality, woven in the loom of Time and Space, is not the Thing in itself, but only its appearance-form. Externally to the thinking subject, this appearance-form, as such, has no existence; it is merely an attribute of our consciousness, bounded, as the latter is, by manifold conditions, indeed, depending on an organic function.

The view of things as above stated—that all plurality is only apparent, that in the endless series of individuals, passing simultaneously and successively into and out of life, generation after generation, age after age, there is but one and the same entity really existing, which is present and identical in all alike—this theory, I say, was of course known long before Kant; indeed, it may be carried back to the remotest antiquity. It is the alpha and omega of the oldest book in the world, the sacred Vedas, whose dogmatic part, or rather esoteric teaching, is found in the Upanishads. There, in almost every page this profound doctrine lies enshrined; with tireless repetition, in countless adaptations, by many varied parables and similes it is expounded and inculcated. That such was, moreover, the fount whence Pythagoras drew his wisdom cannot be doubted, despite the scanty knowledge we possess of what he taught. That it formed practically the central point in the whole philosophy of the Eleatic School is likewise a familiar fact. [. . .] In the ninth century we find it unexpectedly appearing in Europe. It kindles the spirit of no less a divine than Johannes Scotus Erigena, who endeavors to clothe it with the forms and terminology of the Christian religion. Among the Mohammedans we detect it again in the rapt mysticism of the Sufi. In the West, Giordano Bruno cannot resist the impulse to utter it aloud; but his reward is a death of shame and torture. And at the same time we find the Christian Mystics losing themselves in it, against their own will and intention, whenever and wherever we read of them! Spinoza's name is identified with it. Lastly, in our own days, after Kant had annihilated the old dogmatism, and the world stood aghast at its smoking ruins, the same teaching was revived in Schelling's eclectic philosophy. The latter took all the systems of Plotinus, Spinoza, Kant, and Jakob Böhme, and mixing them together with the results of modern natural science, speedily served up a dish sufficient to satisfy for the moment the pressing needs of his contemporaries; and then proceeded to perform a series of variations on the original theme. The consequence is that in the learned circles of Germany this line of thought has come to be generally accepted; indeed even among people of ordinary education, it is almost universally diffused. [. . .]

Now, if plurality and difference belong only to the appearance-form, if there is but one and the same Entity manifested in all living things, it follows that, when we obliterate the distinction between the ego and the non-ego, we are not the sport of an illusion. Rather are we so, when we maintain the reality of individuation, a thing the Hindus call Maya, that is, a deceptive vision, a phantasma. The former theory we have found to be the actual source of the phenomenon of Compassion; indeed Compassion is nothing but its translation into definite expression. This, therefore, is what I should regard as the metaphysical foundation of Ethics, and should describe it as the sense which identifies the ego with the non-ego, so that the individual directly recognizes in another his own self, his true and very being. From this standpoint the profoundest teaching of theory pushed to its furthest limits may be shown in the end to harmonize perfectly with the rules of justice and loving-kindness, as exercised; and conversely, it will be clear that practical philosophers, that is, the upright, the beneficent, the magnanimous, do but declare through their acts the same truth as the man of speculation wins by laborious research, by the loftiest flights of intellect. Meanwhile moral excellence stands higher than all theoretical sapience. The latter is at best nothing but a very unfinished and partial structure, and only by the circuitous path of reasoning attains the goal which the former reaches in one step. He who is morally noble, however deficient in mental penetration, reveals by his conduct the deepest insight, the truest wisdom, and puts to shame the most accomplished and learned genius, if the latter's acts betray that his heart is yet a stranger to this great principle—the metaphysical unity of life.

"Individuation is real. The *principium individuationis*, with the consequent distinction of individuals, is the order of things in themselves. Each living unit is an entity radically different from all others. In my own self alone I have my true being; everything outside it belongs to the non-ego, and is foreign to me." This is the creed to the truth of which flesh and bone bear witness: which is at the root of all egoism, and which finds its objective expression in every loveless, unjust, or malicious act.

"Individuation is merely an appearance, born of Space and Time; the latter being nothing else than the forms under which the external world necessarily manifests itself to me, conditioned as they are by my brain's faculty of perception. Hence also the plurality and difference of individuals is but a phenomenon, that is, exists only as my mental picture. My true inmost being subsists in every living thing, just as really, as directly as in my own consciousness it is evidenced only to myself." This is the higher knowledge: for which there is in

Sanskrit the standing formula *tat tvam asi*, "that art thou." Out of the depths of human nature it wells up in the shape of Compassion, and is therefore the source of all genuine, that is, disinterested virtue, being, so to say, incarnate in every good deed. It is this which in the last resort is invoked whenever we appeal to gentleness, to loving-kindness; whenever we pray for mercy instead of justice. For such appeal, such prayer is in reality the effort to remind a fellow-being of the ultimate truth that we are all one and the same entity. On the other hand, Egoism and its derivatives, envy, hatred, the spirit of persecution, hardness of heart, revenge, pleasure at the sight of suffering, and cruelty, all claim support from the other view of things, and seek their justification in it. The emotion and joy we experience when we hear of, still more, when we see, and most of all, when we ourselves do, a noble act, are at bottom traceable to the feeling of certainty such a deed gives, that, beyond all plurality and distinction of individuals, which the *principium individuationis*, like a kaleidoscope, shows us in ever-shifting evanescent forms, there is an underlying unity, not only truly existing, but actually accessible to us; for lo! in tangible, objective form, it stands before our sight.

Of these two mental attitudes, according as the one or the other is adopted, so the Love or the Hatred of Empedocles appears between man and man. If any one [. . .] could forcibly break in upon his most detested foe, and compel him to lay bare the inmost recesses of his heart; to his surprise, he would find again in the latter his very self. For just as in dreams, all the persons that appear to us are but the masked images of ourselves; so in the dream of our waking life, it is our own being which looks on us from out our neighbors' eyes, though this is not equally easy to discern. Nevertheless, *tat tvam asi*.

The preponderance of either mode of viewing life not only determines single acts; it shapes a man's whole nature and temperament. Hence the radical difference of mental habit between the good character and the bad. The latter feels everywhere that a thick wall of partition hedges him off from all others. For him the world is an absolute non-ego, and his relation to it an essentially hostile one; consequently, the keynote of his disposition is hatred, suspicion, envy, and pleasure in seeing distress. The good character, on the other hand, lives in an external world homogeneous with his own being; the rest of mankind is not in his eyes a non-ego; he thinks of it rather as "myself once more." He therefore stands on an essentially amicable footing with everyone: he is conscious of being, in his inmost nature, akin to the whole human race, takes direct interest in their weal and woe, and confidently assumes in their case the same interest in him. This is the source of his deep inward peace, and of that happy, calm, contented manner, which goes out on those around him, and is as the "presence of a good diffused." Whereas the bad character in time of trouble has no trust in the help of his fellow-creatures. If he invokes aid, he does so without confidence: obtained, he feels no real gratitude for it; because he can hardly discern therein anything but the effect of others' folly. For he is simply incapable of recognizing his own self in some one else; and this, even after it has furnished the most incontestable signs of existence in that other person: on which fact the repulsive nature of all unthankfulness in reality depends. The moral isolation, which thus naturally and inevitably encompasses the bad man, is often the cause of his becoming the victim of despair. The good man, on the contrary, will appeal to his neighbors for assistance, with an assurance equal to the consciousness he has of being ready himself to help them. As I have said: to the one type, humanity is a non-ego; to the other, "myself once more." The magnanimous character, who forgives his enemy, and returns good for evil, rises to the sublime, and receives the highest meed of praise; because he recognizes his real self even there where it is most conspicuously disowned.

Every purely beneficent act, all help entirely and genuinely un-selfish, being, as such, exclusively inspired by another's distress is, in fact, if we probe the matter to the bottom, a dark enigma, a piece of mysticism put into practice; inasmuch as it springs out of, and finds its only true explanation in, the same higher knowledge that consti-tutes the essence of whatever is mystical. For how, otherwise than metaphysically, are we to account for even the smallest offering of alms made with absolutely no other object than that of lessening the want which afflicts a fellow creature? Such an act is only conceivable, only possible, insofar as the giver knows that it is his very self which stands before him, clad in the garments of suffering; in other words, so far as he recognizes the essential part of his own being, under a form not his own. It now becomes apparent, why [. . .] I have called Compassion the great mystery of Ethics.

He who goes to meet death for his fatherland has freed himself from the illusion which limits a man's existence to his own person. Such a one has broken the fetters of the *principium individuationis*. In his widened, enlightened nature he embraces all his countrymen, and in them lives on and on. Nay, he reaches forward to, and merges himself in the generations yet unborn, for whom he works; and he regards death as a wink of the eyelids, so momentary that it does not interrupt the sight.

We may here sum up the characteristics of the two human types above indicated. To the Egoist all other people are uniformly and in-trinsically strangers. In point of fact, he considers nothing to be truly real, except his own person, and regards the rest of mankind practi-cally as troops of phantoms, to whom he assigns merely a relative existence, so far as they may be instruments to serve, or barriers to obstruct, his purposes; the result being an immeasurable difference, a vast gulf between his ego on the one side, and the non-ego on the other. In a word, he lives exclusively centered in his own individuality, and on his death-day he sees all reality, indeed the whole world, coming to an end along with himself. Whereas the Altruist discerns in all other persons, in every living thing, his own entity, and feels therefore that his being is commingled, is identical with the being of whatever is alive. By death he loses only a small part of himself. Putting off the narrow limitations of the individual, he passes into the larger life of all mankind, in whom he always recognized, and, recognizing, loved, his very self; and the illusion of Time and Space, which separated his consciousness from that of others, vanishes. These two opposite modes of viewing the world are probably the chief, though not indeed the sole, cause of the indifference we find between very good and exceptionally bad men, as to the manner in which they meet their last hour.

In all ages Truth, poor thing, has been put to shame for being paradoxical; and yet it is not her fault. She cannot assume the form of Error seated on his throne of world-wide sovereignty. So then, with a sigh, she looks up to her tutelary god, Time, who nods assurance to her of future victory and glory, but whose wings beat the air so slowly with their mighty strokes that the individual perishes awaiting the day of triumph. Hence I, too, am perfectly aware of the paradox which this metaphysical explanation of the ultimate ethical phenomenon must present to Western minds, accustomed, as they are, to very different methods of providing Morals with a basis. Nevertheless, I cannot offer violence to the truth. All that is possible for me to do, out of consideration for European blindness, is to assert once more, and demonstrate by actual quotation, that the Metaphysics of Ethics, which I have here suggested, was thousands of years ago the fundamental principle of Indian wisdom. And to this wisdom I point back, as Copernicus did to the Pythagorean cosmic system, which was suppressed by Aristotle and Ptolemaeus. In the Bhagavad Gita, according to A. W. von Schlegel's translation, we find the following passage: "That man is endowed with true insight who sees that the same ruling power is inherent in all things, and that when these perish, it perishes not. For if he discerns the same ruling power everywhere present he does not degrade himself by his own fault: thence he passes to the highest path."

With these hints towards the elaboration of a metaphysical basis for Ethics I must close, although an important step still remains to be taken. The latter would presuppose a further advance in Moral Science itself, and this can hardly be made, because in the West the highest aim of Ethics is reached in the theory of justice and virtue. What lies beyond is unknown, or at any rate ignored. The omission, therefore, is unavoidable; and the reader need feel no surprise if the above slight outline of the Metaphysics of Ethics does not bring into view—even remotely—the cornerstone of the whole metaphysical edifice, nor reveal the connection of all the parts composing the *Divina Commedia*. Such a presentment, moreover, is involved neither in the question set, nor in my own plan. A man cannot say everything in one day, and should not answer more than he is asked. He who tries to promote human knowledge and insight is destined to always encounter the opposition of his age, which is like the deadweight of some mass that has to be dragged along: there on the ground it lies, a huge inert deformity, defying all efforts to quicken its shape with new life. But such a one must take comfort from the certainty that, although prejudices beset his path, yet the truth is with him. And Truth does but wait for her ally, Time, to join her; once he is at her side, she is perfectly sure of victory, which, if today delayed, will be won tomorrow.

Sixteen

Eternal and Temporal Justice

We have learned to recognize *temporal justice*, which has its seat in the State, as requiting or punishing, and have seen that this becomes justice with regard only to the *future*. For without such regard, all punishing and requital of an outrage would remain without justification, would indeed be a mere addition of a second evil to that which had happened, without sense or significance. But it is quite different with *eternal justice*, which has been previously mentioned, and which rules not the State but the world; this is not dependent on human institutions, not subject to chance and deception, not uncertain, wavering, and erring, but infallible, firm, and certain. The concept of retaliation implies time, therefore *eternal justice* cannot be a retributive justice, and hence cannot, like that, admit respite and reprieve, and require time in order to succeed, balancing the evil deed against the evil consequence only by means of time. Here the punishment must be so linked with the offense that the two are one. [. . .] Now that such an eternal justice is actually to be found in the inner nature of the world will soon become perfectly clear to the reader who has grasped in its entirety the thought that we have so far developed.

The phenomenon, the objectivity of the one will-to-live, is the world in all the plurality of its parts and forms. Existence itself, and the kind of existence, in the totality as well as in every part, is only from the will. The will is free; it is almighty. The will appears in everything, precisely as it determines itself in itself and outside time. The world is only the mirror of this willing; and all finiteness, all suffering, all miseries that it contains, belong to the expression of what the will wills, are as they are because the will so wills. Accordingly, with the strictest right, every being supports existence in general, and the existence of its species and of its characteristic individuality, entirely as it is and in surroundings as they are, in a world such as it is, swayed by chance and error, fleeting, transient, always suffering; and in all that happens or indeed can happen to the individual, justice is always done to it. For the will belongs to it; and as the will is, so is the world. Only this world itself—no other—can bear the responsibility for its existence and its nature; for how could anyone else have assumed this responsibility? If we want to know what human beings, morally considered, are worth as a whole and in general, let us consider their fate as a whole and in general. This fate is want, wretchedness, misery, lamentation, and death. Eternal justice prevails; if they were not as a whole contemptible, their fate as a whole would not be so melancholy. In this sense we can say that the world itself is the tribunal of the world. If we could lay all the misery of the world in one pan of the scales, and all its guilt in the other, the pointer would certainly show them to be in equilibrium.

But of course the world does not exhibit itself to knowledge which has sprung from the will to serve it, and which comes to the individual as such in the same way as it finally discloses itself to the inquirer, namely as the objectivity of the one and only will-to-live, which he himself is. On the contrary, the eyes of the uncultured individual are clouded, as the Indians say, by the veil of Maya. To him is revealed not the thing-in-itself, but only the phenomenon in time and space, in the *principium individuationis*, and in the remaining forms of the principle of sufficient reason. In this form of his limited knowledge he sees not the inner nature of things, which is one, but its phenomena as separated, detached, innumerable, very different, and indeed opposed. For pleasure appears to him as one thing, and pain as quite another; one man as tormentor and murderer, another as martyr and victim; wickedness as one thing, evil as another. He sees one person living in pleasure, abundance, and delights, and at the same time another dying in agony of want and cold at the former's very door. He then asks where retribution is to be found. He himself in the vehement pressure of will, which is his origin and inner nature, grasps the pleasures and enjoyments of life, embraces them firmly, and does not know that, by this very act of his will, he seizes and hugs all the pains and miseries of life, at the sight of which he shudders. He sees the evil, he sees the wickedness in the world; but, far from recognizing that the two are but different aspects of the phenomenon of the one will-to-live, he regards them as very different, indeed as quite opposed. He often tries to escape by wickedness, in other words, by causing another's suffering, from the evil, from the suffering of his own individuality, involved as he is in the *principium individuationis*, deluded by the veil of Maya. Just as the boatman sits in his small boat, trusting his frail craft in a stormy sea that is boundless in every direction, rising and falling with the howling, mountainous waves, so in the midst of a world full of suffering and misery the individual man calmly sits, supported by and trusting the *principium individuationis*, or the way in which the individual knows things as phenomenon. The boundless world, everywhere full of suffering in the infinite past, in the infinite future, is strange to him, is indeed a fiction. His vanishing person, his extensionless present, his momentary gratification, these alone have reality for him; and he does everything to maintain them, so long as his eyes are not opened by a better knowledge. Till then, there lives only in the innermost depths of his consciousness the wholly obscure presentiment that all this is indeed not really so strange to him, but has a connection with him from which the *principium individuationis* cannot protect him. From this presentiment arises that ineradicable *dread*, common to all human beings (and possibly even to the more intelligent animals), which suddenly seizes them, when by any chance they become puzzled over the *principium individuationis*, in that the principle of sufficient reason in one or other of its forms seems to undergo an exception. For example, when it appears that some change has occurred without a cause, or a deceased person exists again; or when in any other way the past or the future is present, or the distant is near. The fearful terror at anything of this kind is based on the fact that they suddenly become puzzled over the forms of knowledge of the phenomenon which alone hold their own individuality separate from the rest of the world. This separation, however, lies only in the phenomenon and not in the thing-in-itself; and precisely on this rests eternal justice. In fact, all temporal happiness stands, and all prudence proceeds, on undermined ground. They protect the person from accidents, and supply it with pleasures, but the person is mere phenomenon, and its difference from other individuals, and exemption from the sufferings they bear, rest merely on the form of the phenomenon, on the *principium individuationis*. According to the true nature of things, everyone has all the sufferings of the world as his own; indeed, he has to look upon all merely possible sufferings as actual for him, so long as he is the firm and constant will-to-live, in other words, affirms life with all his strength. For the knowledge that sees through the *principium individuationis*, a happy life in time, given by chance or won from it by shrewdness, amid the sufferings of innumerable others, is only a beggar's dream, in which he is a king, but from which he must awake, in order to realize that only a fleeting illusion had separated him from the suffering of his life.

Eternal justice is withdrawn from the view that is involved in knowledge following the principle of sufficient reason, in the *principium individuationis*; such a view altogether misses it, unless it vindicates it in some way by fictions. It sees the wicked man, after misdeeds and cruelties of every kind, live a life of pleasure, and quit the world undisturbed. It sees the oppressed person drag out to the end a life full of suffering without the appearance of an avenger or vindicator. But eternal justice will be grasped and comprehended only by the man who rises above that knowledge which proceeds on the guiding line of the principle of sufficient reason and is bound to individual things, who recognizes the Ideas, who sees through the *principium individuationis*, and who is aware that the forms of the phenomenon do not apply to the thing-in-itself. Moreover, it is this man alone who, by dint of the same knowledge, can understand the true nature of virtue, as will soon be disclosed to us in connection with the present discussion, although for the practice of virtue this knowledge in the abstract is by no means required. Therefore, it becomes clear to the man who has reached the knowledge referred to, that, since the will is the in-itself of every phenomenon, the misery inflicted on others and that experienced by himself, the bad and the evil, always concern the one and the same inner being, although the phenomena in which the one and the other exhibit themselves stand out as quite different individuals, and are separated even by wide intervals of time and space. He sees that the difference between the inflicter of suffering and he who must endure it is only phenomenon, and does not concern the thing-in-itself which is the will that lives in both. Deceived by the knowledge bound to its service, the will here fails to recognize itself; seeking enhanced well-being in *one* of its phenomena, it produces great suffering in *another*. Thus in the fierceness and intensity of its desire it buries its teeth in its own flesh, not knowing that it always injures only itself, revealing in this form through the medium of individuation the conflict with itself which it bears in its inner nature. Tormentor and tormented are one. The former is mistaken in thinking he does not share the torment, the latter in thinking he does not share the guilt. If the eyes of both were opened, the inflicter of the suffering would recognize that he lives in everything that suffers pain in the whole wide world, and, if endowed with the faculty of reason, ponders in vain over why it was called into existence for such great suffering, whose cause and guilt it does not perceive. On the other hand, the tormented person would see that all the wickedness that is or ever was perpetrated in the world proceeds from that will which constitutes also *his* own inner being, and appears also in *him*. He would see that, through this phenomenon and its affirmation, he has taken upon himself all the sufferings resulting from such a will, and rightly endures them so long as he is this will. In *Life Is a Dream*, the prophetic poet Calderón speaks from this knowledge:

> For man's greatest offense
> Is that he has been born.

How could it fail to be an offense, as death comes after it in accordance with an eternal law? In that verse Calderón has merely expressed the Christian dogma of original sin.

The vivid knowledge of eternal justice, of the balance inseparably uniting the *malum culpae* with the *malum poenae*, demands the complete elevation above individuality and the principle of its possibility. It will therefore always remain inaccessible to the majority of men, as also will the pure and distinct knowledge of the real nature of all virtue which is akin to it, and which we are about to discuss. Hence the wise ancestors of the Indian people have directly expressed it in the Vedas, permitted only to the three twice-born castes, or in the esoteric teaching, namely insofar as concept and language comprehend it, and insofar as their method of presentation, always pictorial and even rhapsodical, allows it. But in the religion of the people, or in exoteric teaching, they have communicated it only mythically. We find the direct presentation in the Vedas, the fruit of the highest human knowledge and wisdom, the kernel of which has finally come to us in the Upanishads as the greatest gift to the nineteenth century. It is expressed in various ways, but especially by the fact that all beings of the world, living and lifeless, are led past in succession in the presence of the novice, and that over each of them is pronounced the word which has become a formula, and as such has been called the Mahavakya: *tatoumes*, or more correctly, *tat tvam asi*, which means "this art thou." For the people, however, that great truth, insofar as it was possible for them to comprehend it with their limited mental capacity, was translated into the way of knowledge following the principle of sufficient reason. From its nature, this way of knowledge is indeed quite incapable of assimilating that truth purely and in itself; indeed it is even in direct contradiction with it; yet in the form of a myth, it received a substitute for it which was sufficient as a guide to conduct. For the myth makes intelligible the ethical significance of conduct through figurative description in the method of knowledge according to the principle of sufficient reason, which is eternally foreign to this significance. This is the object of religious teachings, since these are all the mythical garments of the truth which is inaccessible to the crude human intellect. In this sense, that myth might be called in Kant's language a postulate of practical reason (*Vernunft*), but, considered as such, it has the great advantage of containing absolutely no elements but those which lie before our eyes in the realm of reality, and thus of being able to support all its concepts with perceptions. What is here meant is the myth of the transmigration of souls. This teaches that all sufferings inflicted in life by man on other beings must be expiated in a following life in this world by precisely the same sufferings. It goes to the length of teaching that a person who kills only an animal will be born as just such an animal at some point in endless time, and will suffer the same death. It teaches that wicked conduct entails a future life in suffering and despised creatures in this world; that a person is accordingly born again in lower castes, or as a woman, or as an animal, as a pariah or Chandala, as a leper, a crocodile, and so on. All the torments threatened by the myth are supported by it with perceptions from the world of reality, through suffering creatures that do not know how they have merited the punishment of their misery; and it does not need to call in the assistance of any other hell. On the other hand, it promises as reward rebirth in better and nobler forms, as Brahmans, sages, or saints. The highest reward awaiting the noblest deeds and most complete resignation, which comes also to the woman who in seven successive lives has voluntarily died on the funeral pyre of her husband, and no less to the person whose pure mouth has never uttered a single lie—such a reward can be expressed by the myth only negatively in the language of this world, namely by the promise, so often occurring, of not being reborn anymore: "You will not again assume phenomenal existence," or as the Buddhists, admitting neither Vedas nor castes, express it: "You shall attain to Nirvana, in other words, to a state or condition in which there are not four things, namely birth, old age, disease, and death."

Never has a myth been, and never will one be, more closely associated with a philosophical truth accessible to so few, than this very ancient teaching of the noblest and oldest of peoples. Degenerate as this race may now be in many respects, this truth still prevails with it as the universal creed of the people, and it has a decided influence on life today, as it had four thousand years ago. Therefore Pythagoras and Plato grasped with admiration that *non plus ultra* of mythical expression, took it over from India or Egypt, revered it, applied it, and themselves believed it, to what extent we know not. We, on the contrary, now send to the Brahmans English clergymen and evangelical linen-weavers, in order out of sympathy to put them right, and to point out to them that they are created out of nothing, and that they ought to be grateful and pleased about it. But it is just the same as if we fired a bullet at a cliff. In India our religions will never at any time take root; the ancient wisdom of the human race will not be supplanted by the events in Galilee. On the contrary, Indian wisdom flows back to Europe, and will produce a fundamental change in our knowledge and thought.

From our description of eternal justice, which is not mythical but philosophical, we will now proceed to the kindred consideration of the ethical significance of conduct, and of conscience, which is merely the felt knowledge of that significance. Here, however, I wish first of all to draw attention to two characteristics of human nature which may help to make clear how the essential nature of that eternal justice and the unity and identity of the will in all its phenomena, on which that justice rests, are known to everyone, at least as an obscure feeling.

After a wicked deed has been done, it affords satisfaction not only to the injured party, who is often filled with a desire for revenge, but also to the completely indifferent spectator, to see that the person who caused pain to another suffers in turn exactly the same measure of pain; and this quite independently of the object (which we have demonstrated) of the State in punishing, which is the basis of criminal law. It seems to me that nothing is expressed here but consciousness of that eternal justice, which, however, is at once misunderstood and falsified by the unpurified mind. Such a mind, involved in the *principium individuationis*, commits an amphiboly of the concepts, and demands of the phenomenon what belongs only to the thing-in-itself. It does not see to what extent the offender and the offended are in themselves one, and that it is the same inner nature which, not recognizing itself in its own phenomenon, bears both the pain and the guilt. On the contrary, it longs to see again the pain in the same individual to whom the guilt belongs. A man might have a very high degree of wickedness, which yet might be found in many others, though not matched with other qualities such as are found in him, namely one who was far superior to others through unusual mental powers, and who, accordingly, inflicted unspeakable sufferings on millions of others—a world conqueror, for instance. Most people would like to demand that such a man should at some time and in some place atone for all those sufferings by an equal amount of pain; for they do not recognize how the tormentor and tormented are in themselves one, and that it is the same will by which these latter exist and live which appears in the former, and precisely through him attains to the most distinct revelation of its inner nature. This will likewise suffers both in the oppressed and in the oppressor, and in the latter indeed all the more, in proportion as the consciousness has greater clearness and distinctness, and the will a greater vehemence. But Christian ethics testifies to the fact that the deeper knowledge, no longer involved in the *principium individuationis*, a knowledge from which all virtue and nobleness of mind proceed, no longer cherishes feelings demanding retaliation. Such ethics positively forbids all retaliation of evil for evil, and lets eternal justice rule in the province of the thing-in-itself which is different from that of the phenomenon ("Vengeance is mine; I will repay, saith the Lord").

A much more striking, but likewise much rarer, characteristic of human nature, which expresses that desire to draw eternal justice into the province of experience, i.e., of individuation, and at the same time indicates a felt consciousness that, as I put it above, the will-to-live acts out the great tragedy and comedy at its own expense, and that the same one will lives in all phenomena—such a characteristic,

I say, is the following. Sometimes we see a man so profoundly indignant at a great outrage, which he has experienced or perhaps only witnessed, that he deliberately and irretrievably stakes his own life in order to take vengeance on the perpetrator of that outrage. We see him search for years for some mighty oppressor, finally murder him, and then himself die on the scaffold, as he had foreseen. Indeed, often he did not attempt in any way to avoid this, since his life was of value to him only as a means for revenge. Such instances are found especially among the Spaniards. Now if we carefully consider the spirit of that mania for retaliation, we find it to be very different from common revenge, which desires to mitigate suffering endured by the sight of suffering caused; indeed, we find that what it aims at deserves to be called not so much revenge as punishment. For in it there is really to be found the intention of an effect on the future through the example, and without any selfish aim either for the avenging individual, who perishes in the attempt, or for a society that secures its own safety through laws. This punishment is carried out by the individual, not by the State; nor is it in fulfillment of a law; on the contrary, it always concerns a deed which the State would not or could not punish, and whose punishment it condemns. It seems to me that the wrath which drives such a man so far beyond the limits of all self-love springs from the deepest consciousness that he himself is the whole will-to-live that appears in all creatures through all periods of time, and that therefore the most distant future, like the present, belongs to him in the same way, and cannot be a matter of indifference to him. Affirming this will, he nevertheless desires that in the drama that presents its inner nature no such monstrous outrage shall ever appear again; and he wishes to frighten every future evildoer by the example of a revenge against which there is no wall of defense, as the fear of death does not deter the avenger. The will-to-live, though it still affirms itself here, no longer depends on the individual phenomenon, on the individual person, but embraces the Idea of man. It desires to keep the phenomenon of this Idea pure from such a monstrous and revolting outrage. It is a rare, significant, and even sublime trait of character by which the individual sacrifices himself, in that he strives to make himself the arm of eternal justice, whose true inner nature he still fails to recognize.

Seventeen

Compassion

In all the observations on human conduct hitherto made, we have been preparing for the final discussion, and have greatly facilitated the task of raising to abstract and philosophical clearness, and of demonstrating as a branch of our main idea, the real ethical significance of conduct which in life is described by the words *good* and *bad*, and is thus made perfectly intelligible.

First of all, however, I wish to trace back to their proper meaning these concepts of *good* and *bad*, which are treated by the philosophical writers of our times in a very odd way as simple concepts, that is, as concepts incapable of any analysis. I will do this so that the reader shall not remain involved in some hazy and obscure notion that they contain more than is actually the case, and that they state in and by themselves all that is here necessary. I am able to do this because in ethics I myself am as little disposed to take refuge behind the word *good* as I was earlier to hide behind the words *beautiful* and *true*, in order that, by an added "-ness," supposed nowadays to have a special solemnity, and hence to be of help in various cases, and by a solemn demeanor, I might persuade people that by uttering three such words I had done more than express three concepts which are very wide and abstract, which therefore contain nothing at all, and are of very different origin and significance. Who is there indeed who has made

himself acquainted with the writings of our times, and has not finally become sick of those three words, admirable as are the things to
which they originally refer, after he has been made to see a thousand
times how those least capable of thinking believe they need only utter
these three words with open mouth and the air of infatuated sheep,
in order to have spoken great wisdom?

The explanation of the concept *true* is already given in my essay
On the Fourfold Root of the Principle of Sufficient Reason. The content
of the concept *beautiful* received for the first time its proper explanation in the whole of our third book of *The World as Will and Representation*. We will now trace the meaning of the concept *good*; this
can be done with very little trouble. This concept is essentially relative, and denotes the *fitness or suitableness of an object to any definite
effort of the will*. Therefore everything agreeable to the will in any one
of its manifestations, and fulfilling the will's purpose, is thought of
through the concept *good*, however different in other respects such
things may be. We therefore speak of good eating, good roads, good
weather, good weapons, good auguries, and so on; in short, we call
everything good that is just as we want it to be. Hence a thing can be
good to one person, and the very opposite to another. The concept
of good is divided into two subspecies, that of the directly present
satisfaction concerning the future, in other words, the agreeable and
the useful. The concept of the opposite, so long as we are speaking of
beings without knowledge, is expressed by the word *bad*, more rarely
and abstractly by the word *evil*, which therefore denotes everything
that is not agreeable to the striving of the will in each case. Like
all other beings that can come into relation with the will, persons
who favor, promote, and befriend aims that happen to be desired are
called *good*, with the same meaning, and always with the retention of
the relative that is seen, for example, in the expression: "This is good
for me, but not for you." Those, however, whose character induces

them generally not to hinder another's efforts of will as such, but rather to promote them, and who are therefore consistently helpful, benevolent, friendly, and charitable, are called *good*, on account of this relation of their mode of conduct to the will of others in general. In the case of beings with knowledge (animals and human beings), the opposite concept is denoted in German, and has been for about a hundred years in French also, by a word different from that used in the case of beings without knowledge, namely *böse*, *méchant* (spiteful, malicious, unkind); whereas in almost all other languages this distinction does not occur. *Malus, cattivo, bad* are used both of human beings and of inanimate things which are opposed to the aims of a definite individual will. Thus, having started entirely from the passive side of the good, the discussion could only later pass to the active side, and investigate the mode of conduct of the man called *good*, in reference no longer to others, but to himself. It could then specially set itself the task of explaining the purely objective esteem produced in others by such conduct, as well as the characteristic contentment with himself obviously engendered in the person, for he purchases this even with sacrifices of another kind. On the other hand, it could also explain the inner pain that accompanies the evil disposition, however many advantages it may bring to the man who cherishes it. Now from this sprang the ethical systems, both the philosophical and those supported by religious teachings. Both always attempt to associate happiness in some way with virtue, the former either by the principle of contradiction, or even by that of sufficient reason, and thus to make happiness either identical with, or the consequence of, virtue, always sophistically; but the latter by asserting the existence of worlds other than the one that can be known to experience. On the other hand, from our discussion, the inner nature of virtue will show itself as a striving in quite the opposite direction to that of happiness, which is that of well-being and life.

It follows from the above remarks that the *good* is according to its concept *something belonging to the relative*, hence every good is essentially relative; for it has its essential nature only in its relation to a desiring will. Accordingly, *absolute good* is a contradiction; highest good, *summum bonum*, signifies the same thing, namely in reality a final satisfaction of the will, after which no fresh willing would occur; a last motive, the attainment of which would give the will an imperishable satisfaction. According to the discussion so far carried on in this fourth book, such a thing cannot be conceived. The will can just as little through some satisfaction cease to will always afresh, as time can end or begin; for the will there is no permanent fulfillment which completely and forever satisfies its craving. It is the vessel of the Danaids; there is no highest good, no absolute good, for it, but always a temporary good only. However, if we wish to give an honorary, or so to speak an emeritus, position to an old expression that from custom we do not like entirely to discard, we may, metaphorically and figuratively, call the complete self-effacement and denial of the will true willlessness, which alone stills and silences forever the craving of the will; which alone gives that contentment that cannot again be disturbed; which alone is world-redeeming; and which we shall now consider at the conclusion of our whole discussion; the absolute good, the *summum bonum*; and we may regard it as the only radical cure for the disease against which all other good things, such as all fulfilled wishes and all attained happiness, are only palliatives, anodynes. In this sense, the Greek *telos* and also *finis bonorum* meet the case even better. So much for the words *good* and *bad*; now to the matter itself.

If a person is always inclined to do *wrong* the moment the inducement is there and no external power restrains him, we call him *bad*. In accordance with our explanation of wrong, this means that such a man not only affirms the will-to-live as it appears in his own body, but in this affirmation goes so far as to deny the will that appears in other individuals. This is shown by the fact that he demands their powers for the service of his own will, and tries to destroy their existence when they stand in the way of the efforts of his will. The ultimate source of this is a high degree of egoism, the nature of which has already been explained. Two different things are at once clear here; *firstly*, that in such a person an excessively vehement will-to-live, going far beyond the affirmation of his own body, expresses itself; and *secondly*, that this knowledge, devoted entirely to the principle of sufficient reason and involved in the *principium individuationis*, definitely confines itself to the complete difference, established by this latter principle, between his own person and all others. He therefore seeks only his own well-being, and is completely indifferent to that of all others. On the contrary, their existence is wholly foreign to him, separated from his by a wide gulf; indeed, he really regards them only as masks without any reality. And these two qualities are the fundamental elements of the bad character.

This great intensity of willing is in and by itself and directly a constant source of suffering, firstly because all willing as such springs from want, and hence from suffering. (Therefore, as will be remembered from the third book, the momentary silencing of all willing, which comes about whenever as pure will-less subject of knowing, the correlative of the Idea, we are devoted to aesthetic contemplation, is a principal element of pleasure in the beautiful.) Secondly because, through the causal connection of things, most desires must remain unfulfilled, and the will is much more often crossed than satisfied. Consequently, much intense willing always entails much intense suffering. For all suffering is simply nothing but unfulfilled and thwarted willing, and even the pain of the body, when this is injured or destroyed, is as such possible only by the fact that the body is nothing but the will itself become object. Now, for the reason that much intense suffering is inseparable from much intense willing, the facial expression of very bad people already bears the stamp of inward suffering. Even when they have obtained every external happiness, they always look unhappy, whenever they are not transported by momentary exultation, or are not pretending. From this inward torment, absolutely and directly essential to them, there finally results even that delight at the suffering of another which has not sprung from egoism, but is disinterested; this is *wickedness* proper, and rises to the pitch of *cruelty*. For this the suffering of another is no longer a means for attaining the ends of its own will, but an end in itself. The following is a more detailed explanation of this phenomenon. Since man is phenomenon of the will illuminated by the clearest knowledge, he is always measuring and comparing the actual and felt satisfaction of his will with the merely possible satisfaction put before him by knowledge. From this springs envy; every privation is infinitely aggravated by the pleasure of others, and relieved by the knowledge that others also endure the same privation. The evils that are common to all and inseparable from human life do not trouble us much, just as little as do those that belong to the climate and to the whole country. The calling to mind of sufferings greater than our own stills their pain; the sight of another's sufferings alleviates our own. Now a person filled with an extremely intense pressure of will wants with burning eagerness to accumulate everything, in order to slake the thirst of egoism. As is inevitable, he is bound to see that all satisfaction is only apparent, and that the attained object never fulfills the promise held out by the desired object, namely the final appeasement of the excessive pressure of will. He sees that, with fulfillment, the wish changes only its form, and now torments under another form; indeed, when at last all wishes are exhausted, the pressure of will itself remains, even without any recognized motive, and makes itself known with terrible pain as a feeling of the most frightful desolation and emptiness. If from all this, which with ordinary degrees of willing is felt only in a smaller measure, and produces only the ordinary degree of dejection, there necessarily arises an excessive inner torment, an eternal unrest, an incurable pain in the case of a person who is the phenomenon of the will reaching to extreme wickedness, he then seeks indirectly the alleviation of which he is incapable directly, in other words, he tries to mitigate his own suffering by the sight of another's, and at the same time recognizes this as an expression of his power. The suffering of another becomes for him an end in itself; it is a spectacle over which he gloats; and so arises the phenomenon of cruelty proper, of bloodthirstiness, so often revealed by history in the Neros and Domitians, in the African deys, in Robespierre and others.

The thirst for revenge is closely related to wickedness. It repays evil with evil, not from regard for the future, which is the character of punishment, but merely on account of what has happened and is past as such, and thus disinterestedly, not as means but as end, in order to gloat over the offender's affliction caused by the avenger himself. What distinguishes revenge from pure wickedness, and to some extent excuses it, is an appearance of right, insofar as the same act that is now revenge, if ordered by law, in other words, according to a previously determined and known rule and in a society that has sanctioned such a rule, would be punishment, and hence justice or right.

Besides the suffering described, and inseparable from wickedness, as having sprung from a single root, namely a very intense will, there is associated with wickedness another particular pain quite different from this. This pain is felt in the case of every bad action, whether it be mere injustice arising out of egoism, or pure wickedness; and according to the length of its duration it is called the *sting of conscience* or the *pangs of conscience*. Now he who remembers, and has present in his mind, the foregoing contents of this fourth book, especially the truth explained at its beginning, namely that life itself is always sure and certain to the will-to-live as its mere copy or mirror, and also the discussion on eternal justice, will find that, in accordance with those remarks, the sting of conscience can have no other meaning than the following; in other words, its content, expressed in the abstract, is as follows, in which two parts are distinguished, but again these entirely coincide, and must be thought of as wholly united.

However densely the veil of Maya envelops the mind of the bad person, in other words, however firmly involved he is in the *principium individuationis*, according to which he regards his person as absolutely different from every other and separated from it by a wide gulf, a knowledge to which he adheres with all his might, since it alone suits and supports his egoism, so that knowledge is almost always corrupted by the will, there is nevertheless roused in the innermost depths of his consciousness the secret presentiment that such an order of things is only phenomenon, but that, in themselves, things are quite different. He has a presentiment that, however much time and space separate him from other individuals and the innumerable miseries they suffer, indeed suffer through him; however much time and space present these as quite foreign to him, yet in themselves and apart from the representation and its forms, it is the one will-to-live appearing in them all which, failing to recognize itself here, turns its weapons against itself, and, by seeking increased well-being in one of its phenomena, imposes the greatest suffering on another. He dimly sees that he, the bad person, is precisely this whole will; that in consequence he is not only the tormentor but also the tormented, from whose suffering he is separated and kept free only by a delusive dream, whose form is space and time. But this dream vanishes, and he sees that in reality he must pay for the pleasure with the pain, and that all suffering which he knows only as possible actually concerns him as the will-to-live, since possibility and actuality, near and remote in time and space, are different only for the knowledge of the individual, only by means of the *principium individuationis*, and not in themselves. It is this truth which mythically, in other words, adapted to the principle of sufficient reason, is expressed by the transmigration of souls, and is thus translated into the form of the phenomenon. Nevertheless it has its purest expression, free from all admixture, precisely in that obscurely felt but inconsolable misery called the pangs of conscience. But this also springs from a *second* immediate knowledge closely associated with the first, namely knowledge of the strength with which the will-to-live affirms itself in the wicked individual, extending as it does far beyond his individual phenomenon to the complete denial of the same will as it appears in individuals foreign to him. Consequently, the wicked man's inward alarm at his own deed, which he tries to conceal from himself, contains that presentiment of the nothingness and mere delusiveness of the *principium individuationis*, and of the distinction established by this principle between him and others. At the same time it contains the knowledge of the vehemence of his own will, of the strength with which he has grasped life and attached himself firmly to it, this very life whose terrible side he sees before him in the misery of those he oppresses, and with which he is nevertheless so firmly entwined that, precisely in this way, the most terrible things come from himself as a means to the fuller affirmation of his own will. He recognizes himself as the concentrated phenomenon of the will-to-live; he feels to what degree he is given up to life, and therewith also to the innumerable sufferings essential to it, for it has infinite time and infinite space to abolish the distinction between possibility and actuality, and to change all the sufferings as yet merely *known* by him into those *felt and experienced* by him. The millions of years of constant rebirth certainly continue merely in conception, just as the whole of the past and future exists only in conception. Occupied time, the form of the phenomenon of the will, is only the present, and time for the individual is always new; he always finds himself as newly sprung into existence. For life is inseparable from the will-to-live, and its form is only the Now. Death (the repetition of the comparison must be excused) is like the setting of the sun, which is only apparently engulfed by the night, but actually, itself the source of all light, burns without intermission, brings new days to new worlds, and is always rising and always setting. Beginning and end concern only the individual by means of time, of the form of this phenomenon for the representation. Outside time lie only the will, Kant's thing-in-itself, and its adequate objectivity, namely Plato's Idea. Suicide, therefore, affords no escape; what everyone *wills* in his innermost being, that must he *be*; and what everyone *is*, is just what he *wills*. Therefore, besides the merely felt knowledge of the delusiveness and nothingness of the forms of the representation that separate individuals, it is the self-knowledge of one's own will and of its degree that gives conscience its sting. The course of life brings out the picture of the empirical character, whose original is the intelligible character, and the wicked person is horrified at this picture. It is immaterial whether the picture is produced in large characters, so that the world shares his horror, or in characters so small that he alone sees it; for it directly concerns him alone. The past would be a matter of indifference as mere phenomenon, and could not disturb or alarm the conscience, did not the character feel itself free from all time and incapable of alteration by it, so long as it does not deny itself. For this reason, things that happened long ago still continue to weigh heavily on the conscience. The prayer "Lead me not into temptation" means "Let me not see who I am." In the strength with which the wicked person affirms life, and which is exhibited to him in the suffering he perpetrates on others, he estimates how far he is from the surrender and denial of that very will, from the only possible deliverance from the world and its miseries. He sees to what extent he belongs to the world, and how firmly he is bound to it. The *known* suffering of others has not been able to move him; he is given up to life and to *felt or experienced* suffering. It remains doubtful whether this will ever break and overcome the vehemence of his will.

This explanation of the significance and inner nature of the *bad*, which as mere feeling, i.e., *not* as distinct, abstract knowledge, is the content of the *pangs of conscience*, will gain even more clarity and completeness from a consideration of the *good* carried out in precisely the same way. This will consider the *good* as a quality of the human will, and finally of complete resignation and holiness that result from this quality, when it has reached the highest degree. For opposites always elucidate each other, and the day simultaneously reveals both itself and the night, as Spinoza has admirably said.

Morality without argumentation and reasoning, that is, mere moralizing, cannot have any effect, because it does not motivate. But a morality that *does* motivate can do so only by acting on self-love. Now what springs from this has no moral worth. From this it follows that no genuine virtue can be brought about through morality and abstract knowledge in general, but that such virtue must spring from the intuitive knowledge that recognizes in another's individuality the same inner nature as in one's own.

For virtue does indeed result from knowledge, but not from abstract knowledge communicable through words. If this were so, virtue could be taught, and by expressing here in the abstract its real nature and the knowledge at its foundation, we should have ethically improved everyone who comprehended this. But this is by no means the case. On the contrary, we are as little able to produce a virtuous person by ethical discourses or sermons as all the systems of aesthetics from Aristotle's downwards have ever been able to produce a poet. For the concept is unfruitful for the real inner nature of virtue, just as it is for art; and only in a wholly subordinate position can it serve as an instrument in elaborating and preserving what has been ascertained and inferred in other ways. Willing cannot be taught. In fact, abstract dogmas are without influence on virtue, i.e., on goodness of disposition; false dogmas do not disturb it, and true ones hardly support it. Actually, it would be a bad business if the principal thing in a man's life, his ethical worth that counts for eternity, depended on something whose attainment was so very much subject to chance as are dogmas, religious teachings, and philosophical arguments. For morality dogmas have merely the value that the man who is virtuous from another kind of knowledge shortly to be discussed has in them a scheme or formula. According to this, he renders to his own faculty of reason an account, for the most part only fictitious, of his non-egoistical actions, the nature of which it, in other words he himself, does not *comprehend*. With such an account he has been accustomed to rest content.

Dogmas can of course have a powerful influence on *conduct*, on outward actions, and so can custom and example (the latter, because the ordinary man does not trust his judgment, of whose weakness he is conscious, but follows only his own or someone else's experience); but the disposition is not altered in this way. All abstract knowledge gives only motives, but, as was shown above, motives can alter only the direction of the will, never the will itself. But all communicable knowledge can affect the will as motive only; therefore, however the will is guided by dogmas, what a person really and generally wills still always remains the same. He has obtained different ideas merely of the ways in which it is to be attained, and imaginary motives guide him like real ones. Thus, for instance, it is immaterial, as regards his ethical worth, whether he makes donations to the destitute, firmly persuaded that he will receive everything back tenfold in a future life, or spends the same sum on improving an estate that will bear interest, late certainly, but all the more secure and substantial. And the man who, for the sake of orthodoxy, commits the heretic to the flames, is just as much a murderer as the bandit who earns a reward by killing; indeed, as regards inner circumstances, so also is he who massacres the Turks in the Promised Land, if, like the burner of heretics, he really does it because he imagines he will thus earn a place in heaven. For these are anxious only about themselves, about their egoism, just like the bandit, from whom they differ only in the absurdity of their means. As we have already said, the will can be reached from outside only through motives; but these alter merely the way in which it manifests itself, never the will itself. Willing cannot be taught.

In the case of good deeds, however, the doer of which appeals to dogmas, we must always distinguish whether these dogmas are really the motive for them, or whether, as I said above, they are nothing more than the delusive account by which he tries to satisfy his own faculty of reason about a good deed that flows from quite a different source. He performs such a deed because he is *good*, but he does not understand how to explain it properly, since he is not a philosopher, and yet he would like to think something with regard to it. But the distinction is very hard to find, since it lies in the very depths of our inner nature. Therefore we can hardly ever pronounce a correct moral judgment on the actions of others, and rarely on our own. The deeds and ways of acting of the individual and of a nation can be very much modified by dogmas, example, and custom. In themselves, however, all deeds (*opera operata*) are merely empty figures, and only the disposition that leads to them gives them moral significance. But this disposition can be actually quite the same, in spite of a very different external phenomenon. With an equal degree of wickedness one person can die on the wheel, and another peacefully in the bosom of his family. It can be the same degree of wickedness that expresses itself in one nation in the crude characteristics of murder and cannibalism, and in another finely and delicately in miniature, in court intrigues, oppressions, and subtle machinations of every kind; the inner nature remains the same. It is conceivable that a perfect State, or even perhaps a complete dogma of rewards and punishments after death firmly believed in, might prevent every crime. Politically much would be gained in this way; morally, absolutely nothing; on the contrary, only the mirroring of the will through life would be checked.

Genuine goodness of disposition, disinterested virtue, and pure nobleness of mind, therefore, do not come from abstract knowledge; yet they do come from knowledge. But it is a direct and intuitive knowledge that cannot be reasoned away or arrived at by reasoning; a knowledge that, just because it is not abstract, cannot be communicated, but must dawn on each of us. It therefore finds its real and adequate expression not in words, but simply and solely in deeds, in conduct, in the course of a man's life. We who are here looking for the theory of virtue, and who thus have to express in abstract terms the inner nature of the knowledge lying at its foundation, shall nevertheless be unable to furnish that knowledge itself in this expression, but only the concept of that knowledge. We thus always start from conduct, in which alone it becomes visible, and refer to such conduct as its only adequate expression. We only interpret and explain this expression, in other words, express in the abstract what really takes place in it.

Now before we speak of the *good* proper, in contrast to the *bad* that has been described, we must touch on the mere negation of the bad as an intermediate stage; this is *justice*. We have adequately explained above what right and wrong are; therefore we can briefly say here that the man who voluntarily recognizes and accepts that merely moral boundary between wrong and right, even where no State or other authority guarantees it, and who consequently, according to our explanation, never in the affirmation of his own will goes to the length of denying the will that manifests itself in another individual, is *just*. Therefore, in order to increase his own well-being, he will not inflict suffering on others; that is to say, he will not commit any crime; he will respect the rights and property of everyone. We now see that for such a just man the *principium individuationis* is no longer an absolute partition as it is for the bad; that he does not, like the bad man, affirm merely his own phenomenon of will and deny all others; that others are not for him mere masks, whose inner nature is quite different from his. On the contrary, he shows by his way of acting that he *again recognizes* his own inner being, namely the will-to-live as thing-in-itself, in the phenomenon of another given to him merely as representation. Thus he finds himself again in that phenomenon up to a certain degree, namely that of doing no wrong, i.e., of not injuring. Now in precisely this degree he sees through the *principium individuationis*, the veil of Maya. To this extent he treats the inner being outside himself like his own; he does not injure it.

If we examine the innermost nature of this justice, there is to be found in it the intention not to go so far in the affirmation of one's own will as to deny the phenomena of will in others by compelling them to serve one's own will. We shall therefore want to provide for others just as much as we benefit from them. The highest degree of this justice of disposition, which, however, is always associated with goodness proper, the character of this last being no longer merely negative, extends so far that a person questions his right to inherited property, desires to support his body only by his own powers, mental and physical, feels every service rendered by others, every luxury, as a reproach, and finally resorts to voluntary poverty. Thus we see how Pascal would not allow the performance of any more services when he turned to asceticism, although he had servants enough. In spite of his constant bad health, he made his own bed, fetched his own food from the kitchen, and so on. Quite in keeping with this, it is reported that many Hindus, even rajas, with great wealth, use it merely to support and maintain their families, their courts, and their establishment of servants, and follow with strict scrupulousness the maxim of eating nothing but what they have sown and reaped with their own hands. Yet at the bottom of this there lies a certain misunderstanding, for just because the individual is rich and powerful, he is able to render such important services to the whole of human society that they counterbalance inherited wealth, for the security of which he is indebted to society. In reality, that excessive justice of such Hindus is more than justice, indeed actual renunciation, denial of the will-to-live, asceticism, about which we shall speak last of all. On the other hand, pure idleness and living through the exertions of others with inherited property, without achieving anything, can indeed be regarded as morally wrong, even though it must remain right according to positive laws.

We have found that voluntary justice has its innermost origin in a certain degree of seeing through the *principium individuationis*, while the unjust man remains entirely involved in this principle. This seeing through can take place not only in the degree required for justice, but also in the higher degree that urges a man to positive benevolence and well-doing, to philanthropy. Moreover, this can happen however strong and energetic the will that appears in such an individual may be in itself. Knowledge can always counterbalance it, can teach a man to resist the temptation to do wrong, and can even produce every degree of goodness, indeed of resignation. Therefore the good man is in no way to be regarded as an originally weaker phenomenon of will than the bad, but it is knowledge that masters in him the blind craving of will. Certainly there are individuals who merely seem to be good-natured on account of the weakness of the will that appears in them; but what they are soon shows itself in the fact that they are not capable of any considerable self-conquest, in order to perform a just or good deed.

Now if, as a rare exception, we come across a man who possesses a considerable income, but uses only a little of it for himself, and gives all the rest to persons in distress, whilst he himself forgoes many pleasures and comforts, and we try to make clear to ourselves the action of this man, we shall find, quite apart from the dogmas by which he himself will make his action intelligible to his faculty of reason, the simplest general expression and the essential character of his way of acting to be that he *makes less distinction than is usually made between himself and others*. This very distinction is in the eyes of many so great, that the suffering of another is a direct pleasure for the wicked, and a welcome means to their own well-being for the unjust. The merely just person is content not to cause it; and generally most people know and are acquainted with innumerable sufferings of others in their vicinity, but do not decide to alleviate them, because to do so they would have to undergo some privation. Thus a strong distinction seems to prevail in each of all these between his own ego and another's. On the other hand, to the noble person, whom we have in mind, this distinction is not so significant. The *principium individuationis*, the form of the phenomenon, no longer holds him so firmly in its grasp, but the suffering he sees in others touches him almost as closely as does his own. He therefore tries to strike a balance between the two, denies himself pleasures, undergoes privations, in order to alleviate another's suffering. He perceives that the distinction between himself and others, which to the wicked man is so great a gulf, belongs only to a fleeting, deceptive phenomenon. He recognizes immediately, and without reasons or arguments, that the in-itself of his own phenomenon is also that of others, namely that will-to-live which constitutes the inner nature of everything, and lives in all; in fact, he recognizes that this extends even to the animals and to the whole of nature; he will therefore not cause suffering even to an animal.

He is now just as little able to let others starve, while he himself has enough to spare, as anyone would one day be on short commons, in order on the following day to have more than he can enjoy. For the veil of Maya has become transparent for the person who performs works of love, and the deception of the *principium individuationis* has left him. Himself, his will, he recognizes in every creature, and hence in the sufferer also. He is free from the perversity with which the will-to-live, failing to recognize itself, here in one individual enjoys fleeting and delusive pleasures, and there in another individual suffers and starves in return for these. Thus this will inflicts misery and endures misery, not knowing that, like Thyestes, it is eagerly devouring its own flesh. Then it here laments its unmerited suffering, and there commits an outrage without the least fear of Nemesis, always merely because it fails to recognize itself in the phenomenon of another, and thus does not perceive eternal justice, involved as it is in the *principium individuationis*, and so generally in that kind of knowledge which is governed by the principle of sufficient reason. To be cured of this delusion and deception of Maya and to do works of love are one and the same thing; but the latter is the inevitable and infallible symptom of that knowledge.

The opposite of the sting of conscience, whose origin and significance were explained above, is the *good conscience*, the satisfaction we feel after every disinterested deed. It springs from the fact that such a deed, as arising from the direct recognition of our own inner being-in-itself in the phenomenon of another, again affords us the verification of this knowledge, of the knowledge that our true self exists not only in our own person, in this particular phenomenon, but in everything that lives. In this way, the heart feels itself enlarged, just as by egoism it feels contracted. For just as egoism concentrates our interest on the particular phenomenon of our own individuality, and then knowledge always presents us with the innumerable perils that continually threaten this phenomenon, whereby anxiety and care become the keynote of our disposition, so the knowledge that every living thing is just as much our own inner being-in-itself as is our own person, extends our interest to all that lives; and in this way the heart is enlarged. Thus through the reduced interest in our own self, the anxious care for that self is attacked and restricted at its root; hence the calm and confident serenity afforded by a virtuous disposition and a good conscience, and the more distinct appearance of this with every good deed, since this proves to ourselves the depth of that disposition. The egoist feels himself surrounded by strange and hostile phenomena, and all his hope rests on his own well-being. The good person lives in a world of friendly phenomena; the well-being of any of these is his own well-being. Therefore, although the knowledge of the lot of man generally does not make his disposition a cheerful one, the permanent knowledge of his own inner nature in everything that lives nevertheless gives him a certain uniformity and even serenity of disposition. For the interest extended over innumerable phenomena cannot cause such anxiety as that which is concentrated on one phenomenon. The accidents that concern the totality of individuals equalize themselves, while those that befall the individual entail good or bad fortune.

Therefore, although others have laid down moral principles which they gave out as precepts for virtue and laws necessarily to be observed, I cannot do this, as I have said already, because I have no "ought" or law to hold before the eternally free will. On the other hand, in reference to my discussion, what corresponds and is analogous to that undertaking is that purely theoretical truth, and the whole of my argument can be regarded as a mere elaboration thereof, namely that the will is the in-itself of every phenomenon, but itself as such is free from the forms of that phenomenon, and so from plurality. In reference to conduct, I do not know how this truth can be more worthily expressed than by the formula of the Vedas already quoted: *tat tvam asi* ("this art thou!"). Whoever is able to declare this to himself with clear knowledge and firm inward conviction about every creature with whom he comes in contact is certain of all virtue and bliss, and is on the direct path to salvation.

Now before I go farther, and show, as the last item in my discussion, how love, whose origin and nature we know to be seeing through the *principium individuationis*, leads to salvation, that is, to the entire surrender of the will-to-live, i.e., of all willing, and also how another path, less smooth yet more frequented, brings man to the same goal, a paradoxical sentence must first be here stated and explained. This is not because it is paradoxical, but because it is true, and is necessary for the completeness of the thought I have to express. It is this: "All love (*caritas*) is compassion or sympathy."

We have seen how, from seeing through the *principium individuationis*, in the lesser degree justice arises, and in the higher degree real goodness of disposition, a goodness that shows itself as pure, i.e., disinterested, affection towards others. Now, where this becomes complete, the individuality and fate of others are treated entirely like one's own. It can never go farther, for no reason exists for preferring another's individuality to one's own. Yet the great number of the other individuals whose whole well-being or life is in danger can outweigh the regard for one's own particular well-being. In such a case, the character that has reached the highest goodness and perfect magnanimity will sacrifice its well-being and its life completely for the well-being of many others. So died Codrus, Leonidas, Regulus, Decius Mus, and Arnold von Winkelried; so does everyone die who voluntarily and consciously goes to certain death for his friends, or for his native land. And everyone also stands at this level who willingly takes suffering and death upon himself for the maintenance of what conduces and rightfully belongs to the welfare of all mankind,

in other words, for universal, important truths, and for the eradication of great errors. So died Socrates and Giordano Bruno; and so did
many a hero of truth meet his death at the stake at the hands of the
priests.

Now, with reference to the paradox above expressed, I must call
to mind the fact that we previously found suffering to be essential
to and inseparable from life as a whole, and that we saw how every
desire springs from a need, a want, a suffering, and that every satisfaction is therefore only a pain removed, not a positive happiness
brought. We saw that the joys certainly lie to the desire in stating
that they are a positive good, but that in truth they are only of a
negative nature, and only the end of an evil. Therefore, whatever
goodness, affection, and magnanimity do for others is always only an
alleviation of their sufferings; and consequently what can move them
to good deeds and to works of affection is always only *knowledge of
the suffering of others*, directly intelligible from one's own suffering,
and put on a level therewith. It follows from this, however, that pure
affection (*caritas*) is of its nature sympathy or compassion. The suffering alleviated by it, to which every unsatisfied desire belongs, may
be great or small. We shall therefore have no hesitation in saying
that the mere concept is as unfruitful for genuine virtue as it is for
genuine art; that all true and pure affection is sympathy or compassion, and all love that is not sympathy is selfishness. All this will be in
direct contradiction to Kant, who recognizes all true goodness and all
virtue as such only if they have resulted from abstract reflection, and
in fact from the concept of duty and the categorical imperative, and
who declares felt sympathy to be weakness, and by no means virtue.
Selfishness is *eros*, sympathy or compassion is *agape*. Combinations of
the two occur frequently; even genuine friendship is always a mixture
of selfishness and sympathy. Selfishness lies in the pleasure in the
presence of the friend, whose individuality corresponds to our own,

and it almost invariably constitutes the greatest part; sympathy shows itself in a sincere participation in the friend's weal and woe, and in the disinterested sacrifices made for the latter. Even Spinoza in his *Ethics* says: "Benevolence is nothing but a desire sprung from compassion." [. . .] As confirmation of our paradoxical sentence, it may be observed that the tone and words of the language and the caresses of pure love entirely coincide with the tone of sympathy or compassion. Incidentally, it may be observed also that sympathy and pure love are expressed in Italian by the same word, *pietà*.

This is also the place to discuss one of the most striking peculiarities of human nature, *weeping*, which, like laughter, belongs to the manifestations that distinguish man from the animal. Weeping is by no means a positive manifestation of pain, for it occurs where pains are least. In my opinion, we never weep directly over pain that is felt, but always only over its repetition in reflection. Thus we pass from the felt pain, even when it is physical, to a mere mental picture or representation of it; we then find our own state so deserving of sympathy that, if another were the sufferer, we are firmly and sincerely convinced that we would be full of sympathy and love to help him. Now we ourselves are the object of our own sincere sympathy; with the most charitable disposition, we ourselves are most in need of help. We feel that we endure more than we could see another endure, and in this peculiarly involved frame of mind, in which the directly felt suffering comes to perception only in a doubly indirect way, pictured as the suffering of another and sympathized with as such, and then suddenly perceived again as directly our own; in such a frame of mind nature finds relief through that curious physical convulsion. Accordingly, *weeping is sympathy with ourselves*, or sympathy thrown back to its starting-point. It is therefore conditioned by the capacity for affection and sympathy, and by the imagination. Therefore people who are either hard-hearted or without imagination do not readily weep; indeed weeping is always regarded as a sign of a certain degree of goodness of character, and it disarms anger. This is because it is felt that whoever is still able to weep must also necessarily be capable of affection, i.e., of sympathy towards others, for this enters in the way described into that mood that leads to weeping. The description which Petrarch gives of the rising of his own tears, naively and truly expressing his feeling, is entirely in accordance with the explanation that has been given: "As I wander deep in thought, so strong a *sympathy with myself* comes over me, that I must often weep aloud, a thing I am otherwise not accustomed to do."

What has been said is also confirmed by the fact that children who have been hurt generally cry only when they are pitied, and hence not on account of the pain, but on account of the conception of it. That we are moved to tears not by our own sufferings, but by those of others, happens in the following way; either in imagination we put ourselves vividly in the sufferer's place, or we see in his fate the lot of the whole of humanity, and consequently above all our own fate. Thus in a very roundabout way, we always weep about ourselves; we feel sympathy with ourselves. This seems also to be a main reason for the universal, and hence natural, weeping in cases of death. It is not the mourner's loss over which he weeps; he would be ashamed of such egoistical tears, instead of sometimes being ashamed of not weeping. In the first place, of course, he weeps over the fate of the deceased; yet he weeps also when for the deceased death was a desirable deliverance after long, grave, and incurable sufferings. In the main, therefore, he is seized with sympathy over the lot of the whole of mankind that is given over to finiteness. In consequence of this, every life, however ambitious and often rich in deeds, must become extinct and nothing. In this lot of mankind, however, the mourner sees first of all his own lot, and this the more, the more closely he was related to the deceased, and most of all therefore when the deceased was his father. Although to this father life was a misery through age and sickness, and through his helplessness a heavy burden to the son, the son nevertheless weeps bitterly over the death of his father for the reason already stated.

Eighteen

Mystics, Saints, Ascetics

After this digression on the identity of pure love with sympathy, the turning back of sympathy onto our own individuality having as its symptom the phenomenon of weeping, I take up again the thread of our discussion of the ethical significance of conduct, to show how, from the same source from which all goodness, affection, virtue, and nobility of character spring, there ultimately arises also what I call denial of the will-to-live.

Just as previously we saw hatred and wickedness conditioned by egoism, and this depending on knowledge being entangled in the *principium individuationis*, so we found as the source and essence of justice, and, when carried farther to the highest degrees, of love and magnanimity, that penetration of the *principium individuationis*. This penetration alone, by abolishing the distinction between our own individuality and that of others, makes possible and explains perfect goodness of disposition, extending to the most disinterested love, and the most generous self-sacrifice for others.

Now, if seeing through the *principium individuationis*, if this direct knowledge of the identity of the will in all its phenomena, is present in a high degree of distinctness, it will at once show an influence on the will which goes still farther. If that veil of Maya, the *principium individuationis*, is lifted from the eyes of a man to such an extent that he no longer makes the egoistical distinction between himself and the person of others, but takes as much interest in the sufferings of other individuals as in his own, and thus is not only benevolent and charitable in the highest degree, but even ready to sacrifice his own individuality whenever several others can be saved thereby, then it follows automatically that such a man, recognizing in all beings his own true and innermost self, must also regard the endless sufferings of all that lives as his own, and thus take upon himself the pain of the whole world. No suffering is any longer strange or foreign to him. All the miseries of others, which he sees and is so seldom able to alleviate, all the miseries of which he has indirect knowledge, and even those he recognizes merely as possible, affect his mind just as do his own. It is no longer the changing weal and woe of his person that he has in view, as is the case with the man still involved in egoism, but, as he sees through the *principium individuationis*, everything lies equally near to him. He knows the whole, comprehends its inner nature, and finds it involved in a constant passing away, a vain striving, an inward conflict, and a continual suffering. Wherever he looks, he sees suffering humanity and the suffering animal world, and a world that passes away. Now all this lies just as near to him as only his own person lies to the egoist. Now how could he, with such knowledge of the world, affirm this very life through constant acts of will, and precisely in this way bind himself more and more firmly to it, press himself to it more and more closely? Thus, whoever is still involved in the *principium individuationis*, in egoism, knows only particular things and their relation to his own person, and these then become ever renewed *motives* of his willing. On the other hand, that knowledge of the whole, of the inner nature of the thing-in-itself, which has been described, becomes the *quieter* of all and every willing. The will now turns away from life; it shudders at the pleasures in which it recognizes the affirmation of life. Man attains to the state of voluntary renunciation, resignation, true composure, and complete will-lessness. At times, in the hard experience of our own sufferings or in the vividly recognized suffering of others, knowledge of the vanity and bitterness of life comes close to us who are still enveloped in the veil of Maya. We would like to deprive desires of their sting, close the entry to all suffering, purify and sanctify ourselves by complete and final resignation. But the illusion of the phenomenon soon ensnares us again, and its motives set the will in motion once more; we cannot tear ourselves free. The allurements of hope, the flattery of the present, the sweetness of pleasures, the well-being that falls to the lot of our person amid the lamentations of a suffering world governed by chance and error, all these draw us back to it and rivet the bonds anew. Therefore Jesus says: "It is easier for a camel to go through the eye of a needle, than for a rich man to enter into the Kingdom of God."

If we compare life to a circular path of red-hot coals having a few cool places, a path that we have to run over incessantly, then the man entangled in delusion is comforted by the cool place on which he is just now standing, or which he sees near him, and sets out to run over the path. But the man who sees through the *principium individuationis*, and recognizes the true nature of things-in-themselves, and thus the whole, is no longer susceptible of such consolation; he sees himself in all places simultaneously, and withdraws. His will turns about; it no longer affirms its own inner nature, mirrored in the phenomenon, but denies it. The phenomenon by which this becomes manifest is the transition from virtue to *asceticism*. In other words, it is no longer enough for him to love others like himself, and to do as much for them as for himself, but there arises in him a strong aversion to the inner nature whose expression is his own phenomenon, to the will-to-live, the kernel and essence of that world recognized as full of misery. He therefore renounces precisely this inner nature, which appears in him and is expressed already by his body, and his action gives the lie to his phenomenon, and appears in open contradiction thereto. Essentially nothing but phenomenon of the will, he ceases to will anything, guards against attaching his will to anything, tries to establish firmly in himself the greatest indifference to all things. His body, healthy and strong, expresses the sexual impulse through the genitals, but he denies the will, and gives the lie to the body; he desires no sexual satisfaction on any condition. Voluntary and complete chastity is the first step in asceticism or the denial of the will-to-live. It thereby denies the affirmation of the will which goes beyond the individual life, and thus announces that the will, whose phenomenon is the body, ceases with the life of this body. Nature, always true and naive, asserts that, if this maxim became universal, the human race would die out; and after what was said in the second book about the connection of all phenomena of will, I think I can assume that, with the highest phenomenon of will, the weaker reflection of it, namely the animal world, would also be abolished, just as the half-shades vanish with the full light of day. With the complete abolition of knowledge the rest of the world would of itself also vanish into nothing, for there can be no object without a subject. Here I would like to refer to a passage in the Vedas where it says: "As in this world hungry children press round their mother, so do all beings await the holy oblation." [. . .] Sacrifice signifies resignation generally, and the rest of nature has to expect its salvation from man, who is at the same time priest and sacrifice. In fact, it is worth mentioning as extremely remarkable that this thought has also been expressed by the admirable and immeasurably profound Angelus Silesius in the little poem entitled "Man Brings All to God"; it runs:

> Man! all love you; great is the throng around you:
> All flock to you that they may attain to God.

But an even greater mystic, Meister Eckhart [. . .] says wholly in the sense here discussed: "I confirm this with Christ, for he says: 'I, if I be lifted up from the earth, will draw all things [men] unto me.' So shall the good man draw all things up to God, to the source whence they first came. The masters certify to us that all creatures are made for the sake of man. This is proved in all creatures by the fact that one creature makes use of another; the ox makes use of the grass, the fish of the water, the bird of the air, the animals of the forest. Thus all creatures come to the profit of the good man. A good man bears to God one creature in the other." He means that because, in and with himself, man also saves the animals, he makes use of them in this life.

Even in Buddhism there is no lack of expressions of this matter; for example, when the Buddha, while still a Bodhisattva, has his horse saddled for the last time, for the flight from his father's house into the wilderness, he says to the horse in verse: "Long have you existed in life and in death, but now you shall cease to carry and to draw. Bear me away from here just this once, O Kantakana, and when I have attained the Law (have become Buddha), I shall not forget you."

Asceticism shows itself further in voluntary and intentional poverty, which arises not only by accident, since property is given away to alleviate the sufferings of others, but which is here an end in itself; it is to serve as a constant mortification of the will, so that satisfaction of desires, the sweets of life, may not again stir the will, of which self-knowledge has conceived a horror. He who has reached this point still always feels, as living body, as concrete phenomenon of will, the natural tendency to every kind of willing; but he deliberately suppresses it, since he compels himself to refrain from doing all that he would like to do, and on the other hand to do all that he would not like to do, even if this has no further purpose than that of serving to mortify the will. As he himself denies the will that appears in his own person, he will not resist when another does the same thing, in other words, inflicts wrong on him. Therefore, every suffering that comes to him from outside through chance or the wickedness of others is welcome to him; every injury, every ignominy, every outrage. He gladly accepts them as the opportunity for giving himself the certainty that he no longer affirms the will, but gladly sides with every enemy of the will's phenomenon that is his own person. He therefore endures such ignominy and suffering with inexhaustible patience and gentleness, returns good for all evil without ostentation, and allows the fire of anger to rise again within him as little as he does the fire of desires. Just as he mortifies the will itself, so does he mortify its visibility, its objectivity, the body. He nourishes it sparingly, lest its vigorous flourishing and thriving should animate afresh and excite more strongly the will, of which it is the mere expression and mirror. Thus he resorts to fasting, and even to self-castigation and self-torture, in order that, by constant privation and suffering, he may more and more break down and kill the will that he recognizes and abhors as the source of his own suffering existence and of the world's. Finally, if death comes, which breaks up the phenomenon of this will, the essence of such will having long since expired through free denial of itself except for the feeble residue which appears as the vitality of this body, then it is most welcome, and is cheerfully accepted as a longed-for deliverance.

It is not merely the phenomenon, as in the case of others, that comes to an end with death, but the inner being itself that is abolished; this had a feeble existence merely in the phenomenon. This last slender bond is now severed; for him who ends thus, the world has at the same time ended. This idea is expressed by a fine simile in the ancient Sanskrit philosophical work the Sankhya Karika: "Yet the soul remains for a time clothed with the body, just as the potter's wheel continues to spin after the pot has been finished, in consequence of the impulse previously given to it. Only when the inspired soul separates itself from the body and nature ceases for it does its complete salvation take place." And what I have described here with feeble tongue, and only in general terms, is not some philosophical fable, invented by myself and only of today. No, it was the enviable life of so many saints and great souls among the Christians, and even more among the Hindus and Buddhists, and also among the believers of other religions. Different as were the dogmas that were impressed on their faculty of reason, the inner, direct, and intuitive knowledge from which alone all virtue and holiness can come is nevertheless expressed in precisely the same way in the conduct of life. For here also is seen the great distinction between intuitive and abstract knowledge, a distinction of such importance and of general application in the whole of our discussion, and one which hitherto has received too little notice. Between the two is a wide gulf; and, in regard to knowledge of the inner nature of the world, this gulf can be crossed only by philosophy. Intuitively, or *in concreto*, every man is really conscious of all philosophical truths; but to bring them into his abstract knowledge, into reflection, is the business of the philosopher, who neither ought to nor can do more than this.

Thus it may be that the inner nature of holiness, of self-renunciation, of mortification of one's own will, of asceticism, is here for the first time expressed in abstract terms and free from everything mythical, as *denial of the will-to-live*, which appears after the complete knowledge of its own inner being has become for it the quieter of all willing. On the other hand, it has been known directly and expressed in deed by all those saints and ascetics who, in spite of the same inner knowledge, used very different language according to the dogmas which their faculty of reason had accepted, and in consequence of which an Indian, a Christian, or a Lamaist saint must each give a very different account of his own conduct; but this is of no importance at all as regards the fact. A saint may be full of the most absurd superstition, or, on the other hand, may be a philosopher; it is all the same. His conduct alone is evidence that he is a saint; for, in a moral regard, it springs not from abstract knowledge, but from intuitively apprehended, immediate knowledge of the world and of its inner nature, and is expressed by him through some dogma only for the satisfaction of his faculty of reason. It is therefore just as little necessary for the saint to be a philosopher as for the philosopher to be a saint; just as it is not necessary for a perfectly beautiful person to be a great sculptor, or for a great sculptor to be himself a beautiful person. In general, it is a strange demand on a moralist that he should commend no other virtue than that which he himself possesses. To repeat abstractly, universally, and distinctly in concepts the whole inner nature of the world, and thus to deposit it as a reflected image in permanent concepts always ready for the faculty of reason, this and nothing else is philosophy.

But my description, given above, of the denial of the will-to-live, or of the conduct of a beautiful soul, of a resigned and voluntarily expiating saint, is only abstract and general, and therefore cold. As the knowledge from which results the denial of the will is intuitive and not abstract, it finds its complete expression not in abstract concepts, but only in the deed and in conduct. Therefore, in order to understand more fully what we express philosophically as denial of the will-to-live, we have to learn to know examples from experience and reality. Naturally we shall not come across them in daily experience: "For all that is excellent and eminent is as difficult as it is rare," as Spinoza admirably says in his *Ethics*. Therefore, unless we are made eyewitnesses by a specially favorable fate, we shall have to content ourselves with the biographies of such persons. Indian literature, as we see from the little that is so far known to us through translations, is very rich in descriptions of the lives of saints, penitents, Samanas, Sannyasis, and so on. [. . .] Among Christians there is also no lack of examples affording us the illustrations that we have in mind. Let us see the biographies, often badly written, of those persons sometimes called saintly souls, sometimes pietists, quietists, pious enthusiasts, and so on. Collections of such biographies have been made at various times. [. . .] To this category very properly belongs the life of Saint Francis of Assisi, that true personification of asceticism and proto-type of all mendicant friars. [. . .]

We also see how immaterial it is whether it proceeds from a the-istic or from an atheistic religion. But as a special and extremely full example and actual illustration of the conceptions I advance, I can particularly recommend the *Autobiography* of Madame de Guyon. To become acquainted with that great and beautiful soul, whose remem-brance always fills me with reverence, and to do justice to the excel-lence of her disposition while making allowances for the superstition of her faculty of reason, must be gratifying to every person of the better sort, just as with common thinkers, in other words the major-ity, that book will always stand in bad repute. For everyone, always and everywhere, can appreciate only that which is to some extent analogous to him, and for which he has at any rate a feeble gift; this holds good of the ethical as well as of the intellectual. To a certain extent we might regard even the well-known French biography of Spinoza as a case in point, if we use as the key to it that excellent introduction to his very inadequate essay *De Emendatione Intellectus*. At the same time, I can recommend this passage as the most effec-tive means known to me of stilling the storm of the passions. Finally, even the great Goethe, Greek as he was, did not regard it as beneath his dignity to show us this most beautiful side of humanity in the elucidating mirror of the poetic art, since he presented to us in an idealized form the life of Fräulein Klettenberg in the *Confessions of a Beautiful Soul*, and later, in his own biography, gave us also a his-torical account of it. Besides this, he twice narrated the life of Saint

Philip Neri. The history of the world will, and indeed must, always keep silence about the persons whose conduct is the best and only adequate illustration of this important point of our investigation. For the material of world history is quite different therefrom, and indeed opposed to it; thus it is not the denial and giving up of the will-to-live, but its affirmation and manifestation in innumerable individuals in which its dissension with itself at the highest point of its objectification appears with perfect distinctness, and brings before our eyes, now the superior strength of the individual through his shrewdness, now the might of the many through their mass, now the ascendancy of chance personified as fate, always the vanity and futility of the whole striving and effort. But we do not follow here the thread of phenomena in time, but, as philosophers, try to investigate the ethical significance of actions, and take this as the only criterion of what is significant and important for us. No fear of the always permanent majority of vulgarity and shallowness will prevent us from acknowledging that the greatest, the most important, and the most significant phenomenon that the world can show is not the conqueror of the world, but the overcomer of the world, and so really nothing but the quiet and unobserved conduct in the life of such a man. On this man has dawned the knowledge in consequence of which he gives up and denies that will-to-live that fills everything, and strives and strains in all. The freedom of this will first appears here in him alone, and by it his actions now become the very opposite of the ordinary. For the philosopher, therefore, in this respect those accounts of the lives of saintly, self-denying persons, badly written as they generally are, and mixed up with superstition and nonsense, are through the importance of the material incomparably more instructive and important than even Plutarch and Livy.

Further, a more detailed and complete knowledge of what we express in abstraction and generality through our method of presentation as denial of the will-to-live, will be very greatly facilitated by a consideration of the ethical precepts given in this sense and by people who were full of this spirit. These will at the same time show how old our view is, however new its purely philosophical expression may be. In the first place, Christianity is nearest at hand, the ethics of which is entirely in the spirit we have mentioned, and leads not only to the highest degrees of charity and human kindness, but also to renunciation. The germ of this last side is certainly distinctly present in the writings of the Apostles, yet only later is it fully developed and explicitly expressed. We find commanded by the Apostles love for our neighbor as for ourselves, returning of hatred with love and good actions, patience, meekness, endurance of all possible affronts and injuries without resistance, moderation in eating and drinking for suppressing desire, resistance to the sexual impulse, even complete if possible for us. Here we see the first stages of asceticism or of real denial of the will; this last expression denotes what is called in the Gospels denying the self and taking of the cross upon oneself. This tendency was soon developed more and more, and was the origin of penitents, anchorites, and monasticism, an origin that in itself was pure and holy, but, for this very reason, quite unsuitable to the great majority of people. Therefore what developed out of it could be only hypocrisy and infamy, for "the worst is the abuse of the best." In more developed Christianity, we see that seed of asceticism unfold into full flower in the writings of the Christian saints and mystics. Besides the purest love, these preach also complete resignation, voluntary and ab-solute poverty, true composure, complete indifference to all worldly things, death to one's own will and regeneration in God, entire for-getting of one's own person and absorption in the contemplation of God. [. . .] But the spirit of this development of Christianity is cer-tainly nowhere so perfectly and powerfully expressed as in the writ-ings of the German mystics, e.g., those of Meister Eckhart, and the justly famous book *Theologia Germanica*. In his introduction to this last, Luther wrote that, with the exception of the Bible and Saint Augustine, he had learnt more from it of what God, Christ, and man are than from any other book. [. . .] The precepts and doctrines given in it are the most perfect explanation, springing from deep inward conviction, of what I have described as the denial of the will-to-live. One has therefore to make a closer study of it before dogmatizing about it with Jewish-Protestant assurance. Tauler's *Nachfolgung des armen Leben Christi*, together with his *Medulla animae*, are written in the same admirable spirit, although not quite equal in value to that work. In my opinion, the teachings of these genuine Christian mystics are related to those of the New Testament as alcohol is to wine; in other words, what becomes visible to us in the New Testament as if through a veil and mist stands before us in the works of the mystics without cloak or disguise, in full clearness and distinctness. Finally, we might also regard the New Testament as the first initiation, the mystics as the second—small and great mysteries.

But we find what we have called denial of the will-to-live still further developed, more variously expressed, and more vividly presented in the ancient works in the Sanskrit language than could be the case in the Christian Church and the Western world. That this important ethical view of life could attain here to a more far-reaching development and a more decided expression is perhaps to be ascribed mainly to the fact that it was not restricted by an element quite foreign to it, as the Jewish doctrine of faith is in Christianity. The sublime founder of Christianity had necessarily to adapt and accommodate himself, partly consciously, partly, it may be, unconsciously, to this doctrine; and so Christianity is composed of two very heterogeneous elements. Of these I should like to call the purely ethical element preferably, indeed exclusively, the Christian, and to distinguish it from the Jewish dogmatism with which it is found. If, as has often been feared, and especially at the present time, that excellent and salutary religion should completely decline, then I would look for the reason for this simply in the fact that it does not consist of one simple element, but of two originally heterogeneous elements, brought into combination only by means of world events. In such a case, dissolution would necessarily result through the breakup of these elements, which arises from their different relationship and reaction to the advanced spirit of the times. Yet after this dissolution, the purely ethical part would still be bound always to remain intact, because it is indestructible. However imperfect our knowledge of Hindu literature still is, as we now find it most variously and powerfully expressed in the ethics of the Hindus, in the Vedas, Puranas, poetical works, myths, legends of their saints; in aphorisms, maxims, and rules of conduct, we see that it ordains love of one's neighbor with complete denial of all self-love; love in general, not limited to the human race, but embracing all that lives; charitableness even to the giving away of one's hard-won daily earnings; boundless patience towards all offenders; return of all evil, however bad it may be, with goodness and love; voluntary and cheerful endurance of every insult and ignominy; abstinence from all animal food; perfect chastity and renunciation of all sensual pleasure for him who aspires to real holiness; the throwing away of all property; the forsaking of every dwelling-place and of all kinsfolk; deep unbroken solitude spent in silent contemplation with voluntary penance and terrible slow self-torture for the complete mortification of the will, ultimately going as far as voluntary death by starvation, or facing crocodiles, or jumping over the consecrated precipice in the Himalaya, or being buried alive, or flinging oneself under the wheels of the huge car that drives round with the images of the gods amid the singing, shouting, and dancing of bayaderes. These precepts, whose origin reaches back more than four thousand years, are still lived up to by individuals even to the utmost extreme, degenerate as that race is in many respects. That which has remained in practice for so long in a nation embracing so many millions, while it imposes the heaviest sacrifices, cannot be an arbitrarily invented freak, but must have its foundation in the very nature of mankind. But besides this, we cannot sufficiently wonder at the harmony we find, when we read the life of a Christian penitent or saint and that of an Indian. In spite of such fundamentally different dogmas, customs, and circumstances, the endeavor and the inner life of both are absolutely the same; and it is also the same with the precepts for both. For example, Tauler speaks of the complete poverty which one should seek, and which consists in giving away and divesting oneself entirely of everything from which one might draw some comfort or worldly pleasure, clearly because all this always affords new nourishment to the will, whose complete mortification is intended. As the Indian counterpart of this, we see in the precepts of Fo that the Sannyasi, who is supposed to be without dwelling and entirely without property, is finally enjoined not to lie down too often under the same tree, lest he acquire a preference or inclination for it. The Christian mystics and the teachers of the Vedanta philosophy agree also in regarding all outward works and religious practices as superfluous for the man who has attained perfection. So much agreement, in spite of such different ages and races, is a practical proof that here is expressed not an eccentricity and craziness of the mind, as optimistic shallowness and dullness like to assert, but an essential side of human nature which appears rarely only because of its superior quality.

I have now mentioned the sources from which we can obtain a direct knowledge, drawn from life, of the phenomena in which the denial of the will-to-live exhibits itself. To a certain extent, this is the most important point of our whole discussion; yet I have explained it only quite generally, for it is better to refer to those who speak from direct experience, than to increase the size of this book unnecessarily by repeating more feebly what they say.

I wish to add only a little more to the general description of their state. We saw above that the wicked man, by the vehemence of his willing, suffers constant, consuming, inner torment, and finally that, when all the objects of willing are exhausted, he quenches the fiery thirst of his willfulness by the sight of others' pain. On the other hand, the man in whom the denial of the will-to-live has dawned, however poor, cheerless, and full of privation his state may be when looked at from outside, is full of inner cheerfulness and true heavenly peace. It is not the restless and turbulent pressure of life, the jubilant delight that has keen suffering as its preceding or succeeding condition, such as constitute the conduct of the man attached to life, but it is an unshakable peace, a deep calm and inward serenity, a state that we cannot behold without the greatest longing, when it is brought before our eyes or imagination, since we at once recognize it as that which alone is right, infinitely outweighing everything else, at which our better spirit cries to us the great "bring yourself to be reasonable." We then feel that every fulfillment of our wishes won from the world is only like the alms that keep the beggar alive today so that he may starve again tomorrow. Resignation, on the other hand, is like the inherited estate; it frees its owner from all care and anxiety forever.

It will be remembered [. . .] that aesthetic pleasure in the beautiful consists, to a large extent, in the fact that, when we enter the state of pure contemplation, we are raised for the moment above all willing, above all desires and cares; we are, so to speak, rid of ourselves. We are no longer the individual that knows, in the interest of its constant willing, the correlative of the particular thing to which objects become motives, but the eternal subject of knowing purified of the will, the correlative of the Idea. And we know that these moments, when, delivered from the fierce pressure of the will, we emerge, as it were, from the heavy atmosphere of the earth, are the most blissful that we experience. From this we can infer how blessed must be the life of a man whose will is silenced not for a few moments, as in the enjoyment of the beautiful, but forever, indeed completely extinguished, except for the last glimmering spark that maintains the body and is extinguished with it. Such a man who, after many bitter struggles with his own nature, has at last completely conquered, is then left only as pure knowing being, as the undimmed mirror of the world. Nothing can distress or alarm him anymore; nothing can any longer move him; for he has cut all the thousand threads of willing which hold us bound to the world, and which as craving, fear, envy, and anger drag us here and there in constant pain. He now looks back calmly and with a smile on the phantasmagoria of this world which was once able to move and agonize even his mind, but now stands before him as indifferently as chessmen at the end of a game, or as fancy dress cast off in the morning, the form and figure of which taunted and disquieted us on the carnival night. Life and its forms merely float before him as a fleeting phenomenon, as a light morning dream to one half-awake, through which reality already shines, and which can no longer deceive; and, like this morning dream, they too finally vanish without any violent transition. From these considerations we can learn to understand what Madame de Guyon means when, towards the end of her *Autobiography*, she often expresses herself thus: "Everything is indifferent to me; I *cannot* will anything more; often I do not know whether I exist or not." In order to express how, after the dying-away of the will, the death of the body (which is indeed only the phenomenon of the will, and thus with the abolition of the will loses all meaning) can no longer have anything bitter, but is very welcome, I may be permitted to record here that holy penitent's own words, although they are not very elegantly turned: "The noonday of glory; a day no longer followed by night; a life that no longer fears death, even in death itself, because death has overcome death, and because whoever has suffered the first death will no longer feel the second."

However, we must not imagine that, after the denial of the will-to-live has once appeared through knowledge that has become a quieter of the will, such denial no longer wavers or falters, and that we can rest on it as on an inherited property. On the contrary, it must always be achieved afresh by constant struggle. For as the body is the will itself only in the form of objectivity, or as phenomenon in the world as representation, that whole will-to-live exists potentially so long as the body lives, and is always striving to reach actuality and to burn afresh with all its intensity. We therefore find in the lives of saintly persons that peace and bliss we have described, only as the blossom resulting from the constant overcoming of the will; and we see the constant struggle with the will-to-live as the soil from which it shoots up; for on earth no one can have lasting peace. We therefore see the histories of the inner life of saints full of spiritual conflicts, temptations, and desertion from grace, in other words, from that kind of knowledge which, by rendering all motives ineffectual, as a universal quieter silences all willing, gives the deepest peace, and opens the gate to freedom. Therefore we see also those who have once attained to denial of the will strive with all their might to keep to this path by self-imposed renunciations of every kind, by a penitent and hard way of life, and by looking for what is disagreeable to them; all this in order to suppress the will that is constantly springing up afresh. Finally, therefore, because they already know the value of salvation, their anxious care for the retention of the hard-won blessing, their scruples of conscience in the case of every innocent enjoyment or with every little excitement of their vanity; this is also the last thing to die, the most indestructible, the most active, and the most foolish of all man's inclinations. By the expression *asceticism*, which I have already used so often, I understand in the narrower sense this *deliberate* breaking of the will by refusing the agreeable and looking for the disagreeable, the voluntarily chosen way of life of penance and self-chastisement, for the constant mortification of the will.

Now, if we see this practiced by persons who have already attained to denial of the will, in order that they may keep to it, then
suffering in general, as it is inflicted by fate, is also a second way
of attaining to that denial. Indeed, we may assume that most men
can reach it only in this way, and that it is the suffering personally
felt, not the suffering merely known, which most frequently produces
complete resignation, often only at the approach of death. For only
in the case of a few is mere knowledge sufficient to bring about the
denial of the will, the knowledge namely that sees through the *principium individuationis*, first producing perfect goodness of disposition
and universal love of mankind, and finally enabling them to recognize as their own all the sufferings of the world. Even in the case of
the individual who approaches this point, the tolerable condition of
his own person, the flattery of the moment, the allurement of hope,
and the satisfaction of the will offering itself again and again, i.e., the
satisfaction of desire, are almost invariably a constant obstacle to the
denial of the will, and a constant temptation to a renewed affirmation of it. For this reason, all those allurements have in this respect
been personified as the devil. Therefore in most cases the will must
be broken by the greatest personal suffering before its self-denial appears. We then see the man suddenly retire into himself after he is
brought to the verge of despair through all the stages of increasing
affliction with the most violent resistance. We see him know himself
and the world, change his whole nature, rise above himself and above
all suffering, as if purified and sanctified by it, in inviolable peace,
bliss, and sublimity, willingly renounce everything he formerly desired with the greatest vehemence, and gladly welcome death. It is
the gleam of silver that suddenly appears from the purifying flame
of suffering, the gleam of the denial of the will-to-live, of salvation.
Occasionally we see even those who were very wicked purified to this
degree by the deepest grief and sorrow; they have become different,

and are completely converted. Therefore, their previous misdeeds no longer trouble their consciences, yet they gladly pay for such misdeeds with death, and willingly see the end of the phenomenon of that will that is now foreign to and abhorred by them. The great Goethe has given us a distinct and visible description of this denial of the will, brought about by great misfortune and by the despair of all deliverance, in his immortal masterpiece *Faust*, in the story of the sufferings of Gretchen. I know of no other description in poetry. It is a perfect specimen of the second path, which leads to the denial of the will not, like the first, through the mere knowledge of the suffering of a whole world which one acquires voluntarily, but through the excessive pain felt in one's own person. It is true that very many tragedies bring their violently willing heroes ultimately to this point of complete resignation, and then the will-to-live and its phenomenon usually end at the same time. But no description known to me brings to us the essential point of that conversion so distinctly and so free from everything extraneous as the one mentioned in *Faust*.

In real life we see those unfortunate persons who have to drink to the dregs the greatest measure of suffering, face a shameful, violent, and often painful death on the scaffold with complete mental vigor, after they are deprived of all hope; and very often we see them converted in this way. We should not, of course, assume that there is so great a difference between their character and that of most men, as their fate seems to suggest; we have to ascribe the latter for the most part to circumstances; yet they are guilty and, to a considerable degree, bad. But we see many of them converted in the way mentioned, after the appearance of complete hopelessness. They now show actual goodness and purity of disposition, true abhorrence of committing any deed in the least degree wicked or uncharitable. They forgive their enemies, even those through whom they innocently suffered; and not merely in words and from a kind of hypocritical fear of the judges of the netherworld, but in reality and with inward earnestness, and with no wish for revenge. Indeed, their suffering and dying in the end become agreeable to them, for the denial of the will-to-live has made its appearance. They often decline the deliverance offered them, and die willingly, peacefully, and blissfully. The last secret of life has revealed itself to them in the excess of pain, the secret, namely, that evil and wickedness, suffering and hatred, the tormented and the tormentor, different as they may appear to knowledge that follows the principle of sufficient reason, are in themselves one, phenomenon of the one will-to-live that objectifies its conflict with itself by means of the *principium individuationis*. They have learned to know both sides in full measure, the wickedness and the evil; and since they ultimately see the identity of the two, they reject them both at the same time; they deny the will-to-live. As we have said, it is a matter of complete indifference by what myths and dogmas they account to their faculty of reason for this intuitive and immediate knowledge, and for their conversion.

Matthias Claudius was undoubtedly a witness to a change of mind of this sort, when he wrote the remarkable essay which appears in the *Wandsbecker Bote* under the title "History of the Conversion of . . ." which has the following ending: "Man's way of thinking can pass over from a point of the periphery to the opposite point, and back again to the previous point, if circumstances trace out for him the curved path to it. And these changes are not really anything great and interesting in man. But that *remarkable, catholic, transcendental change*, where the whole circle is irreparably torn up and all the laws of psychology become vain and empty, where the coat of skins is taken off, or at any rate turned inside out, and man's eyes are opened, is such that everyone who is conscious to some extent of the breath in his nostrils, forsakes father and mother, if he can hear and experience something certain about it."

The approach of death and hopelessness, however, are not absolutely necessary for such a purification through suffering. Even without them, the knowledge of the contradiction of the will-to-live with itself can, through great misfortune and suffering, violently force itself on us, and the vanity of all endeavor can be perceived. Hence men who have led a very adventurous life under the pressure of passions, men such as kings, heroes, or adventurers, have often been seen suddenly to change, resort to resignation and penance, and become hermits and monks. To this class belong all genuine accounts of conversion, for instance that of Raymond Lull, who had long wooed a beautiful woman, was at last admitted to her chamber, and was looking forward to the fulfillment of all his desires, when, opening her dress, she showed him her bosom terribly eaten away with cancer. From that moment, as if he had looked into hell, he was converted; leaving the court of the King of Majorca, he went into the wilderness to do penance. [. . .] If we consider how [. . .] the transition from the pleasure to the horror of life was the occasion, this gives us an explanation of the remarkable fact that it is the French nation, the most cheerful, merry, gay, sensual, and frivolous in Europe, in which by far the strictest of all monastic orders, namely the Trappist, arose [. . .] and maintains itself even to the present day in all its purity and fearful strictness, in spite of revolutions, changes in the Church, and the encroachments of infidelity.

However, a knowledge of the above-mentioned kind of the nature of this existence may depart again simultaneously with its occasion, and the will-to-live, and with it the previous character, may reappear. Thus we see that the passionate Benvenuto Cellini was converted in such a way, once in prison and again during a serious illness, but relapsed into his old state after the suffering had disappeared. In general, the denial of the will by no means results from suffering with the necessity of effect from cause; on the contrary, the will remains free. For here is just the one and only point where its freedom enters directly into the phenomenon; hence the astonishment so strongly expressed by Asmus (Matthais Claudius) about the "transcendental change." For every case of suffering, a will can be conceived which surpasses it in intensity, and is unconquered by it. Therefore, Plato speaks in the *Phaedo* of persons who, up to the moment of their execution, feast, carouse, drink, indulge in sexual pleasures, affirming life right up to the death. Shakespeare in Cardinal Beaufort presents to us the fearful end of a wicked ruffian who dies full of despair, since no suffering or death can break his will that is vehement to the extreme point of wickedness.

The more intense the will, the more glaring the phenomenon of its conflict, and hence the greater the suffering. A world that was the phenomenon of an incomparably more intense will-to-live than the present one is would exhibit so much the greater suffering; thus it would be a *hell*.

Since all suffering is a mortification and a call to resignation, it has potentially a sanctifying force. By this is explained the fact that great misfortune and deep sorrow in themselves inspire one with a certain awe. But the sufferer becomes wholly an object of reverence to us only when, surveying the course of his life as a chain of sorrows, or mourning a great and incurable pain, he does not really look at the concatenation of circumstances which plunged just his life into mourning; he does not stop at that particular great misfortune that befell him. For up till then, his knowledge still follows the principle of sufficient reason, and clings to the particular phenomenon; he still continues to will life, only not on the conditions that have happened to him. He is really worthy of reverence only when his glance has been raised from the particular to the universal, and when he regards his own suffering merely as an example of the whole and for him; for in an ethical respect he becomes inspired with genius, one case holds good for a thousand, so that the whole of life, conceived as essential suffering, then brings him to resignation. For this reason it is worthy of reverence when in Goethe's *Torquato Tasso* the princess speaks of how her own life and that of her relations have always been sad and cheerless, and here her regard is wholly towards the universal.

We always picture a very noble character to ourselves as having a certain trace of silent sadness that is anything but constant peevishness over daily annoyances (that would be an ignoble trait, and might lead us to fear a bad disposition). It is a consciousness that has resulted from knowledge of the vanity of all possessions and of the suffering of all life, not merely of one's own. Such knowledge, however, may first of all be awakened by suffering personally experienced, especially by a single great suffering, just as a single wish incapable of fulfillment brought Petrarch to that resigned sadness concerning the whole of life which appeals to us so pathetically in his works; for the Daphne he pursued had to vanish from his hands, in order to leave behind for him the immortal laurel instead of herself. If the will is to a certain extent broken by such a great and irrevocable denial of fate, then practically nothing more is desired, and the character shows itself as mild, sad, noble, and resigned. Finally, when grief no longer has any definite object, but is extended over the whole of life, it is then to a certain extent a self-communion, a withdrawal, a gradual disappearance of the will, the visibility of which, namely the body, is imperceptibly but inwardly undermined by it, so that the person feels a certain loosening of his bonds, a mild foretaste of the death that proclaims itself to be the dissolution of the body and of the will at the same time. A secret joy therefore accompanies this grief; and I believe it is this that the most melancholy of all nations has called "the joy of grief." Here, however, lies the danger of *sentimentality*, both in life itself and in its description in poetry; namely when a person is always mourning and wailing without standing up courageously and rising to resignation. In this way heaven and earth are both lost, and only a watery sentimentality is retained. Only when suffering assumes the form of pure knowledge, and then this knowledge, as a *quieter of the will*, produces true resignation, is it the path to salvation, and thus worthy of reverence. But in this respect, we feel on seeing any very unfortunate person a certain esteem akin to that which virtue and nobility of character force from us; at the same time, our own fortunate condition seems like a reproach. We cannot help but regard every suffering, both those felt by ourselves and those felt by others, as at least a possible advance towards virtue and holiness, and pleasures and worldly satisfactions, on the other hand, as a departure therefrom. This goes so far that every man who undergoes great bodily or mental suffering, indeed everyone who performs a physical labor demanding the greatest exertion in the sweat of his brow and with evident exhaustion, yet does all this with patience and without grumbling, appears, when we consider him with close attention, somewhat like a sick man who applies a painful cure. Willingly, and even with satisfaction, he endures the pain caused by the cure, since he knows that the more he suffers, the more is the substance of the disease destroyed; and thus the present pain is the measure of his cure.

It follows from all that has been said that the denial of the will-to-live, which is the same as what is called complete resignation or holiness, always proceeds from that quieter of the will; and this is the knowledge of its inner conflict and its essential vanity, expressing themselves in the suffering of all that lives. The difference, which we have described as two paths, is whether that knowledge is called forth by suffering which is merely and simply *known* and freely appropriated by our seeing through the *principium individuationis*, or by suffering immediately felt by ourselves. True salvation, deliverance from life and suffering, cannot even be imagined without complete denial of the will. Till then, everyone is nothing but this will itself, whose phenomenon is an evanescent existence, an always vain and constantly frustrated striving, and the world full of suffering as we have described it. All belong to this irrevocably and in like manner. For we found previously that life is always certain to the will-to-live, and its sole actual form is the present from which they never escape, since birth and death rule in the phenomenon. The Indian myth expresses this by saying that "they are born again." The great ethical difference of characters means that the bad man is infinitely remote from attaining that knowledge, whose result is the denial of the will, and is therefore in truth *actually* abandoned to all the miseries which appear in life as *possible*. For even the present fortunate state of his person is only a phenomenon brought about by the *principium individuationis*, and the illusion of Maya, the happy dream of a beggar. The sufferings that in the vehemence and passion of his pressing will he inflicts on others are the measure of the sufferings, the experience of which in his own person cannot break his will and lead to final denial. On the other hand, all true and pure affection, and even all free justice, result from seeing through the *principium individuationis*; when this penetration occurs in all its force, it produces perfect sanctification and salvation, the phenomenon of which are the state of resignation previously described, the unshakable peace accompanying this, and the highest joy and delight in death.

Nineteen

Death and Rebirth

Death is the real inspiring genius [. . .] of philosophy, and for this reason Socrates defined philosophy as "preparation for death." Indeed, without death there would hardly have been any philosophizing. [. . .]

The animal lives without any real knowledge of death; therefore the individual animal immediately enjoys the absolute imperishableness and immortality of the species, since it is conscious of itself only as endless. With man the terrifying certainty of death necessarily appeared along with the faculty of reason. But just as everywhere in nature a remedy, or at any rate a compensation, is given for every evil, so the same reflection that introduced the knowledge of death also assists us in obtaining *metaphysical* points of view. Such views console us concerning death, and the animal is neither in need of nor capable of them. All religions and philosophical systems are directed principally to this end, and are thus primarily the antidote to the certainty of death which reflecting reason produces from its own resources. The degree in which they attain this end is, however, very different, and *one* religion or philosophy will certainly enable man, far more than the others will, to look death calmly in the face. Brahmanism and Buddhism, which teach man to regard himself as Brahman, as the original being himself, to whom all arising and passing away are essentially foreign, will achieve much more in this respect than will those religions that represent man as being made out of nothing and as actually beginning at his birth the existence he has received from another. In keeping with this we find in India a confidence and a contempt for death of which we in Europe have no conception. It is indeed a ticklish business to force on man through early impression weak and untenable notions in this important respect, and thus to render him forever incapable of adopting more correct and stable views. For example, to teach him that he came but recently from nothing, that consequently he has been nothing throughout an eternity, and yet for the future is to be imperishable and immortal, is just like teaching him that, although he is through and through the work of another, he shall nevertheless be responsible to all eternity for his commissions and omissions. Thus if with a mature mind and with the appearance of reflection the untenable nature of such doctrines forces itself on him, he has nothing better to put in their place; in fact, he is no longer capable of understanding anything better, and in this way is deprived of the consolation that nature had provided for him as compensation for the certainty of death. In consequence of such a development, we now (1844) see in England the Socialists among the demoralized and corrupted factory workers, and in Germany the young Hegelians among the demoralized and corrupted students, sink to the absolutely physical viewpoint. This leads to the result: "Eat and drink, after death there is no more rejoicing," and to this extent can be described as bestiality.

According, however, to all that has been taught about death, it cannot be denied that, at any rate in Europe, the opinion of men, often in fact even of the same individual, very frequently vacillates afresh between the conception of death as absolute annihilation and the assumption that we are, so to speak, with skin and hair, immortal. Both are equally false, but we have not so much to find a correct mean as rather to gain the higher standpoint from which such views disappear of themselves.

With these considerations, I wish to start first of all from the entirely empirical viewpoint. Here we have primarily before us the undeniable fact that, according to natural consciousness, man not only fears death for his own person more than anything else, but also weeps violently over the death of his friends and relations. It is evident, indeed, that he does this not egoistically over his own loss, but out of sympathy for the great misfortune that has befallen them. He therefore censures as hard-hearted and unfeeling those who in such a case do not weep and show no grief. Parallel with this is the fact that, in its highest degrees, the thirst for revenge seeks the death of the adversary as the greatest evil that can be inflicted on him. Opinions change according to time and place, but the voice of nature remains always and everywhere the same, and is therefore to be heeded before everything else. Now here it seems clearly to assert that death is a great evil. In the language of nature, death signifies annihilation; and that death is a serious matter could already be inferred from the fact that, as everyone knows, life is no joke. Indeed we must not deserve anything better than these two.

The fear of death is, in fact, independent of all knowledge, for the animal has it, although it does not know death. Everything that is born already brings this fear into the world. Such fear of death, however, is *a priori* only the reverse side of the will-to-live, which indeed we all are. Therefore in every animal the fear of its own destruction, like the care for its maintenance, is inborn. Thus it is this fear of death, and not the mere avoidance of pain, that shows itself in the anxious care and caution with which the animal seeks to protect itself, and still more its brood, from everyone who might become dangerous. Why does the animal flee, tremble, and try to conceal itself? Because it is simply the will-to-live, but as such it is forfeit to death and would like to gain time. By nature, man is just the same. The greatest of evils, the worst thing that can threaten anywhere, is death; the greatest anxiety is the anxiety of death. Nothing excites us so irresistibly to the most lively interest as does danger to the lives of others; nothing is more dreadful than an execution. Now the boundless attachment to life which appears here cannot have sprung from knowledge and reflection. To these, on the contrary, it appears foolish, for the objective value of life is very uncertain, and it remains at least doubtful whether existence is to be preferred to nonexistence; in fact, if experience and reflection have their say, nonexistence must certainly win. If we knocked on the graves and asked the dead whether they would like to rise again, they would shake their heads. In Plato's *Apology* this is also the opinion of Socrates, and even the cheerful and amiable Voltaire cannot help saying: "We like life, but all the same nothingness also has its good points. [. . .] I do not know what eternal life is, but this present life is a bad joke." Moreover, in any case life must end soon, so that the few years which possibly we have still to exist vanish entirely before the endless time when we shall be no more. Accordingly, to reflection it appears even ludicrous for us to be so very anxious about this span of time, to tremble so much when our own life or another's is endangered, and to write tragedies whose terrible aspect has as its main theme merely the fear of death. Consequently, this powerful attachment to life is irrational and blind; it can be explained only from the fact that our whole being-in-itself is the will-to-live, to which life therefore must appear as the highest good, however embittered, short, and uncertain it may be; and that that will is originally and in itself without knowledge and blind. Knowledge, on the contrary, far from being the origin of that attachment to life, even opposes it, since it discloses life's worthlessness, and in this way combats the fear of death. When it is victorious, and man accordingly faces death courageously and calmly,

this is honored as great and noble. Therefore we then extol the triumph of knowledge over the blind will-to-live which is nevertheless
the kernel of our own inner being. In the same way we despise him
in whom knowledge is defeated in that conflict, who therefore clings
unconditionally to life, struggles to the utmost against approaching
death, and receives it with despair. Cicero observes: "In gladiatorial
conflicts we usually abhor and abominate the cowards who beg and
implore us to let them live. On the other hand, we seek to preserve
the lives of the brave, the courageous, and those who of their own
free will impetuously face death." Yet in him is expressed only the
original inner being of our own self and of nature. Incidentally, it
may here be asked how the boundless love of life and the endeavor to
maintain it in every way as long as possible could be regarded as base
and contemptible, and likewise considered by the followers of every
religion as unworthy thereof, if life were the gift of the good gods
to be acknowledged with thanks. How then could it appear great
and noble to treat it with contempt? Meanwhile, these considerations
confirm for us: (1) that the will-to-live is the innermost essence of
man; (2) that in itself the will is without knowledge and blind; (3)
that knowledge is an adventitious principle, originally foreign to the
will; (4) that knowledge conflicts with the will, and our judgment
applauds the triumph of knowledge over the will.

If what makes death seem so terrible to us were the thought of
nonexistence, we should necessarily think with equal horror of the
time when as yet we did not exist. For it is irrefutably certain that
nonexistence after death cannot be different from nonexistence
before birth, and is therefore no more deplorable than that is. An
entire infinity ran its course when we did *not yet exist*, but this in
no way disturbs us. On the other hand, we find it hard, and even
unendurable, that after the momentary intermezzo of an ephemeral
existence, a second infinity should follow in which we shall exist

no longer. Now could this thirst for existence possibly have arisen through our having tasted it and found it so very delightful? As was briefly set forth above, certainly not; the experience gained would far rather have been capable of causing an infinite longing for the lost paradise of nonexistence. To the hope of immortality of the soul there is always added that of a "better world": an indication that the present world is not worth much. Notwithstanding all this, the question of our state after death has certainly been discussed verbally and in books ten thousand times more often than that of our state before birth. Theoretically, however, the one is a problem just as near at hand and just as legitimate as the other; moreover, he who answered the one would likewise be fully enlightened about the other. We have fine declamations about how shocking it would be to think that the mind of man, which embraces the world and has so many excellent ideas, should sink with him into the grave; but we hear nothing about this mind having allowed a whole infinity of time to elapse before it arose with these its qualities, and how for just as long a time the world had to manage without it. Yet to knowledge uncorrupted by the will no question presents itself more naturally than this, namely: An infinite time has run its course before my birth; what was I throughout all that time? Metaphysically, the answer might perhaps be: "I was always I; that is, all who throughout that time said I, were just I." But let us turn away from this to our present entirely empirical point of view, and assume that I did not exist at all. But I can then console myself for the infinite time after my death when I shall not exist, with the infinite time when I did not as yet exist, as a quite customary and really very comfortable state. For the infinity "after life" without me cannot be any more fearful than the infinity "before life" without me, since the two are not distinguished by anything except by the intervention of an ephemeral life-dream. All proofs of continued existence after death may also be applied just as well before life, where they then demonstrate existence before life, in assuming which the Hindus and Buddhists therefore show themselves to be very consistent. Only Kant's ideality of time solves all these riddles; but we are not discussing this at the moment. But this much follows from what has been said, namely that to mourn for the time when we shall no longer exist is just as absurd as it would be to mourn for the time when we did not as yet exist; for it is all the same whether the time our existence does not fill is related to that which it does fill as future or as past.

But quite apart even from these considerations of time, it is in and by itself absurd to regard nonexistence as an evil; for every evil, like every good, presupposes existence, indeed even consciousness. But this ceases with life, as well as in sleep and in a fainting fit; therefore the absence of consciousness is well known and familiar to us as a state containing no evil at all; in any case, its occurrence is a matter of a moment. Epicurus considered death from this point of view, and therefore said quite rightly, "Death does not concern us," with the explanation that when we are, death is not, and when death is, we are not. To have lost what cannot be missed is obviously no evil; therefore we ought to be just as little disturbed by the fact that we shall not exist as by the fact that we did not exist. Accordingly, from the standpoint of knowledge, there appears to be absolutely no ground for fearing death; but consciousness consists in knowing, and thus for consciousness death is no evil. Moreover, it is not really this *knowing* part of our *ego* that fears death, but *fuga mortis* comes simply and solely from the blind *will*, with which every living thing is filled. But, as already mentioned, this *fuga mortis* is essential to it, just because it is the will-to-live, whose whole inner nature consists in a craving for life and existence. Knowledge is not originally inherent in it, but appears only in consequence of the will's objectification in animal individuals. Now, if by means of knowledge the will beholds death as the end of the phenomenon with which it has identified itself, and to which it therefore sees itself limited, its whole nature struggles against this with all its might. We shall investigate later on whether it really has anything to fear from death, and shall then remember the real source of the fear of death which is indicated here with a proper distinction between the willing and knowing part of our true nature.

According to this, what makes death so terrible for us is not so much the end of life—for this cannot seem to anyone specially worthy of regret—as the destruction of the organism, really because this organism is the will itself manifested as body. But actually, we feel this destruction only in the evils of illness or of old age; on the other hand, for the *subject*, death itself consists merely in the moment when consciousness vanishes, since the activity of the brain ceases. The extension of the stoppage to all the other parts of the organism which follows this is really already an event after death. Therefore, in a subjective respect, death concerns only consciousness. Now from going to sleep everyone can, to some extent, judge what the vanishing of consciousness may be; and whoever has had a real fainting fit knows it even better. The transition here is not so gradual, nor is it brought about by dreams; but first of all, while we are still fully conscious, the power of sight disappears, and then immediately supervenes the deepest unconsciousness. As far as the accompanying sensation goes, it is anything but unpleasant; and undoubtedly just as sleep is the brother of death, so is the fainting fit its twin brother. Violent death also cannot be painful, for, as a rule, even severe wounds are not felt at all till some time afterwards, and are often noticed only from their external symptoms. If they are rapidly fatal, consciousness will vanish before this discovery; if they result in death later, it is the same as with other illnesses. All who have lost consciousness in water, through charcoal fumes, or through hanging, also state, as is well known, that it happened without pain. And finally, even death through natural causes proper, death through old age, euthanasia, is a gradual vanishing and passing out of existence in an imperceptible manner. In old age, passions and desires, together with the susceptibility to their objects, are gradually extinguished; the emotions no longer find any excitement, for the power to make representations or mental pictures becomes weaker and weaker, and its images feebler. The impressions no longer stick to us, but pass away without a trace; the days roll by faster and faster; events lose their significance; everything grows pale. The old man, stricken in years, totters about or rests in a corner, now only a shadow, a ghost, of his former self. What still remains there for death to destroy? One day a slumber is his last, and his dreams are— They are the dreams that Hamlet asks about in the famous monologue. I believe that we dream them just now.

I have still to observe that, although the maintenance of the life process has a metaphysical basis, it does not take place without resistance, and hence without effort. It is this to which the organism yields every evening, for which reason it then suspends the brain function, and diminishes certain secretions, respiration, pulse, and the development of heat. From this it may be concluded that the entire cessation of the life process must be a wonderful relief for its driving force. Perhaps this is partly responsible for the expression of sweet contentment on the faces of most of the dead. In general, the moment of dying may be similar to that of waking from a heavy nightmare.

So far, the result for us is that death cannot really be an evil, however much it is feared, but that it often appears even as a good thing, as something desired, as a friend. All who have encountered insuperable obstacles to their existence or to their efforts, who suffer from incurable disease or from inconsolable grief, have the return into the womb of nature as the last resource that is often open to them as a matter of course. Like everything else, they emerged from this womb for a short time, enticed by the hope of more favorable conditions of existence than those that have fallen to their lot, and from this the same path always remains open to them. That return is the "surrender of property" of the living. Yet even here it is entered into only after a physical or moral conflict, so hard does everyone struggle against returning to the place from which he came forth so readily and willingly to an existence that has so many sorrows and so few joys to offer. To Yama, the god of death, the Hindus give two faces, one very fearful and terrible, one very cheerful and benevolent. This is already explained in part from the observations we have just made.

From the empirical standpoint, at which we are still placed, the following consideration is one which presents itself automatically, and therefore merits being defined accurately by elucidation, and thus kept within its limits. The sight of a corpse shows me that sensibility, irritability, blood circulation, reproduction, and so on in it have ceased. From this I conclude with certainty that that which previously actuated them, which was nevertheless something always unknown to me, now actuates them no longer, and so has departed from them. But if I now wished to add that this must have been just what I have known only as consciousness, and consequently as intelligence (soul), this would be a conclusion not merely unjustified, but obviously false. For consciousness has always shown itself to me not as the cause, but as a product and result of organic life, since it rose and sank in consequence thereof at the different periods of life, in health and sickness, in sleep, in a faint, in awaking, and so on. Thus it always appeared as the effect, never as a cause, of organic life, always showed itself as something arising and passing away and again arising, so long as the conditions for this still exist, but not apart from them. Indeed, I may also have seen that the complete derangement of consciousness, madness, far from dragging down with it and depressing the other forces, or even endangering life, greatly enhances these, especially irritability or muscular force, and lengthens rather than shortens life, if there are no other competing causes. Then I knew individuality as a quality or attribute of everything organic, and when this was a self-conscious organism, of consciousness also. But there exists no occasion for concluding now that individuality is inherent in that vanished principle which imparts life and is wholly unknown to me; the less so, as everywhere in nature I see each particular phenomenon to be the work of a universal force active in thousands of similar phenomena. But on the other hand there is just as little occasion for concluding that, because organized life has here ceased, the force that actuated it hitherto has also become nothing; just as little as there is to infer from the stopping of the spinning wheel the death of the spinner. If, by finding its center of gravity again, a pendulum finally comes to rest, and thus its individual apparent life has ceased, no one will suppose that gravitation is annihilated, but everyone sees that now as always it is active in innumerable phenomena. Of course, it might be objected to this comparison that even in the pendulum gravitation has not ceased to be active, but has merely given up manifesting its activity visibly. He who insists on this may think, instead, of an electrical body in which, after its discharge, electricity has really ceased to be active. I wished only to show by this that we directly attribute an eternity and ubiquity even to the lowest forces of nature; and the transitoriness of their fleeting phenomena does not for a moment confuse us with regard thereto. So much the less, therefore, should it occur to us to regard the cessation of life as the annihilation of the living principle, and thus death as the entire destruction of man. Because the strong arm that three thousand years ago bent the bow of Ulysses no longer exists, no reflective and well-regulated understanding will look upon the force that acted so energetically in it as entirely annihilated. Therefore, on further reflection, it will not be assumed that the force that bends the bow today first began to exist with that arm. Much nearer to us is the idea that the force that formerly actuated a life now vanished is the same force that is active in the life now flourishing; indeed this thought is almost inevitable. However, we certainly know that, as was explained in the second book of *The World as Will and Representation*, only that is perishable which is involved in the causal chain; but merely the states and forms are so involved. Untouched, however, by the change of these, which is produced by causes, there remain matter on the one hand, and the natural forces on the other; for both are the presupposition of all those changes. But the principle that gives us life must first be conceived at any rate as a force of nature, until a profounder investigation may perhaps let us know what it is in itself. Thus, taken already as a force of nature, vital force remains entirely untouched by the change of forms and states, which the bond of cause and effect introduces and carries off again, and which alone are subject to arising and passing away, just as these processes lie before us in experience. To this extent, therefore, the imperishableness of our true inner nature could already be certainly demonstrated. But this, of course, will not satisfy the claims usually made on proofs of our continued existence after death, nor will it afford the consolation expected from such proofs. Yet it is always something, and whoever fears death as his absolute annihilation cannot afford to disdain the perfect certainty that the innermost principle of his life remains untouched by it. In fact, we might advance the paradox that that second thing which, like the forces of nature, remains untouched by the continuous change of states under the guidance of causality, i.e., matter, also assures us through its absolute permanence of an indestructibility; and by virtue of this, he who might be incapable of grasping any other could yet be confident of a certain imperishability.

But it will be asked: "How is the permanence of mere dust, of crude matter, to be regarded as a continuance of our true inner nature?" Oh! do you know this dust, then? Do you know what it is and what it can do? Learn to know it before you despise it. This matter, now lying there as dust and ashes, will soon form into crystals when dissolved in water; it will shine as metal; it will then emit electric sparks. By means of its galvanic tension it will manifest a force which, decomposing the strongest and firmest combinations, reduces earths to metals. It will, indeed of its own accord, form itself into plant and animal; and from its mysterious womb it will develop that life, about the loss of which you in your narrowness of mind are so nervous and anxious. Is it, then, so absolutely and entirely nothing to continue to exist as such matter? Indeed, I seriously assert that even this permanence of matter affords evidence of the indestructibility of our true inner being, although only as in an image and simile, or rather only as in a shadowy outline. To see this, we need only recall [. . .] that mere formless matter—this basis of the world of experience, never perceived by itself alone, but assumed as always permanent—is the immediate reflection, the visibility in general, of the thing-in-itself, that is, of the will. Therefore, what absolutely pertains to the will in itself holds good of matter under the conditions of experience, and it reproduces the true eternity of the will under the image of temporal imperishability. Because, as we have already said, nature does not lie, no view which has sprung from a purely objective comprehension of her, and has been logically thought out, can be absolutely and entirely false; in the worst case it is only very one-sided and imperfect. But such a view is unquestionably consistent materialism, for instance that of Epicurus, just as is the absolute idealism opposed to it, like that of Berkeley, and generally every fundamental view of philosophy which has come from a correct *aperçu* and has been honestly worked out. Only they are all extremely one-sided interpretations, and therefore, in spite of their contrasts, are *simultaneously* true, each from a definite point of view. But as soon as we rise

above this point, they appear to be true only relatively and conditionally. The highest standpoint alone, from which we survey them all
and recognize them in their merely relative truth, and also beyond
this in their falseness, can be that of absolute truth, insofar as such
a truth is in general attainable. Accordingly, as was shown above, we
see even in the really very crude, and therefore very old, fundamental
view of materialism the indestructibility of our true inner being-in-
itself still represented as by a mere shadow of it, namely through the
imperishability of matter; just as in the already higher naturalism of
an absolute physics we see it represented by the ubiquity and eternity
of natural forces, among which vital force is at least to be reckoned.
Hence even these crude fundamental views contain the assertion that
the living being does not suffer any absolute annihilation through
death, but continues to exist in and with the whole of nature.

The considerations which have brought us to this point, and with
which the further discussions are connected, started from the remarkable fear of death which affects all living beings. But now we
wish to alter the point of view, and to consider how, in contrast to individual beings, the *whole* of nature behaves with regard to death; yet
here we still remain always on the ground and soil of the empirical.

We know, of course, of no higher gamble than that for life and
death. We watch with the utmost attention, interest, and fear every
decision concerning them; for in our view all in all is at stake. On the
other hand, *nature*, which never lies, but is always frank and sincere,
speaks quite differently on this theme, as Krishna does in the Bhagavad Gita. Her statement is that the life or death of the individual is of
absolutely no consequence. She expresses this by abandoning the life
of every animal, and even of man, to the most insignificant accidents
without coming to the rescue. Consider the insect on your path; a
slight unconscious turning of your foot is decisive as to its life or
death. Look at the wood-snail that has no means of flight, of defense,

of practicing deception, of concealment, a ready prey to all. Look at the fish carelessly playing in the still open net; at the frog prevented by its laziness from the flight that could save it; at the bird unaware of the falcon soaring above it; at the sheep eyed and examined from the thicket by the wolf. Endowed with little caution, all these go about guilelessly among the dangers which at every moment threaten their existence. Now, since nature abandons without reserve her organisms constructed with such inexpressible skill, not only to the predatory instinct of the stronger, but also to the blindest chance, the whim of every fool, and the mischievousness of every child, she expresses that the annihilation of these individuals is a matter of indifference to her, does her no harm, is of no significance at all, and that in these cases the effect is of no more consequence than is the cause. Nature states this very clearly, and she never lies; only she does not comment on her utterances, but rather expresses them in the laconic style of the oracle. Now if the universal mother carelessly sends forth her children without protection to a thousand threatening dangers, this can be only because she knows that, when they fall, they fall back into her womb, where they are safe and secure; therefore their fall is only a jest. With man she does not act otherwise than she does with the animals; hence her declaration extends also to him; the life or death of the individual is a matter of indifference to her. Consequently, they should be, in a certain sense, a matter of indifference to us; for in fact, we ourselves are nature. If only we saw deeply enough, we should certainly agree with nature, and regard life or death as indifferently as does she. Meanwhile, by means of reflection, we must attribute nature's careless and indifferent attitude concerning the life of individuals to the fact that the destruction of such a phenomenon does not in the least disturb its true and real inner being.

As we have just been considering, not only are life and death dependent on the most trifling accidents, but the existence of organic beings generally is also ephemeral; animal and plant arise today and tomorrow pass away; birth and death follow in quick succession, whereas to inorganic things, standing so very much lower, an incomparably longer duration is assured, but an infinitely long one only to absolutely formless matter, to which we attribute this even *a priori*. Now if we ponder over all this, I think the merely empirical, but objective and unprejudiced, comprehension of such an order of things must be followed as a matter of course by the thought that this order is only a superficial phenomenon, that such a constant arising and passing away cannot in any way touch the root of things, but can be only relative, indeed only apparent. The true inner being of everything, which, moreover, evades our glance everywhere and is thoroughly mysterious, is not affected by that arising and passing away, but rather continues to exist undisturbed thereby. Of course, we can neither perceive nor comprehend the way in which this happens, and must therefore think of it only generally as a kind of "conjuring trick" that took place here. For whereas the most imperfect thing, the lowest, the inorganic, continues to exist unassailed, it is precisely the most perfect beings, namely living things with their infinitely complicated and inconceivably ingenious organizations, which were supposed always to arise afresh from the very bottom, and after a short span of time to become absolutely nothing, in order to make room once more for new ones like them coming into existence out of nothing. This is something so obviously absurd that it can never be the true order of things, but rather a mere veil concealing such an order, or more correctly a phenomenon conditioned by the constitution of our intellect. In fact, the entire existence and nonexistence of these individual beings, in reference to which life and death are opposites, can be only relative. Hence the language of nature, in which it is given to us as something absolute, cannot be the true and ultimate expression of the quality and constitution of things and of the order of the world, but really only a provincial dialect, in other words, something merely relatively true, something self-styled, to be understood "with a grain of salt," or properly speaking, something conditioned by our intellect. I say that an immediate, intuitive conviction of the kind I have here tried to describe in words will force itself on everyone, of course only on everyone whose mind is not of the utterly common species. Such common minds are capable of knowing absolutely only the particular thing, simply and solely as such, and are strictly limited to knowledge of individuals, after the manner of the animal intellect. On the other hand, whoever, through an ability of an only somewhat higher power, even just begins to see in individual beings their universal, their Ideas, will also to a certain extent participate in that conviction, a conviction indeed that is immediate and therefore certain. Indeed, it is also only small, narrow minds that quite seriously fear death as their annihilation; those who are specially favored with decided capacity are entirely remote from such terrors. Plato rightly founded the whole of philosophy on knowledge of the doctrine of Ideas, in other words, on the perception of the universal in the particular. But the conviction here described and arising directly out of the apprehension of nature must have been extremely lively in those sublime authors of the Upanishads of the Vedas, who can scarcely be conceived as mere human beings. For this conviction speaks to us so forcibly from an immense number of their utterances that we must ascribe this immediate illumination of their mind to the fact that, standing nearer to the origin of our race as regards time, these sages apprehended the inner essence of things more clearly and profoundly than the already enfeebled race, as mortals now are, is capable of doing. But, of course, their comprehension was also assisted by the natural world of India, which is endowed with life in quite a different degree from that in which our northern world is. Thorough reflection, however, as carried through by Kant's great mind, also leads to just the same result by a different path; for it teaches us that our intellect, in which that rapidly changing phenomenal world exhibits itself, does not comprehend the true, ultimate essence of things, but merely its appearance or phenomenon; and indeed, as I add, because originally such an intellect is destined only to present motives to our will, in other words, to be serviceable to it in the pursuit of its paltry aims.

But let us continue still farther our objective and unprejudiced consideration of nature. If I kill an animal, be it a dog, a bird, a frog, or even only an insect, it is really inconceivable that this being, or rather the primary and original force by virtue of which such a marvelous phenomenon displayed itself only a moment before in its full energy and love of life, could through my wicked or thoughtless act have become nothing. Again, on the other hand, the millions of animals of every kind which come into existence at every moment in endless variety, full of force and drive, can never have been absolutely nothing before the act of their generation, and can never have arrived from nothing to an absolute beginning. If in this way I see one of these creatures withdraw from my sight without my ever knowing where it goes to, and another appear without my ever knowing where it comes from; moreover, if both still have the same form, the same inner nature, the same character, but not the same matter, which they nevertheless continue to throw off and renew during their existence; then of course the assumption that what vanishes and what appears in its place are one and the same thing, which has experienced only a slight change, a renewal of the form of its existence, and consequently that death is for the species what sleep is for the individual—this assumption, I say, is so close at hand, that it is impossible for it not to occur to us, unless our minds, perverted in early youth by the impression of false fundamental views, hurry it out of the way, even from afar, with superstitious fear. But the opposite assumption that an animal's birth is an arising out of nothing, and accordingly that its death is an absolute annihilation, and this with the further addition that man has also come into existence out of nothing, yet has an individual and endless future existence, and that indeed with consciousness, whereas the dog, the ape, and the elephant are annihilated by death—is really something against which the sound mind must revolt, and must declare to be absurd. If, as is often enough repeated, the comparison of a system's result with the utterances of common sense is supposed to be a touchstone of its truth, I wish that the adherents of that fundamental view, handed down by Descartes to the pre-Kantian eclectics, and indeed still prevalent even now among the great majority of cultured people in Europe, would once apply this touchstone here.

The genuine symbol of nature is universally and everywhere the circle, because it is the schema or form of recurrence; in fact, this is the most general form in nature. She carries it through in everything from the course of the constellations down to the death and birth of organic beings. In this way alone, in the restless stream of time and its content, a continued existence, i.e., a nature, becomes possible.

In autumn we observe the tiny world of insects, and see how one prepares its bed, in order to sleep the long, benumbing winter sleep; another spins a cocoon, in order to hibernate as a chrysalis, and to awake in spring rejuvenated and perfected; finally, how most of them, intending to rest in the arms of death, carefully arrange a suitable place for depositing their eggs, in order one day to come forth from these renewed. This is nature's great doctrine of immortality, which tries to make it clear to us that there is no radical difference between sleep and death, but that the one endangers existence just as little as the other. The care with which the insect prepares a cell, or hole, or nest, deposits therein its egg, together with food for the larva that will emerge from it in the following spring, and then calmly dies, is just like the care with which a person in the evening lays out his clothes and his breakfast ready for the following morning, and then calmly goes to bed; and at bottom it could not take place at all, unless the insect that dies in autumn were in itself and according to its true essence just as identical with the insect hatched in spring as the person who lies down to sleep is with the one who gets up.

After these considerations, we now return to ourselves and our species; we then cast our glance forward far into the future, and try to picture to ourselves future generations with the millions of their individuals in the strange form of their customs and aspirations. But then we interpose with the question: Whence will all these come? Where are they now? Where is the abundant womb of that nothing which is pregnant with worlds, and which still conceals them, the coming generations? Would not the smiling and true answer to this be: Where else could they be but there where alone the real always was and will be, namely in the present and its content?—hence with you, the deluded questioner, who in this mistaking of his own true nature is like the leaf on the tree. Fading in the autumn and about to fall, this leaf grieves over its own extinction, and will not be consoled by looking forward to the fresh green which will clothe the tree in spring, but says as a lament: "I am not these! These are quite different leaves!" Oh, foolish leaf! Whither do you want to go? And whence are the others supposed to come? Where is the nothing, the abyss of which you fear? Know your own inner being, precisely that which is so filled with the thirst for existence; recognize it once more in the inner, mysterious, sprouting force of the tree. This force is always *one* and the same in all the generations of leaves, and it remains untouched by arising and passing away. And now "as the leaves on the tree, so are the generations of human beings." Whether the fly now buzzing round me goes to sleep in the evening and buzzes again the following morning, or whether it dies in the evening and in spring another fly buzzes which has emerged from its egg, this in itself is the same thing. But then the knowledge that presents these as two fundamentally different things is not unconditioned, but relative, a knowledge of the phenomenon, not of the thing-in-itself. In the morning the fly exists again; it also exists again in the spring. For the fly what distinguishes the winter from the night? [. . .]

Thus everything lingers only for a moment, and hurries on to death. The plant and the insect die at the end of the summer, the animal and man after a few years; death reaps unweariedly. But despite all this, in fact as if this were not the case at all, everything is always there and in its place, just as if everything were imperishable. The plant always flourishes and blooms, the insect hums, animal and man are there in evergreen youth, and every summer we again have before us the cherries that have already been a thousand times enjoyed. Nations also exist as immortal individuals, though sometimes they change their names. Even their actions, what they do and suffer, are always the same, though history always pretends to relate something different; for it is like the kaleidoscope that shows us a new configuration at every turn, whereas really we always have the same thing before our eyes. Therefore, what forces itself on us more irresistibly than the thought that that arising and passing away do not concern the real essence of things, but that this remains untouched by them, hence is imperishable, consequently that each and every thing that *wills* to exist actually does exist continuously and without end? Accordingly, at every given point of time all species of animals, from the gnat to the elephant, exist together complete. They have already renewed themselves many thousands of times, and withal have remained the same. They know nothing of others like them who have lived before them, or who will live after them; it is the species that always lives, and the individuals cheerfully exist in the consciousness of the imperishability of the species and their identity with it. The will-to-live manifests itself in an endless present, because this is the form of the life of the species, which therefore does not grow old, but remains always young. Death is for the species what sleep is for the individual, or winking for the eye; when the Indian gods appear in human form, they are recognized by their not winking. Just as at nightfall the world vanishes, yet does not for a moment cease to exist, so man and animal apparently pass away through death, yet their true inner being continues to exist just as undisturbed. Let us now picture to ourselves that alternation of birth and death in infinitely rapid vibrations, and we have before us the persistent and enduring objectification of the will, the permanent Ideas of beings, standing firm like the rainbow on the waterfall. This is temporal immortality. In consequence of this, in spite of thousands of years of death and decay, there is still nothing lost, no atom of matter, still less anything of the inner being exhibiting itself as nature. Accordingly, we can at any moment cheerfully exclaim: "In spite of time, death, and decay, we are still all together!"

Perhaps an exception would have to be made of the man who should once have said from the bottom of his heart with regard to this game: "I no longer like it." But this is not yet the place to speak of that.

Attention, however, must indeed be drawn to the fact that the pangs of birth and the bitterness of death are the two constant conditions under which the will-to-live maintains itself in its objectification, in other words, our being-in-itself, untouched by the course of time and by the disappearance of generations, exists in an everlasting present, and enjoys the fruit of the affirmation of the will-to-live. This is analogous to our being able to remain awake during the day only on condition that we sleep every night; indeed, this is the commentary furnished by nature for an understanding of that difficult passage. For the suspension of the animal functions is sleep; that of the organic functions is death.

The substratum or filling out, the material of the *present*, is really the same through all time. The impossibility of directly recognizing this identity is just *time*, a form and limitation of our intellect. The fact that by virtue of it, for example, the future event does not as yet exist, rests on a delusion of which we become aware when the event has come to pass. The essential form of our intellect produces such a delusion, and this is explained and justified from the fact that the intellect has come forth from the hands of nature by no means for the purpose of comprehending the inner being of things, but merely for the purpose of comprehending motives, and hence to serve an individual and temporal phenomenon of will. There is only *one present*, and this always exists: for it is the sole form of actual existence. We must arrive at the insight that the *past* is not *in itself* different from the present, but is so only in our apprehension. This has *time* as its form, by virtue of which alone the present shows itself as different from the past. To make this insight easier, let us imagine all the events and scenes of human life, good and bad, fortunate and unfortunate, delightful and dreadful, which are presented to us successively in the course of time and variety of places, in the most motley multifariousness and succession, as existing *all at once and simultaneously* and forever, in the *Nunc stans*, whereas only apparently now this now that exists; then we shall understand what the objectification of the will-to-live really means. Our pleasure in genre pictures is also due mainly to their fixing the fleeting scenes of life. The dogma of metempsychosis resulted from the feeling of the truth just expressed.

If we comprehend the observations that concern us here, we shall also understand the true meaning of the paradoxical doctrine of the Eleatics, that there is no arising and passing away at all, but that the whole stands firm and immovable: "Parmenides and Melissus denied arising and passing away, because they believed the universe to be immovable." In the same way light is also thrown here on the fine passage of Empedocles, which Plutarch has preserved for us:

> Foolish and lacking farsighted reflection are they
> Who imagine there could arise what had not already been,
> Or that it could pass away and become entirely nothing . . .
> Never will such things occur to the sage,
> That so long as we live—what is thus described as life—
> Only for so long also are we subject to good and bad,
> And that before birth and after death we are nothing.

The very remarkable passage in Diderot's *Jacques le fataliste*, which in its place is surprising, deserves just as much to be mentioned: "An immense castle over the front entrance of which one read: 'I belong to no one, and I belong to all the world; you were in it before you entered it, and you will still be in it when you have gone out of it.'" Of course in *that* sense in which he arises out of nothing when he is begotten, man becomes nothing through death. But really to become so thoroughly acquainted with this nothing would be very interesting, for it requires only moderate discernment to see that this empirical nothing is by no means an absolute nothing, in other words, such as would be nothing in every sense. We are already led to this insight by the empirical observation that all the features and characteristics of the parents are found once again in their children, and have thus surmounted death. [. . .]

There is no greater contrast than that between the ceaseless, irresistible flight of time carrying its whole content away with it, and the rigid immobility of what is actually existing, which is at all times one and the same; and if, from this point of view, we fix our really objective glance on the immediate events of life, the *Nunc stans* becomes clear and visible to us in the center of the wheel of time. To the eye of a being who lived an incomparably longer life and took in at a single glance the human race in its whole duration, the constant alternation of birth and death would present itself merely as a continuous vibration. Accordingly, it would not occur to it at all to see in it a constantly new coming out of nothing and passing into nothing, but, just as to our glance the rapidly turning spark appears as a continuous circle, the rapidly vibrating spring as a permanent triangle, the vibrating cord as a spindle, so to its glance the species would appear as that which is and remains, birth and death as vibrations.

We shall have false notions about the indestructibility of our true nature through death, so long as we do not make up our minds to study it first of all in the animals, and claim for ourselves alone a class apart from them under the boastful name of immortality. But it is this presumption alone and the narrowness of view from which it proceeds, on account of which most people struggle so obstinately against recognizing the obvious truth that, essentially and in the main, we are the same as the animals; in fact that such people recoil at every hint of our relationship with these. Yet it is this denial of the truth which, more than anything else, bars to them the way to real knowledge of the indestructibility of our true nature. For if we seek anything on a wrong path, we have in so doing forsaken the right; and on the wrong path we shall never attain to anything in the end but belated disillusionment. Therefore, pursue truth straight away, not according to preconceived freaks and fancies, but guided by the hand of nature! First of all learn to recognize, when looking at every young animal, the never-aging existence of the species, which, as a reflection of its own eternal youth, bestows on every new individual a temporal youth, and lets it step forth as new, as fresh, as if the world were of today. Ask yourself honestly whether the swallow of this year's spring is an entirely different one from the swallow of the first spring, and whether actually between the two the miracle of creation out of nothing has been renewed a million times, in order to work just as often into the hands of absolute annihilation. I know quite well that anyone would regard me as mad if I seriously assured him that the cat, playing just now in the yard, is still the same one that did the same jumps and tricks there three hundred years ago; but I also know that it is much more absurd to believe that the cat of today is through and through and fundamentally an entirely different one from that cat of three hundred years ago. We need only become sincerely and seriously engrossed in the contemplation of one of these higher vertebrates, in order to become distinctly conscious that this unfathomable inner being, taken as a whole as it exists, cannot possibly become nothing, and yet, on the other hand, we know its transitoriness. This rests on the fact that in this animal the eternity of its Idea (species) is distinctly marked in the finiteness of the individual. For in a certain sense it is of course true that in the individual we always have before us a different being, namely in the sense resting on the principle of sufficient reason, under which are also included time and space; these constitute the *principium individuationis*. But in another it is not true, namely in the sense in which reality belongs only to the permanent forms of things, to the Ideas, and which was so clearly evident to Plato that it became his fundamental thought, the center of his philosophy; the comprehension of it became his criterion for the ability to philosophize generally.

Just as the spraying drops of the roaring waterfall change with lightning rapidity, while the rainbow, of which they are the supporter, remains immovably at rest, quite untouched by that restless change, so every *Idea*, i.e., every *species* of living beings remains entirely untouched by the constant change of its individuals. But it is the *Idea* or the species in which the will-to-live is really rooted and manifests itself; therefore the will is really concerned only in the continuance of the species. For example, the lions that are born and that die are like the drops of the waterfall; but *leonitas*, the *Idea* or form or shape of the lion, is like the unshaken and unmoved rainbow on the waterfall. Plato therefore attributed real and true being only to the *Ideas*, i.e., to the species; but to the individuals he attributed only a restless arising and passing away. From the deepest consciousness of his imperishable nature there also spring the confidence and serenity with which every animal and even every human individual move along lightheartedly amid a host of chances and hazards that may annihilate them at any moment, and moreover move straight on to death. Out of his eyes, however, there glances the peace of the species, which is unaffected and untouched by that destruction and extinction. Not even to man could this peace and calm be vouchsafed by uncertain and changing dogmas. As I have said, however, the sight of every animal teaches us that death is no obstacle to the kernel of life, the will in its manifestation. Yet what an unfathomable mystery lies in every animal! Look at the nearest one; look at your dog, and see how cheerfully and calmly he stands there! Many thousands of dogs have had to die before it was this dog's turn to live; but the death and extinction of those thousands have not affected the *Idea* of the dog. This Idea has not in the least been disturbed by all that dying. Therefore the dog stands there as fresh and endowed with original force as if this day were his first and none could be his last, and out of his eyes there shines the indestructible principle in him, the *archaeus*. Now what has died throughout those thousands of years? Not the dog; he stands there before us intact and unscratched; merely his shadow, his image or copy in our manner of knowing, which is bound to time. Yet how can we ever believe that that passes away which exists forever and ever, and fills all time? The matter is, of course, explainable empirically, namely according as death destroyed the individuals, generation brought forth new ones. This empirical explanation, however, is only an apparent explanation;

it puts one riddle in place of the other. Although a metaphysical understanding of the matter is not to be had so cheaply, it is nevertheless the only true and satisfactory one.

In his subjective method, Kant brought to light the great though negative truth that time cannot belong to the thing-in-itself, because it lies preformed in our apprehension. Now death is the temporal end of the temporal phenomenon; but as soon as we take away time, there is no longer any end at all, and the word has lost all meaning. But here, on the objective path, I am now trying to show the positive aspect of the matter, namely that the thing-in-itself remains untouched by time and by that which is possible only through time, that is, by arising and passing away, and that the phenomena in time could not have even that restless, fleeting existence that stands next to nothingness, unless there were in them a kernel of eternity. It is true that *eternity* is a concept having no perception as its basis; for this reason, it is also of merely negative content, and thus implies a timeless existence. *Time*, however, is a mere image of eternity, "time is a copy or image of eternity," as Plotinus has it; and in just the same way, our temporal existence is the mere image of our true inner being. This must lie in eternity, just because time is only the form of our knowing; but by virtue of this form alone we know our own existence and that of all things as transitory, finite, and subject to annihilation.

In the second book of *The World as Will and Representation, Vol. I*, I have explained that the adequate objectivity of the will as thing-in-itself is the (Platonic) *Idea* at each of its grades. Similarly in the third book I have shown that the Ideas of beings have as their correlative the pure subject of knowing, consequently that the knowledge of them appears only by way of exception and temporarily under specially favorable conditions. For individual knowledge, on the other hand, and hence in time, the *Idea* exhibits itself under the form of the *species*, and this is the Idea drawn apart by entering into time. The *species* is therefore the most immediate objectification of the thing-in-itself, i.e., of the will-to-live. Accordingly, the innermost being of every animal and of man also lies in the *species*; thus the will-to-live, which is so powerfully active, has its root in the species, not really in the individual. On the other hand, immediate consciousness is to be found only in the individual; therefore it imagines itself to be different from the species, and thus fears death. The will-to-live manifests itself in reference to the individual as hunger and fear of death; in reference to the species, as sexual impulse and passionate care for the offspring. In agreement with this, we find nature, as being free from that delusion of the individual, just as careful for the maintenance of the species as she is indifferent to the destruction of the individuals; for her the latter are always only means, the former the end. Therefore, a glaring contrast appears between her niggardliness in the equipment of individuals and her lavishness when the species is at stake. From *one* individual often a hundred thousand seeds or more are obtained annually, for example, from trees, fish, crabs, termites, and many others. In the case of her niggardliness, on the other hand, only barely enough in the way of strength and organs is given to each to enable it with ceaseless exertion to maintain a bare living. If, therefore, an animal is crippled or weakened, it must, as a rule, die of starvation. And where an occasional economy was possible, through the circumstance that a part could be dispensed with in an emergency, it has been withheld, even out of order. Hence, for example, many caterpillars are without eyes; the poor animals grope about in the dark from leaf to leaf, and in the absence of antennae they do this by moving three quarters of their body to and fro in the air, till they come across an object. In this way they often miss their food that is to be found close at hand. But this happens in consequence of the parsimonious law of nature, to the expression of which "nature does nothing in vain and creates nothing superfluous"; can still be added "and she gives away nothing." The same tendency of nature shows itself also in the fact that the fitter an individual is for propagation by virtue of his age, the more powerfully does the "healing power of nature" manifest itself in him. His wounds, therefore, heal easily, and he easily recovers from illnesses. This diminishes with the power of procreation, and sinks low after this power is extinguished; for in the eyes of nature the individual has now become worthless.

Now, if we cast a glance at the scale of beings together with the gradation of consciousness that accompanies them, from the polyp to man, we see this wonderful pyramid kept in ceaseless oscillation certainly by the constant death of the individuals, yet enduring in the species throughout the endlessness of time by means of the bond of generation. Now, whereas, as was explained above, the *objective*, the species, manifests itself as indestructible, the *subjective*, consisting merely in the self-consciousness of these beings, seems to be of the shortest duration, and to be incessantly destroyed, in order just as often to come forth again out of nothing in an incomprehensible way. But a man must really be very shortsighted to allow himself to be deceived by this appearance, and not to understand that, although the form of temporal permanence belongs only to the objective, the subjective—i.e., the *will*, living and appearing in everything, and with it the subject of *knowing* in which this exhibits itself—must be no less indestructible. For the permanence of the objective, or the external, can indeed be only the phenomenal appearance of the indestructibility of the subjective, or the internal, since the former cannot possess anything that it had not received in fee from the latter; it cannot be essentially and originally something objective, a phenomenon, and then secondarily and accidentally something subjective, a thing-in-itself, something conscious of itself. For obviously, the former as phenomenon or appearance presupposes something that appears, just as being-for-another presupposes being-for-self, and object presupposes subject; but not conversely, since everywhere the root of things must lie in that which they are by themselves, hence in the subjective, not in the objective, not in that which they are only for others, not in the consciousness of another. Accordingly, we found in the first book that the correct starting point for philosophy is essentially and necessarily the subjective, i.e., the idealistic, just as the opposite starting point, proceeding from the objective, leads to materialism. Fundamentally, however, we are far more at one with the world than we usually think; its inner nature is our will, and its phenomenal appearance our representation. The difference between the continuance of the external world after his death and his own continuance after death would vanish for anyone who could bring this unity or identity of being to distinct consciousness; the two would present themselves to him as one and the same thing; in fact, he would laugh at the delusion that could separate them. For an understanding of the indestructibility of our true nature coincides with that of the identity of macrocosm and microcosm. Meanwhile, we can elucidate what has here been said by a peculiar experiment that is to be carried out by means of the imagination, and might be called metaphysical. Let a person attempt to present vividly to his mind the time, not in any case very distant, when he will be dead. He then thinks himself away, and allows the world to go on existing; but soon, to his own astonishment, he will discover that nevertheless he still exists. For he imagined he made a mental representation of the world without himself; but the I or ego is in consciousness that which is immediate, by which the world is first brought about, and for which alone the world exists. This center of all existence, this kernel of all reality, is to be abolished, and yet the world is to be allowed to go on existing; it is an idea that may, of course, be conceived in the abstract, but not realized. The endeavor to achieve this, the attempt to think the secondary without the primary, the conditioned without the condition, the supported without the supporter, fails every time, much in the same way as the attempt fails to conceive an equilateral right-angled triangle, or an arising and passing away of matter, and similar impossibilities. Instead of what was intended, the feeling here forces itself on us that the world is no less in us than we are in it, and that the source of all reality lies within ourselves. The result is really that the time when I shall not be will come objectively; but subjectively it can never come. Indeed, it might therefore be asked how far anyone in his heart actually believes in a thing that he cannot really conceive at all; or whether, since the deep consciousness of the indestructibility of our real inner nature is associated with that merely intellectual experiment that has, however, already been carried out more or less distinctly by everyone, whether, I say, our own death is not perhaps for us at bottom the most incredible thing in the world.

The deep conviction of the impossibility of our extermination by death, which, as the inevitable qualms of conscience at the approach of death also testify, everyone carries at the bottom of his heart, depends entirely on the consciousness of our original and eternal nature; therefore Spinoza expresses it thus: "We feel and experience that we are *eternal*." For a reasonable person can think of himself as imperishable only insofar as he thinks of himself as beginningless, as eternal, in fact as timeless. On the other hand, he who regards himself as having come out of nothing must also think that he becomes nothing again; for it is a monstrous idea that an infinity of time elapsed before he was, but that a second infinity has begun throughout which he will never cease to be. Actually the most solid ground for our imperishable nature is the old aphorism: "Nothing comes out of nothing, and nothing can again become nothing." Therefore, Theophrastus Paracelsus says very pertinently: "The soul in me has come from something, therefore it does not come to nothing; for it comes out of something." He states the true reason. But he who regards man's birth as his absolute beginning must regard death as his absolute end. For both are what they are in the same sense; consequently everyone can think of himself as *immortal* only insofar as he also thinks of himself as *unborn*, and in the same sense. What birth is, that also is death, according to its true nature and significance; it is the same line drawn in two directions. If the former is an actual arising out of nothing, the latter is also an actual annihilation. In truth, however, it is only by means of the *eternity* of our real inner nature that an imperishableness of it is conceivable; consequently such an imperishableness is not temporal. The assumption that man is created out of nothing necessarily leads to the assumption that death is his absolute end. In this respect, therefore, the Old Testament is quite consistent; for no doctrine of immortality is appropriate to a creation out of nothing. New Testament Christianity has such a doctrine, because it is Indian in spirit, and therefore, more than probably Indian in origin, although only indirectly, through Egypt. Such a doctrine, however, is as little suited to the Jewish stem on which that Indian wisdom had to be grafted in the Holy Land as the freedom of the will is to the will's being created or, as Horace says, "[as] if a painter wanted to join a human head to the neck of a horse."

It is always bad if we are not allowed to be thoroughly original and to carve out of the whole wood. Brahmanism and Buddhism, on the other hand, quite consistently with a continued existence after death, have an existence before birth, and the purpose of this life is to atone for the guilt of that previous existence. The following passage from Colebrooke's *Essays on the Religion and Philosophy of the Hindus* shows also how clearly conscious they are of the necessary consistency in this: "Against the system of the Bhagavatas, which is but partially heretical, the objection upon which the chief stress is laid by Vyasa is, that the soul would not be eternal, if it were a production, and consequently had a beginning." Further, in Upham's *Doctrine of Buddhism* it is said: "The lot in hell of impious persons call'd Deitty is the most severe: these are they who, discrediting the evidence of Buddha, adhere to the heretical doctrine, that all living beings had their beginning in the mother's womb, and will have their end in death."

He who conceives his existence as merely accidental must certainly be afraid of losing it through death. On the other hand, he who sees, even only in a general way, that his existence rests on some original necessity, will not believe that this necessity, which has produced so wonderful a thing, is limited to such a brief span of time, but that it is active at all times. But whoever reflects that up till now, when he exists, an infinite time, and thus an infinity of changes, has run its course, but yet notwithstanding this he exists, will recognize his existence as a necessary one. Therefore the entire possibility of all states and conditions has exhausted itself already without being able to eliminate his existence. *If ever he could not be, he would already not be now.* For the infinity of the time that has already elapsed, with the exhausted possibility of its events in it, guarantees that what *exists necessarily exists.* Consequently, everyone has to conceive himself as a necessary being, in other words, as a being whose existence would follow from its true and exhaustive definition, if only we had this. Actually, in this train of thought is to be found the only immanent proof of the imperishableness of our real inner nature, that is to say, the only proof that keeps within the sphere of empirical data. Existence must be inherent in this inner nature, since it shows itself to be independent of all states or conditions that can possibly be brought about through the causal chain; for these states have already done what they could, and yet our existence has remained just as unshaken thereby, as the ray of light is by the hurricane that it cuts through. If from its own resources time could bring us to a happy state, we should already have been there long ago; for an infinite time lies behind us.

But likewise, if time could lead us to destruction, we should already long ago have ceased to exist. It follows from the fact that we now exist, if the matter is well considered, that we are bound to exist at all times. For we ourselves are the inner nature that time has taken up into itself, in order to fill up its void; therefore this inner nature fills the *whole* of time, present, past, and future, in the same way; and it is just as impossible for us to fall out of existence as it is for us to fall out of space. If we carefully consider this, it is inconceivable that what once exists in all the force of reality could ever become nothing, and then not exist throughout an infinite time. From this have arisen the Christian doctrine of the restoration of all things, the Hindu doctrine of the constantly renewed creation of the world by Brahma, together with similar dogmas of the Greek philosophers. The great mystery of our existence and nonexistence, to explain which these and all kindred dogmas were devised, ultimately rests on the fact that the same thing that objectively constitutes an infinite course of time is subjectively a point, an indivisible, ever-present present-moment; but who comprehends it? It has been most clearly expounded by Kant in his immortal doctrine of the ideality of time and of the sole reality of the thing-in-itself. For it follows from this that what is really essential in things, in man, in the world, lies permanently and enduringly in the *Nunc stans*, firm and immovable; and that the change of phenomena and of events is a mere consequence of our apprehension of it by means of our perception-form of time. Accordingly, instead of saying to men: "Ye have arisen through birth, but are immortal," one should say: "Ye are not nothing," and teach them to understand this in the sense of the saying attributed to Hermes Trismegistus: "For that which is must always be." Yet if this does not succeed, but the anxious heart breaks out into its old lament: "I see all beings arise out of nothing through birth, and again after a brief term return to nothing; even my existence, now in the present, will soon lie in the remote past, and I shall be nothing!" then the right answer is: "Do you not exist? Do you not possess the precious present, to which you children of time all aspire so eagerly, actually at this moment? And do you understand how you have attained to it? Do you know the paths which have led you to it, that you could see them barred to you by death? An existence of yourself after the destruction of your body is not possibly conceivable to you; but can it be more inconceivable to you than are your present existence and the way you have attained to it? Why should you doubt that the secret paths that stood open to you up to this present will not also stand open to you to every future present?"

Therefore, if considerations of this kind are certainly calculated to awaken the conviction that there is something in us that death cannot destroy, this nevertheless happens only by our being raised to a point of view from which birth is not the beginning of our existence. It follows from this, however, that what is proved to be indestructible through death is not really the individual. Moreover, having arisen through generation and carrying within himself the qualities of the father and mother, this individual exhibits himself as a mere difference of the species, and as such can be only finite. Accordingly, just as the individual has no recollection of his existence before his birth, so can he have no recollection of his present existence after death. Everyone, however, places his I or ego in *consciousness*; therefore this seems to him to be tied to individuality. Moreover, with individuality there disappears all that which is peculiar to him, as to this, and which distinguishes him from others. Therefore his continued existence without individuality becomes for him indistinguishable from the continuance of all other beings, and he sees his I or ego become submerged. Now he who thus links his existence to the identity of *consciousness*, and therefore desires for this an endless existence after death, should bear in mind that in any case he can attain to this only at the price of just as endless a past before birth. For as he has no recollection of an existence before birth, and so his consciousness begins with birth, he must look upon his birth as an arising of his existence out of nothing. But then he purchases the endless time of his existence after death for just as long a time before birth; in this way the account is balanced without any profit to him. On the other hand, if the existence left untouched by death is different from that of individual consciousness, then it must be independent of birth just as it is of death. Accordingly, with reference to it, it must be equally true to say "I shall always be" and "I have always been," which then gives us two infinities for one. However, the greatest equivocation really lies in the word *I*, as will be seen at once by anyone who calls to mind the contents of our second book and the separation there carried out of the willing part of our true inner nature from the knowing part. According as I understand this word, I can say: "Death is my entire end"; or else: "This my personal phenomenal appearance is just as infinitely small a part of my true inner nature as I am of the world." But the I or ego is the dark point in consciousness, just as on the retina the precise point of entry of the optic nerve is blind, the brain itself is wholly insensible, the body of the sun is dark, and the eye sees everything except itself. Our faculty of knowledge is directed entirely *outwards* in accordance with the fact that it is the product of a brain function that has arisen for the purpose of mere self-maintenance, and hence for the search for nourishment and the seizing of prey. Therefore everyone knows of himself only as of this individual, just as it exhibits itself in external perception. If, on the other hand, he could bring to consciousness what he is besides and beyond this, he would willingly give up his individuality, smile at the tenacity of his attachment thereto, and say: "What does the loss of this individuality matter to me? for I carry within myself the possibility of innumerable individualities." He would see that, although there is not in store for him a continued existence of his individuality, it is nevertheless just as good as if he had such an existence, since he carries within himself a complete compensation for it. Besides this, however, it might also be taken into consideration that the individuality of most people is so wretched and worthless that they actually lose nothing in it, and that what in them may still have some value is the universal human element; but to this we can promise imperishableness. In fact, even the rigid unalterability and essential limitation of every individuality as such would, in the case of its endless duration, inevitably and necessarily produce ultimately such great weariness by its monotony, that we should prefer to become nothing, merely in order to be relieved of it. To desire immortality for the individual is really the same as wanting to perpetuate an error forever; for at bottom every individuality is really only a special error, a false step, something that it would be better should not be, in fact something from which it is the real purpose of life to bring us back. This also finds confirmation in the fact that most, indeed really all, people are so constituted that they could not be happy, no matter in what world they might be placed. Insofar as such a world would exclude want and hardship, they would become a prey to boredom, and insofar as this was prevented, they would fall into misery, vexation, and suffering. Thus, for a blissful condition of man, it would not be by any means sufficient for him to be transferred to a "better world"; on the contrary, it would also be necessary for a fundamental change to occur in man himself, and hence for him to be no longer what he is, but rather to become what he is not. For this, however, he must first of all cease to be what he is; as a preliminary, this requirement is fulfilled by death, and the moral necessity of this can from this point of view already be seen. To be transferred to another world and to change one's entire nature are at bottom one and the same thing. On this also ultimately rests that dependence of the objective on the subjective which is explained

by the idealism of our first book; accordingly, here is to be found
the point of contact between transcendental philosophy and ethics.
If we bear this in mind, we shall find that the awakening from the
dream of life is possible only through the disappearance along with
it of its whole fundamental fabric as well; but this is its organ itself,
the intellect together with its forms. With this the dream would go
on spinning itself forever, so firmly is it incorporated with that organ.
That which really dreamt the dream is, however, still different from
it, and alone remains over. On the other hand, the fear that with
death everything might be over and finished may be compared to
the case of a person who in a dream should think that there were
mere dreams without a dreamer. But would it even be desirable for
an individual consciousness to be kindled again, after it had once
been ended by death, in order that it might continue forever? For the
most part, often in fact entirely, its content is nothing but a stream of
paltry, earthly, poor ideas, and endless worries and anxieties; let these
then be finally silenced! Therefore with true instinct the ancients
put on their tombstones: "to eternal security," or "to good repose."
But if even here, as has happened so often, we wanted continued
existence of the individual consciousness, in order to connect with
it a reward or punishment in the next world, then at bottom the aim
would be merely the compatibility of virtue with egoism. But these
two will never embrace; they are fundamentally opposed. On the
other hand, the immediate conviction, which the sight of noble actions calls forth, is well founded, that the spirit of love enjoining one
man to spare his enemies, and another, even at the risk of his life,
to befriend a person never previously seen, can never pass away and
become nothing.

The most complete answer to the question of the individual's
continued existence after death is to be found in Kant's great doctrine of the *ideality of time*. Just here does this doctrine show itself to

be especially fruitful and rich in important results, since it replaces dogmas, which lead to the absurd on the one path as on the other, by a wholly theoretical but well-proved insight, and thus at once settles the most exciting of all metaphysical questions. To begin, to end, and to continue are concepts that derive their significance simply and solely from time; consequently they are valid only on the presupposition of time. But time has no absolute existence; it is not the mode and manner of the being-in-itself of things, but merely the form of our *knowledge* of the existence and inner being of ourselves and of all things; and for this reason such knowledge is very imperfect, and is limited to mere phenomena. Thus in reference to this knowledge alone do the concepts of ceasing and continuing find application, not in reference to that which manifests itself in them, namely the being-in-itself of things; applied to this, such concepts therefore no longer have any true meaning. For this is also seen in the fact that an answer to the question arising from those time-concepts becomes impossible, and every assertion of such an answer, whether on the one side or the other, is open to convincing objections. We might indeed assert that our being-in-itself continues after death, because it would be wrong to say that it was destroyed; but we might just as well assert that it is destroyed, because it would be wrong to say that it continues; at bottom, the one is just as true as the other. Accordingly, something like an antinomy could certainly be set up here, but it would rest on mere negations. In it one would deprive the subject of the judgment of two contradictorily opposite predicates, but only because the whole category of these predicates would not be applicable to that subject. But if one deprives it of those two predicates, not together but separately, it appears as if the contradictory opposite of the predicate, denied in each case, were thus proved of the subject of the judgment. This, however, is due to the fact that incommensurable quantities are here compared, inasmuch as the problem removes us to a scene that abolishes time, but yet asks about time-determinations. Consequently, it is equally false to attribute these to the subject and to deny them, which is equivalent to saying that the problem is transcendent. In this sense death remains a mystery.

On the other hand, adhering to that very distinction between phenomenon and thing-in-itself, we can make the assertion that man as phenomenon is certainly perishable, yet his true inner being is not affected by this. Hence this true inner being is indestructible, although, on account of the elimination of the time-concepts which is connected with this, we cannot attribute continuance to it. Accordingly, we should be led here to the concept of an indestructibility that was nevertheless not a continuance. Now this concept is one which, obtained on the path of abstraction, may possibly be thought in the abstract; yet it cannot be supported by any perception; consequently, it cannot really become distinct. On the other hand, we must here keep in mind that we have not, like Kant, absolutely given up the ability to know the thing-in-itself; on the contrary, we know that it is to be looked for in the will. It is true that we have never asserted an absolute and exhaustive knowledge of the thing-in-itself; indeed, we have seen quite well that it is impossible to know anything according to what it may be absolutely in and by itself. For as soon as I *know*, I have a representation, a mental picture; but just because this representation is mine, it cannot be identical with what is known; on the contrary, it reproduces in an entirely different form that which is known by making it a being-for-others out of a being-for-self; hence it is still always to be regarded as the *phenomenal appearance* of this. However, therefore, a *knowing* consciousness may be constituted, there can always be for it only phenomena. This is not entirely obviated even by the fact that my own inner being is that which is known; for, insofar as it falls within my *knowing* consciousness, it is already a reflex of my inner being, something different from this inner being itself, and so already in a certain degree phenomenon. Thus, insofar as I am that which knows, I have even in my own inner being really only a phenomenon; on the other hand, insofar as I am directly this inner being itself, I am not that which knows. For it is sufficiently proved in the second book of *The World as Will and Representation, Vol. 1* that knowledge is only a secondary property of our inner being, and is brought about through the animal nature of this. Strictly speaking, therefore, we know even our own will always only as phenomenon, and not according to what it may be absolutely in and by itself. But in that second book, as well as in my work *On the Will in Nature*, it is fully discussed and demonstrated that if, in order to penetrate into the essence of things, we leave what is given only indirectly and from outside, and stick to the only phenomenon into whose inner nature an immediate insight is accessible to us from within, we quite definitely find in this the will as the ultimate thing and the kernel of reality. In the will, therefore, we recognize the thing-in-itself insofar as it no longer has space, but time for its form; consequently, we really know it only in its most immediate manifestation, and thus with the reservation that this knowledge of it is still not exhaustive and entirely adequate. In this sense, therefore, we here retain the concept of the will as that of the thing-in-itself.

The concept of ceasing to be is certainly applicable to man as phenomenon in time, and empirical knowledge plainly presents death as the end of this temporal existence. The end of the person is just as real as was its beginning, and in just that sense in which we did not exist before birth, shall we no longer exist after death. But no more can be abolished through death than was produced through birth; and so that cannot be abolished by which birth first of all became possible. In this sense "born and unborn" is a fine expression. Now the whole of empirical knowledge affords us mere phenomena; thus only phenomena are affected by the temporal processes of arising and passing away, not that which appears, namely the being-in-itself. For this inner being the contrast, conditioned by the brain, between arising and passing away, does not exist at all; on the contrary, it has lost meaning and significance. This inner being, therefore, remains unaffected by the temporal end of a temporal phenomenon, and always retains that existence to which the concepts of beginning, end, and continuance are not applicable. But insofar as we can follow up this inner being, it is in every phenomenal being its will; so too in man. Consciousness, on the other hand, consists in knowledge; but this, as has been sufficiently demonstrated, belongs, as activity of the brain, and consequently as function of the organism, to the mere phenomenon, and therefore ends therewith. The will alone, of which the work or rather the copy was the body, is what is indestructible. The sharp distinction between will and knowledge, together with the former's primacy, a distinction that constitutes the fundamental characteristic of my philosophy, is therefore the only key to the contradiction that shows itself in many different ways, and always arises afresh in every consciousness, even the crudest. This contradiction is that death is our end, and yet we must be eternal and indestructible; hence it is the "we feel and experience that we are eternal" of Spinoza. All philosophers have made the mistake of placing that which is metaphysical, indestructible, and eternal in man in the *intellect*. It lies exclusively in the *will*, which is entirely different from the intellect, and alone is original. As was most thoroughly explained in the second book, the intellect is a secondary phenomenon, and is conditioned by the brain, and therefore begins and ends with this. The will alone is that which conditions, the kernel of the whole phenomenon; consequently, it is free from the forms of the phenomenon, one of which is time, and hence it is also indestructible. Accordingly, with death consciousness it is certainly lost, but not what produced and maintained consciousness; life is extinguished, but with it not the principle of life which manifested itself in it. Therefore a sure and certain feeling says to everyone that there is in him something positively imperishable and indestructible. Even the freshness and vividness of recollections from earliest times, from early childhood, are evidence that something in us does not pass away with time, does not grow old, but endures unchanged. However, we were not able to see clearly what this imperishable element is. It is not consciousness anymore than it is the body, on which consciousness obviously depends. On the contrary, it is that on which the body together with consciousness depends. It is, however, just that which, by entering into consciousness, exhibits itself as *will*. Of course, we cannot go beyond this most immediate phenomenal appearance of it, because we cannot go beyond consciousness. Therefore the question what that something may be insofar as it does *not* enter into consciousness, in other words, what it is absolutely in itself, remains unanswerable.

In the phenomenon, and by means of its forms time and space, as *principium individuationis*, it is thus evident that the human individual perishes, whereas the human race remains and continues to live. But in the being-in-itself of things which is free from these forms, the whole difference between the individual and the race is also abolished, and the two are immediately one. The entire will-to-live is in the individual, as it is in the race, and thus the continuance of the species is merely the image of the individual's indestructibility.

Now, since the infinitely important understanding of the indestructibility of our true nature by death rests entirely on the difference between phenomenon and thing-in-itself, I wish to put this very difference in the clearest light by elucidating it in the opposite of death, hence in the origin of animal beings, i.e., in *generation*. For this process, that is just as mysterious as death, places most directly before our eyes the fundamental contrast between phenomenon and the being-in-itself of things, i.e., between the world as representation and the world as will, and also shows us the entire heterogeneity of the laws of these two. The act of procreation thus presents itself to us in a twofold manner: firstly for self-consciousness, whose sole object is, as I have often shown, the will with all its affections; and secondly for the consciousness of other things, i.e., of the world of the representation, or the empirical reality of things. Now from the side of the will, and thus inwardly, subjectively, for self-consciousness, that act manifests itself as the most immediate and complete satisfaction of the will, i.e., as sensual pleasure. On the other hand, from the side of the representation, and thus outwardly, objectively, for the consciousness of other things, this act is just the woof of the most ingenious of all fabrics, the foundation of the inexpressibly complicated animal organism which then needs only development in order to become visible to our astonished eyes. This organism, whose infinite complication and perfection are known only to the student of anatomy, is not to be conceived and thought of, from the side of the representation, as other than a system, devised with the most carefully planned combination and carried out with the most consummate skill and precision, the most arduous work of the profoundest deliberation. Now from the side of the will, we know through self-consciousness that the production of the organism is the result of an act the very opposite of all reflection and deliberation, of an impetuous, blind craving, an exceedingly voluptuous sensation. This contrast is exactly akin to the infinite contrast, shown above, between the absolute facility with which nature produces her works, together with the correspondingly boundless carelessness with which she abandons such works to destruction—and the incalculably ingenious and well-thought-out construction of these very works. To judge from these, it must have been infinitely difficult to make them, and therefore to provide for their maintenance with every conceivable care, whereas we have the very opposite before our eyes. Now if, by this naturally very unusual consideration, we have brought together in the sharpest manner the two heterogeneous sides of the world, and so to speak grasped them with one hand, we must now hold them firmly, in order to convince ourselves of the entire invalidity of the laws of the phenomenon, or of the world as representation, for that of the will, or of things-in-themselves. It will then become clearer to us that whereas, on the side of the representation, i.e., in the phenomenal world, there is exhibited to us first an arising out of nothing, then a complete annihilation of what has arisen, from that other side, or in itself, there lies before us an essence or entity, and when the concepts of arising and passing away are applied to it, they have absolutely no meaning. For by going back to the root, where, by means of self-consciousness, the phenomenon and the being-in-itself meet, we have just palpably apprehended, as it were, that the two are absolutely incommensurable. The whole mode of being of the one, together with all the fundamental laws of this being, signifies nothing, and less than nothing, in the other. I believe that this last consideration will be rightly understood only by a few, and that it will be unpleasant and even offensive to all who do not understand it. However, I shall never on this account omit anything that can serve to illustrate my fundamental idea.

At the beginning of this chapter I explained that the great attachment to life, or rather the fear of death, by no means springs from *knowledge*, for in that case it would be the result of the known value of life, but that that fear of death has its root directly in the *will*; it proceeds from the will's original and essential nature, in which that will is entirely without knowledge, and is therefore the blind will-to-live. Just as we are allured into life by the wholly illusory inclination for sensual pleasure, so are we firmly retained in life by the fear of death, certainly just as illusory. Both spring directly from the will that is in itself without knowledge. On the other hand, if man were a merely *knowing* being, death would necessarily be not

only a matter of indifference, but even welcome to him. Now the
consideration we have reached here teaches us that what is affected
by death is merely the *knowing* consciousness; that the *will*, on the
other hand, insofar as it is the thing-in-itself that lies at the root of
every individual phenomenon, is free from everything that depends
on determinations of time, and so is imperishable. Its striving for
existence and manifestation, from which the world results, is always
satisfied, for it is accompanied by this world just as the body is by
the shadow, since the world is merely the visibility of the true inner
nature of the will. Nevertheless, the will in us fears death, and this is
because knowledge presents to this will its true nature merely in the
individual phenomenon. From this there arises for the will the illusion that it perishes with this phenomenon, just as when the mirror
is smashed my image in it seems to be destroyed at the same time.
Therefore this fills the will with horror, because it is contrary to its
original nature, which is a blind craving for existence. It follows from
this that that in us which alone is capable of fearing death, and also
alone fears it, namely the *will*, is not affected by it; and that, on the
other hand, what is affected by it and actually perishes is that which,
by its nature, is not capable of any fear, and generally of any desire or
emotion, and is therefore indifferent to existence and nonexistence.
I refer to the mere subject of knowledge, the intellect, the existence
of which consists in its relation to the world of the representation, in
other words the objective world; it is the correlative of this objective
world, with whose existence its own existence is at bottom identical.
Thus, although the individual consciousness does not survive death,
that survives it which alone struggles against it, the will. From this is
also explained the contradiction that, from the standpoint of knowledge, philosophers have at all times with cogent arguments shown
death to be no evil; yet the fear of death remains impervious to them
all, simply because it is rooted not in knowledge, but in the will alone.

Just because the will alone, not the intellect, is the indestructible element, it follows that all religions and philosophies promise a reward in eternity only to the virtues of the will or heart, not to those of the intellect or head.

The following may also serve to illustrate this consideration. The will, which constitutes our being-in-itself, is of a simple nature; it merely wills and does not know. The subject of knowing, on the other hand, is a secondary phenomenon, arising out of the objectification of the will; it is the point of unity of the nervous system's sensibility, the focus, as it were, in which the rays of activity of all parts of the brain converge. Therefore with this brain the subject of knowing is bound to perish. In self-consciousness, as that which alone knows, the subject of knowing stands facing the will as a spectator, and although it has sprung from the will, it knows that will as something different from itself, something foreign to it, and thus only empirically, in time, piecemeal, in the successive agitations and acts of the will; only *a posteriori* and often very indirectly does it come to know the will's decisions. This is why our own inner being is a riddle to us, in other words, to our intellect, and why the individual regards himself as newly arisen and as perishable, although his inner being-in-itself is something timeless, and therefore eternal. Now just as the *will* does not *know*, so, conversely, the intellect, or the subject of knowledge, is simply and solely *knowing*, without ever willing. This can be proved even physically from the fact that [. . .] the various emotions [. . .] directly affect all parts of the organism and disturb their functions, with the exception of the brain as that which can be affected by them at most indirectly, in other words, in consequence of those very disturbances. Yet it follows from this that the subject of knowing, by itself and as such, cannot take any part or interest in anything, but that the existence or nonexistence of everything, in fact even of itself, is a matter of indifference to it. Now why should this indifferent being be immortal? It ends with the temporal phenomenon of the will, i.e., with the individual, just as it originated therewith. It is the lantern that after it has served its purpose is extinguished. The intellect, like the world of perception which exists in it alone, is mere phenomenon; but the finiteness of both does not affect that of which they are the phenomenal appearance. The intellect is the function of the cerebral nervous system; but this, like the rest of the body, is the objectivity of the *will*. The intellect, therefore, depends on the somatic life of the organism; but this organism itself depends on the will. Thus, in a certain sense, the organic body can be regarded as the link between the will and the intellect; although, properly speaking, the body is only the will itself spatially exhibiting itself in the perception of the intellect. Death and birth are the constant renewal and revival of the will's consciousness. In itself this will is endless and beginningless; it alone is, so to speak, the substance of existence (every such renewal, however, brings a new possibility of the denial of the will-to-live). Consciousness is the life of the subject of knowing, or of the brain, and death is its end. Therefore consciousness is finite, is always new, beginning each time at the beginning. The *will* alone is permanent; but permanence also concerns it alone, for it is the will-to-live. Nothing is of any consequence to the knowing subject by itself; yet the will and the knowing subject are united in the I or ego. In every animal being the will has achieved an intellect, and this is the light by which the will here pursues its ends. Incidentally, the fear of death may also be due partly to the fact that the individual will is so reluctant to separate itself from the intellect that has fallen to its lot through the course of nature, from its guide and guard, without which it knows that it is helpless and blind.

Finally, this explanation agrees also with that daily moral experience, teaching us that the will alone is real, while its objects, on the other hand, as conditioned by knowledge, are only phenomena, mere

froth and vapor, like the wine provided by Mephistopheles in Auer-
bach's cellar; thus after every pleasure of the senses we say: "And yet
it seemed as I were drinking wine" (Goethe's *Faust*).

The terrors of death rest for the most part on the false illusion
that then the I or ego vanishes, and the world remains. But rather is
the opposite true, namely that the world vanishes; on the other hand,
the innermost kernel of the ego endures, the bearer and producer
of that subject in whose representation alone the world had its existence. With the brain the intellect perishes, and with the intellect
the objective world, this intellect's mere representation. The fact that
in other brains a similar world lives and moves, now as before, is a
matter of indifference with reference to the intellect that is perishing. If, therefore, reality proper did not lie in the *will*, and if the *moral*
existence were not that which extended beyond death, then, as the
intellect and with it its world are extinguished, the true essence of
things generally would be nothing more than an endless succession
of short and troubled dreams without connection among themselves;
for the permanence of nature-without-knowledge consists merely
in the time-representation of nature that knows. Therefore a world-
spirit, dreaming without aim or purpose dreams that are often heavy
and troubled, would then be all in all.

When an individual experiences the dread of death, we really
have the strange, and even ludicrous, spectacle of the lord of the
worlds, who fills everything with his true nature, and through whom
alone everything that is has its existence, in despair and afraid of
perishing, of sinking into the abyss of eternal nothingness; whereas,
in truth, everything is full of him, and there is no place where he
would not be, no being in whom he would not live, for existence does
not support him, but he existence. Yet it is he who despairs in the
individual who suffers the dread of death, since he is exposed to the
illusion, produced by the *principium individuationis*, that his existence

is limited to the being that is now dying. This illusion is part of the heavy dream into which he, as will-to-live, has fallen. However, we might say to the dying individual: "You are ceasing to be something which you would have done better never to become."

As long as no denial of that will has taken place, that of us which is left over by death is the seed and kernel of quite another existence, in which a new individual finds himself again so fresh and original that he broods over himself in astonishment. Hence the enthusiastic, visionary, and dreamy disposition of noble youths at the time when this fresh consciousness has just been fully developed. What sleep is for the individual, death is for the will as thing-in-itself. It could not bear to continue throughout endless time the same actions and sufferings without true gain, if memory and individuality were left to it. It throws them off; this is Lethe; and through this sleep of death it reappears as a new being, refreshed and equipped with another intellect; "A new day beckons to a newer shore!" (Goethe, *Faust*)

As the self-affirming will-to-live, man has the root of his existence in the species. Accordingly, death is the losing of one individuality and the receiving of another, and consequently a changing of the individuality under the exclusive guidance of his own will. For in this alone lies the eternal force which was able to produce his existence with his ego, yet, on account of the nature of this ego, is unable to maintain it in existence. For death is the *dementi* that the essence (*essentia*) of everyone receives in its claim to existence (*existentia*), the appearance of a contradiction lying in every individual existence: "for all things, from the Void, called forth, deserve to be destroyed" (Goethe, *Faust*).

Yet an infinite number of just such existences, each with its ego, stands within reach of the same force, that is, of the will, but these again will be just as perishable and transitory. Now as every ego has its separate consciousness, that infinite number of them, in respect of such an ego, is not different from a single one. From this point of view, it does not appear to me accidental that *aevum*, *aion*, signifies both the individual term of life and infinite time; thus it may be seen from this point, though indistinctly, that ultimately and in themselves both are the same. According to this it would really make no difference whether I existed only through my term of life or throughout an infinite time.

But of course we cannot obtain a notion of all that has been said above entirely without time-concepts; yet these should be excluded when we are dealing with the thing-in-itself. But it is one of the unalterable limitations of our intellect that it can never entirely cast off this first and most immediate form of all its representations, in order to operate without it. Therefore we naturally come here on a kind of metempsychosis, though with the important difference that this does not affect the whole psyche, and hence the *knowing* being, but the *will* alone, whereby so many absurdities that accompany the doctrine of metempsychosis disappear; and with the consciousness that the form of time here appears only as an unavoidable accommodation to the limitation of our intellect. If we now call in the assistance of the fact that the character, i.e., the will, is inherited from the father, whereas the intellect comes from the mother, then this agrees very well with our view that the will of man, in itself individual, separates itself in death from the intellect that was obtained from the mother at procreation, and receives a new intellect in accordance with its now modified nature under the guidance of the absolutely necessary course of the world which harmonizes with this nature. With this new intellect, the will would become a new being that would have no recollection of a previous existence; for the intellect, alone having the faculty of recollection, is the mortal part or the form, whereas the will is the eternal part, the substance. Accordingly, the word *palingenesis* is more correct than *metempsychosis* for describing this doctrine. These constant rebirths then constitute the succession of the life-dreams of a will in itself indestructible, until, instructed and improved by so much and such varied and successive knowledge in a constantly new form, it would abolish itself.

The proper and, so to speak, esoteric doctrine of Buddhism, as we have come to know it through the most recent researches, also agrees with this view, since it teaches not metempsychosis, but a peculiar palingenesis resting on a moral basis, and it expounds and explains this with great depth of thought. [. . .] Yet for the great mass of Buddhists this doctrine is too subtle; and so plain metempsychosis is preached to them as a comprehensible substitute. Moreover, it must not be overlooked that even empirical grounds support a palingenesis of this kind. As a matter of fact, there does exist a connection between the birth of the newly appearing beings and the death of those who are decrepit and worn out. It shows itself in the great fertility of the human race, arising as the result of devastating epidemics. When, in the fourteenth century, the Black Death had for the most part depopulated the Old World, a quite abnormal fertility appeared among the human race, and twin births were very frequent. Most remarkable also was the circumstance that none of the children born at this time acquired all their teeth; thus nature, exerting herself to the utmost, was ungenerous in details. This is stated by F. Schnurrer in the *Chronicle of Plagues* (1825). Casper in his book *The Probable Life Duration of Humans* (1835) also confirms the principle that, in a given population, the number of procreations has the most decided influence on the duration of life and on mortality, as it always keeps pace with the mortality; so that, everywhere and at all times, the births and deaths increase and decrease in equal ratio. This he places beyond doubt by accumulated evidence from many countries and their different provinces. And yet there cannot possibly be a *physical* causal connection between my previous death and the fertility of a couple who are strangers to me, or vice versa. Here, then, the meta-physical appears undeniably and in an astonishing way as the im-mediate ground of explanation of the physical. Every newborn being comes fresh and blithe into the new existence, and enjoys it as a gift; but nothing is or can be freely given. Its fresh existence is paid for by the old age and death of a worn-out and decrepit existence which has perished, but which contained the indestructible seed. Out of this seed the new existence arose; the two existences are *one* being. To show the bridge between the two would, of course, be the solution to a great riddle.

The great truth here expressed has never been entirely overlooked, although it could not be reduced to its precise and correct meaning. This becomes possible only through the doctrine of the primacy and metaphysical nature of the will and the secondary, merely organic, nature of the intellect. Thus we find the doctrine of metempsychosis, springing from the very earliest and noblest ages of the human race, always worldwide, as the belief of the great majority of mankind, in fact really as the doctrine of all religions, with the exception of Judaism and the two religions that have arisen from it. But, as already mentioned, we find this doctrine in its subtlest form, and coming nearest to the truth, in Buddhism. Accordingly, while Christians console themselves with the thought of meeting again in another world, in which they regain their complete personality and at once recognize one another, in those other religions the meeting is going on already, though incognito. Thus, in the round of births, and by virtue of metempsychosis or palingenesis, the persons who now stand in close connection or contact with us will also be born simultaneously with us at the next birth, and will have the same, or analogous, relations and sentiments towards us as they now have, whether these are of a friendly or hostile nature. [. . .] Of course, recognition is limited here to an obscure inkling, a reminiscence which is not to be brought to distinct consciousness, and which points to an infinite remoteness; with the exception, however, of the Buddha himself. He has the prerogative of distinctly knowing his own previous births and those of others; this is described in the Jatakas. But, in fact, if at favorable moments we look at the doings and dealings of men in real life in a purely objective way, the intuitive conviction is forced on us that they not only are and remain the same according to the (Platonic) Ideas, but also that the present generation, according to its real kernel, is precisely and substantially identical with every generation that previously existed. The question is only in what this kernel consists; the answer given to it by my teaching is well known. The above-mentioned intuitive conviction can be conceived as arising from the fact that the multiplying glasses, time and space, for a moment lose their effectiveness. With regard to the universal nature of the belief in metempsychosis, Obry rightly says: "This old belief has journeyed round the world, and was so widespread in ancient times that a learned follower of the Anglican Church judged it to be without father, without mother, without genealogy."

Taught already in the Vedas, as in all the sacred books of India, metempsychosis is well known to be the kernel of Brahmanism and Buddhism. Accordingly it prevails even now in the whole of non-Mohammedan Asia, and thus among more than half of the human race, as the firmest of convictions, with an incredibly strong practical influence. It was also the belief of the Egyptians, from whom it was received with enthusiasm by Orpheus, Pythagoras, and Plato; the Pythagoreans in particular held firmly to it. That it was taught also in the mysteries of the Greeks follows undeniably from the ninth book of Plato's *Laws*. Nemesius even says in *De natura hominis*: "Belief in a wandering from one body to another is common to all the Greeks, who declared that the soul was immortal." [. . .] Even a Mohammedan sect in India, the Bohras, of whom Colebrooke gives a detailed account, believe in metempsychosis, and accordingly abstain from all animal food. Among American Indians and Negro tribes, indeed even among the natives of Australia, traces of this belief are found, as appears from an exact description, given in *The Times* of 29 January 1841, of the execution of two Australian savages for arson and murder. It says: "The younger of the 2 prisoners met his end with a dogged and determinate spirit, as it appeared of revenge; the only intelligible expression he made use of conveyed an impression that he would rise up 'a white fellow,' which, it was considered, strengthened his resolution." It is related also that the Papuans of New Holland regarded the whites as their own relations who had returned to the world. As the result of all this, belief in metempsychosis presents itself as the natural conviction of man whenever he reflects at all in an unprejudiced way. Accordingly, it would actually be that which Kant falsely asserts of his three pretended Ideas of reason, namely a philosopheme natural to human reason, and resulting from the forms of that faculty; and where this belief is not found, it would only be supplanted by positive religious doctrines coming from a different source. I have also noticed that it is at once obvious to everyone who hears of it for the first time. Just see how seriously even Lessing defends it in the last seven paragraphs of his *Education of the Human Race*. Lichtenberg also says of himself: "I cannot get rid of the idea that I had died before I was born." Even the exceedingly empirical Hume says in his skeptical essay on immortality: "The metempsychosis is therefore the only system of this kind that philosophy can hearken to." What opposes this belief, which is spread over the whole human race and is evident to the wise as well as to the vulgar, is Judaism, together with the two religions that have sprung from it, inasmuch as they teach man's creation out of nothing. He then has the hard task of connecting this with the belief in an endless future existence *a parte post*. Of course, they have succeeded, with fire and sword, in driving that consoling, primitive belief of mankind out of Europe and of a part of Asia; for how long is still uncertain. The oldest Church history is evidence of precisely how difficult this was. Most of the heretics were attached to that primitive belief; for example, the Simonians, Basilidians, Valentinians, Marcionites, Gnostics, and Manichaeans. The Jews themselves have come to it to some extent, as is reported by Tertullian and Justin (in his dialogues). In the Talmud it is related that Abel's soul passed into the body of Seth, and then into that of Moses. [. . .] However, in Christianity the doctrine of original sin, in other words of atonement for the sin of another individual, has taken the place of the transmigration of souls and of the expiation by means thereof of all the sins committed in a previous life. Thus both identify, and indeed with a moral tendency, the existing person with one who has existed previously; transmigration of souls does this directly, original sin indirectly.

Death is the great reprimand that the will-to-live and, more particularly, the egoism essential thereto receive through the course of nature; and it can be conceived as a punishment for our existence. Death says: You are the product of an act that ought not to have taken place; therefore, to wipe it out, you must die. Death is the painful untying of the knot that generation with sensual pleasure had tied; it is the violent destruction, bursting in from outside, of the fundamental error of our true nature, the great disillusionment. At bottom, we are something that ought not to be; therefore we cease to be. Egoism really consists in man's restricting all reality to his own person, in that he imagines he lives in this alone, and not in others. Death teaches him something better, since it abolishes this person, so that man's true nature, that is his will, will henceforth live only in other individuals. His intellect, however, which itself belonged only to the phenomenon, i.e., to the world as representation, and was merely the form of the external world, also continues to exist in the condition of being representation, in other words, in the *objective* being, *as such*, of things, hence also only in the existence of what was hitherto the external world. Therefore, from this time forward, his whole ego lives only in what he had hitherto regarded as non-ego; for the difference between external and internal ceases. Here we recall that the better person is the one who makes the least difference between himself and others, and does not regard them as absolutely non-ego; whereas to the bad person this difference is great, in fact absolute. I have discussed this at length in the essay *On the Basis of Morality*. The conclusion from the above remarks is that the degree in which death can be regarded as man's annihilation is in proportion to this difference. But if we start from the fact that the difference between outside me and inside me, as a spatial difference, is founded only in the phenomenon, not in the thing-in-itself, and so is not an absolutely real difference, then in the losing of our own individuality we shall see only the loss of a phenomenon, and thus only an apparent loss. However much reality that difference has in empirical consciousness, from the metaphysical standpoint the sentences "I perish, but the world endures," and "The world perishes, but I endure," are not really different at bottom.

But beyond all this, death is the great opportunity no longer to be I; to him, of course, who embraces it. During life, man's will is without freedom; on the basis of his unalterable character, his conduct takes place with necessity in the chain of motives. Now everyone carries in his memory very many things which he has done, about which he is not satisfied with himself. If he were to go on living, he would go on acting in the same way by virtue of the unalterability of his character. Accordingly, he must cease to be what he is, in order to be able to arise out of the germ of his true nature as a new and different being. Death, therefore, loosens those bonds; the will again becomes free, for freedom lies in the *esse*, not in the *operari*. "Whoever beholds

the highest and profoundest has his heart's knot cut, all his doubts
are resolved, and his works come to naught," is a very famous saying
of the Vedas often repeated by all Vedantists. Dying is the moment of
that liberation from the one-sidedness of an individuality which does
not constitute the innermost kernel of our true being, but is rather
to be thought of as a kind of aberration thereof. The true original
freedom again enters at this moment which in the sense stated can
be regarded as a "restoration to the former state." The peace and composure on the countenance of most dead people seem to have their
origin in this. As a rule, the death of every good person is peaceful
and gentle; but to die willingly, to die gladly, to die cheerfully, is the
prerogative of the resigned, of him who gives up and denies the will-
to-live. For he alone wishes to die *actually* and not merely *apparently*,
and consequently needs and desires no continuance of his person. He
willingly gives up the existence that we know; what comes to him instead of it is in our eyes *nothing*, because our existence in reference to
that one is *nothing*. The Buddhist faith calls that existence *Nirvana*,
that is to say, extinction.

The etymology of the word *Nirvana* is given in various ways. According to Colebrooke it comes from *va*, "to blow" like the wind,
with the prefixed negative *nir*; hence it signifies a lull or calm, but
as adjective, "extinguished." Obry says: "Nirvanam in Sanskrit literally means extinction, e.g., as of a fire." According to other sources
it is really *Neravana*, from *nera*, "without," and *vana*, "life," and the
meaning would be annihilation. According to Spence Hardy's *Eastern Monachism*, *Nirvana* is derived from *vana*, "sinful desires," with
the negative *nir*. I. J. Schmidt, in his translation of *The History of the
Eastern Mongolians*, says that the Sanskrit *Nirvana* is translated into
Mongolian by a phrase meaning "departed from misery," "escaped
from misery." According to the same scholar's lectures at the Saint
Petersburg Academy, *Nirvana* is the opposite of *Samsara*, which is the

world of constant rebirths, of craving and desire, of the illusion of the senses, of changing and transient forms, of being born, growing old, becoming sick, and dying. In Burmese the word *Nirvana*, on the analogy of other Sanskrit words, is transformed into *Nieban*, and is translated as "complete vanishing."

Twenty

The Fullness of Nothingness

In now bringing to a conclusion the main points of ethics, and with these the whole development of that one idea the imparting of which was my object, I do not wish by any means to conceal an objection concerning this last part of the discussion. On the contrary, I want to show that this objection lies in the nature of the case, and that it is quite impossible to remedy it. This objection is that, after our observations have finally brought us to the point where we have before our eyes in perfect saintliness the denial and surrender of all willing, and thus a deliverance from a world whose whole existence presented itself to us as suffering, this now appears to us as a transition into empty *nothingness*.

On this I must first of all observe that the concept of *nothing* is essentially relative, and always refers to a definite something that it negates. This quality has been attributed (especially by Kant) merely to the *nihil privativum* indicated by – in contrast to +. This negative sign (–) from the opposite point of view might become +, and, in opposition to this *nihil privativum*, the *nihil negativum* has been set up, which would in every respect be nothing. For this purpose, the logical contradiction that does away with itself has been used as an example. But considered more closely, an absolute nothing, a really proper *nihil negativum*, is not even conceivable, but everything of this kind, considered from a higher standpoint or subsumed under a wider concept, is always only a *nihil privativum*. Every nothing is thought of as such only in relation to something else; it presupposes this relation, and thus that other thing also. Even a logical contradiction is only a relative nothing; it is no thought of our faculty of reason; yet it is not on that account an absolute nothing. For it is a word-combination; it is an example of the unthinkable which is necessarily required in logic to demonstrate the laws of thought. Therefore, if for this purpose we look for such an example, we shall stick to the nonsense as the positive we are just looking for, and skip the sense as the negative. Thus every *nihil negativum* or absolute nothing, if subordinated to a higher concept, will appear as a mere *nihil privativum* or relative nothing, which can always change signs with what it negates, so that that would then be thought of as negation, but it itself as affirmation. This also agrees with the result of the difficult dialectical investigation on the conception of nothing which is given by Plato in the *Sophist*: "It is the nature of *being different*, of which we have demonstrated that it exists and is dispersed piecemeal over all being in *mutual relationship*, and since we opposed to being every single particle of this nature, we have ventured to assert that precisely this is in truth *non-being*."

What is universally assumed as positive, what we call *being*, the negation of which is expressed by the concept *nothing* in its most general significance, is exactly the world as representation, which I have shown to be the objectivity, the mirror, of the will. We ourselves are also this will and this world, and to it belongs the representation in general as one aspect of it. The form of this representation is space and time; and so, for this point of view, everything that exists must be in some place and at some time. Then the concept, the material of philosophy, and finally the word, the sign of the concept, also belong to the representation. Denial, abolition, turning of the will are also abolition and disappearance of the world, of its mirror. If we no longer perceive the will in this mirror, we ask in vain in what direction it has turned, and then, because it no longer has any *where* and any *when*, we complain that it is lost in nothingness.

If a contrary point of view were possible for us, it would cause the signs to be changed, and would show what exists for us as nothing, and this nothing as that which exists. But so long as we ourselves are the will-to-live, this last, namely the nothing as that which exists, can be known and expressed by us only negatively, since the old saying of Empedocles, that like can be known only by like, deprives us here of all knowledge, just as, conversely, on it ultimately rests the possibility of all our actual knowledge, in other words, the world as representation, or the objectivity of the will; for the world is the self-knowledge of the will.

If, however, it should be absolutely insisted on that somehow a positive knowledge is to be acquired of what philosophy can express only negatively as denial of the will, nothing would be left but to refer to that state which is experienced by all who have attained to complete denial of the will, and which is denoted by the names ecstasy, rapture, illumination, union with God, and so on. But such a state cannot really be called knowledge, since it no longer has the form of subject and object; moreover, it is accessible only to one's own experience that cannot be further communicated.

We, however, who consistently occupy the standpoint of philosophy, must be satisfied here with negative knowledge, content to have reached the final landmark of the positive. If, therefore, we have recognized the inner nature of the world as will, and have seen in all its phenomena only the objectivity of the will; and if we have followed these from the unconscious impulse of obscure natural forces up to the most conscious action of man, we shall by no means evade the consequence that, with the free denial, the surrender of the will, all those phenomena also are now abolished. That constant pressure and effort, without aim and without rest, at all grades of objectivity in which and through which the world exists; the multifarious forms succeeding one another in gradation; the whole phenomenon of the will; finally, the universal forms of this phenomenon, time and space, and also the last fundamental form of these, subject and object; all these are abolished with the will. No will: no representation, no world.

Before us there is certainly left only nothing; but that which struggles against this flowing away into nothing, namely our nature, is indeed just the will-to-live which we ourselves are, just as it is our world. That we abhor nothingness so much is simply another way of saying that we will life so much, and that we are nothing but this will and know nothing but it alone. But we now turn our glance from our own needy and perplexed nature to those who have overcome the world, in whom the will, having reached complete self-knowledge, has found itself again in everything, and then freely denied itself, and who then merely wait to see the last trace of the will vanish with the body that is animated by that trace. Then, instead of the restless pressure and effort; instead of the constant transition from desire to apprehension and from joy to sorrow; instead of the never-satisfied and never-dying hope that constitutes the life-dream of the man who wills, we see that peace that is higher than all reason, that ocean-like calmness of the spirit, that deep tranquility, that unshakable confidence and serenity, whose mere reflection in the countenance, as depicted by Raphael and Correggio, is a complete and certain gospel. Only knowledge remains; the will has vanished. We then look with deep and painful yearning at that state, beside which the miserable and desperate nature of our own appears in the clearest light by the contrast. Yet this consideration is the only one that can permanently console us, when, on the one hand, we have recognized incurable suffering and endless misery as essential to the phenomenon of the will, to the world, and on the other see the world melt away with the abolished will, and retain before us only empty nothingness.

In this way, therefore, by contemplating the life and conduct of saints, to meet with whom is of course rarely granted to us in our own experience, but who are brought to our notice by their recorded history, and, vouched for with the stamp of truth by art, we have to banish the dark impression of that nothingness, which as the final goal hovers behind all virtue and holiness, and which we fear as children fear darkness. We must not even evade it, as the Indians do, by myths and meaningless words, such as reabsorption in Brahman, or the Nirvana of the Buddhists. On the contrary, we freely acknowledge that what remains after the complete abolition of the will is, for all who are still full of the will, assuredly nothing. But also conversely, to those in whom the will has turned and denied itself, this very real world of ours with all its suns and galaxies is—nothing. This is also the Prajna-Paramita of the Buddhists, the "beyond all knowledge," in other words, the point where subject and object no longer exist.

Suggested Further Reading

Arthur Hübscher, *The Philosophy of Schopenhauer in Its Intellectual Context: Thinker Against the Tide*. Translated by Joachim T. Baer and David Humphrey. Lewiston, New York: Erwin Mellen Press, 1989.

Dale Jacquette, *The Philosophy of Schopenhauer*. Chesham, UK: Acumen, 2005.

Christopher Janaway, *Schopenhauer*. Oxford: Oxford University Press, 1994.

Christopher Janaway (editor), *The Cambridge Companion to Schopenhauer*. Cambridge: Cambridge University Press, 1999.

Bryan Magee, *The Philosophy of Schopenhauer*. Oxford: Clarendon Press, 1983.

Rüdiger Safranski, *Schopenhauer and the Wild Years of Philosophy*. Translated by Ewald Osers. London: Weidenfeld and Nicolson, 1989.

Wolfgang Schirmacher, "Homo generator." In: *Just Living: Philosophy in Artificial Life*. Translated by Virginia Cutrufelli and Dan Theisen. New York: Atropos Press, 2010.

Sources

A Note on the Translations
Translation based on consulting several translators: E. F. J. Payne, Konstantin Kolenda, and Arthur Brodrick Bullock

Sources
"On the Suffering of the World." In: Arthur Schopenhauer, *Parerga and Paralipomena*. Volume II. Translated by E. F. J. Payne. Oxford: Oxford University Press, 1974, pp. 291–305.

"On the Affirmation of the Will-to-Live." In: Arthur Schopenhauer, *The World as Will and Representation*. Volume II. Translated by E. F. J. Payne. Indian Hills, Colorado: The Falcon's Wing Press, 1958, chapter XLV.

"On the Vanity and Suffering of Life." In: Arthur Schopenhauer, *The World as Will and Representation*. Volume II. Translated by E. F. J. Payne. Indian Hills, Colorado: The Falcon's Wing Press, 1958, chapter XLVI.

"Freedom of the Will." In: Arthur Schopenhauer, *Essay on the Freedom of the Will*. Translated by Konstantin Kolenda. New York: Liberal Arts Press, 1960, pp. 91–103.

"Principle of Sufficient Reason of Knowing." In: Arthur Schopenhauer, *On the Fourfold Root of the Principle of Sufficient Reason*. Translated by E. F. J. Payne. Chicago: Open Court, 1974, pp. 156–163.

"The World as Will." In: Arthur Schopenhauer, *The World as Will and Representation*. Volume I. Translated by E. F. J. Payne. Indian Hills, Colorado: The Falcon's Wing Press, 1958, paragraphs 17–21.

"Knowledge of the Idea." In: Arthur Schopenhauer, *The World as Will and Representation*. Volume I. Translated by E. F. J. Payne. Indian Hills, Colorado: The Falcon's Wing Press, 1958, paragraphs 34–36.

"On the Inner Nature of Art." In: Arthur Schopenhauer, *The World as Will and Representation*. Volume II. Translated by E. F. J. Payne. Indian Hills, Colorado: The Falcon's Wing Press, 1958, chapter XXXIV.

"Metaphysics of the Beautiful and Aesthetics." In: Arthur Schopenhauer, *Parerga and Paralipomena*. Volume II. Translated by E. F. J. Payne. Oxford: Oxford University Press, 1974, pp. 415–442.

"The Artist and the Sublime." In: Arthur Schopenhauer, *The World as Will and Representation*. Volume I. Translated by E. F. J. Payne. Indian Hills, Colorado: The Falcon's Wing Press, 1958, paragraphs 37–39.

"On Education." In: Arthur Schopenhauer, *Parerga and Paralipomena*. Volume II. Translated by E. F. J. Payne. Oxford: Oxford University Press, 1974, pp. 627–633.

"On Noise." In: Arthur Schopenhauer, *Parerga and Paralipomena*. Volume II. Translated by E. F. J. Payne. Oxford: Oxford University Press, 1974, pp. 642–645.

"On Women." In: Arthur Schopenhauer, *Parerga and Paralipomena*. Volume II. Translated by E. F. J. Payne. Oxford: Oxford University Press, 1974, pp. 614–626.

"On Suicide." In: Arthur Schopenhauer, *Parerga and Paralipomena*. Volume II. Translated by E. F. J. Payne. Oxford: Oxford University Press, 1974, pp. 306–311.

"On the Basis of Ethics." In: Arthur Schopenhauer: *The Basis of Morality*. Translated by Arthur Brodrick Bullock. London: Allen & Unwin, 1903, part IV.

"Eternal and Temporal Justice." In: Arthur Schopenhauer, *The World as Will and Representation*. Volume I. Translated by E. F. J. Payne. Indian Hills,

Colorado: The Falcon's Wing Press, 1958, paragraphs 63–64.

"Compassion." In: Arthur Schopenhauer, *The World as Will and Representation*. Volume I. Translated by E. F. J. Payne. Indian Hills, Colorado: The Falcon's Wing Press, 1958, paragraphs 65–67.

"Mystics, Saints, Ascetics." In: Arthur Schopenhauer, *The World as Will and Representation*. Volume I. Translated by E. F. J. Payne. Indian Hills, Colorado: The Falcon's Wing Press, 1958, paragraph 68.

"Death and Rebirth." In: *The World as Will and Representation*. Volume II. Translated by E. F. J. Payne. Indian Hills, Colorado: The Falcon's Wing Press, 1958, chapter XLI.

"The Fullness of Nothingness." In: Arthur Schopenhauer, *The World as Will and Representation*. Volume I. Translated by E. F. J. Payne. Indian Hills, Colorado: The Falcon's Wing Press, 1958, paragraph 71.

Index

HARPER**PERENNIAL** **✕** MODERN**THOUGHT**

THE HOME OF THE MODERN WORLD'S MOST INFLUENTIAL MINDS

ISBN 978-0-06-199046-5

KIERKEGAARD

THE PRESENT AGE

ON THE DEATH OF REBELLION

HARPER**PERENNIAL** MODERN**THOUGHT**

ISBN 978-0-06-199003-8

ISBN 978-0-06-199045-8

ISBN 978-0-06-171327-9

ISBN 978-0-06-162701-9

ISBN 978-0-06-157559-4

Visit DeadPhilosophersClub.com and Twitter@DeadPhilClub

ISBN 978-0-06-171869-4

ISBN 978-0-06-156161-0

ISBN 978-0-06-176631-2

ISBN 978-0-06-155024-9

ISBN 978-0-06-176521-6

ISBN 978-0-06-163265-5

ISBN 978-0-06-176824-8

ISBN 978-0-06-187599-1

ISBN 978-0-06-120919-2

Available wherever books are sold, or call 1-800-311-3761 to order.